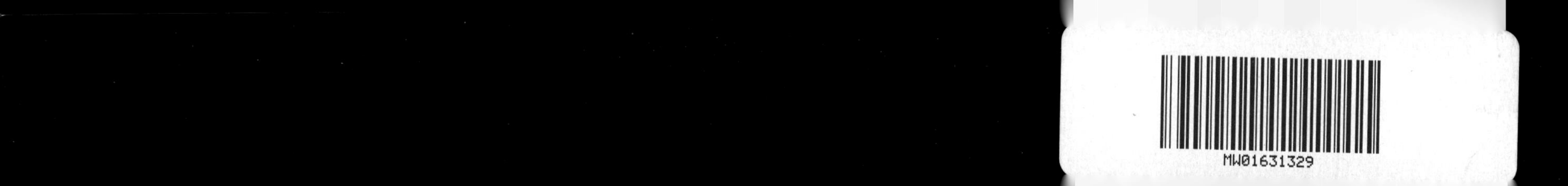
MW01631329

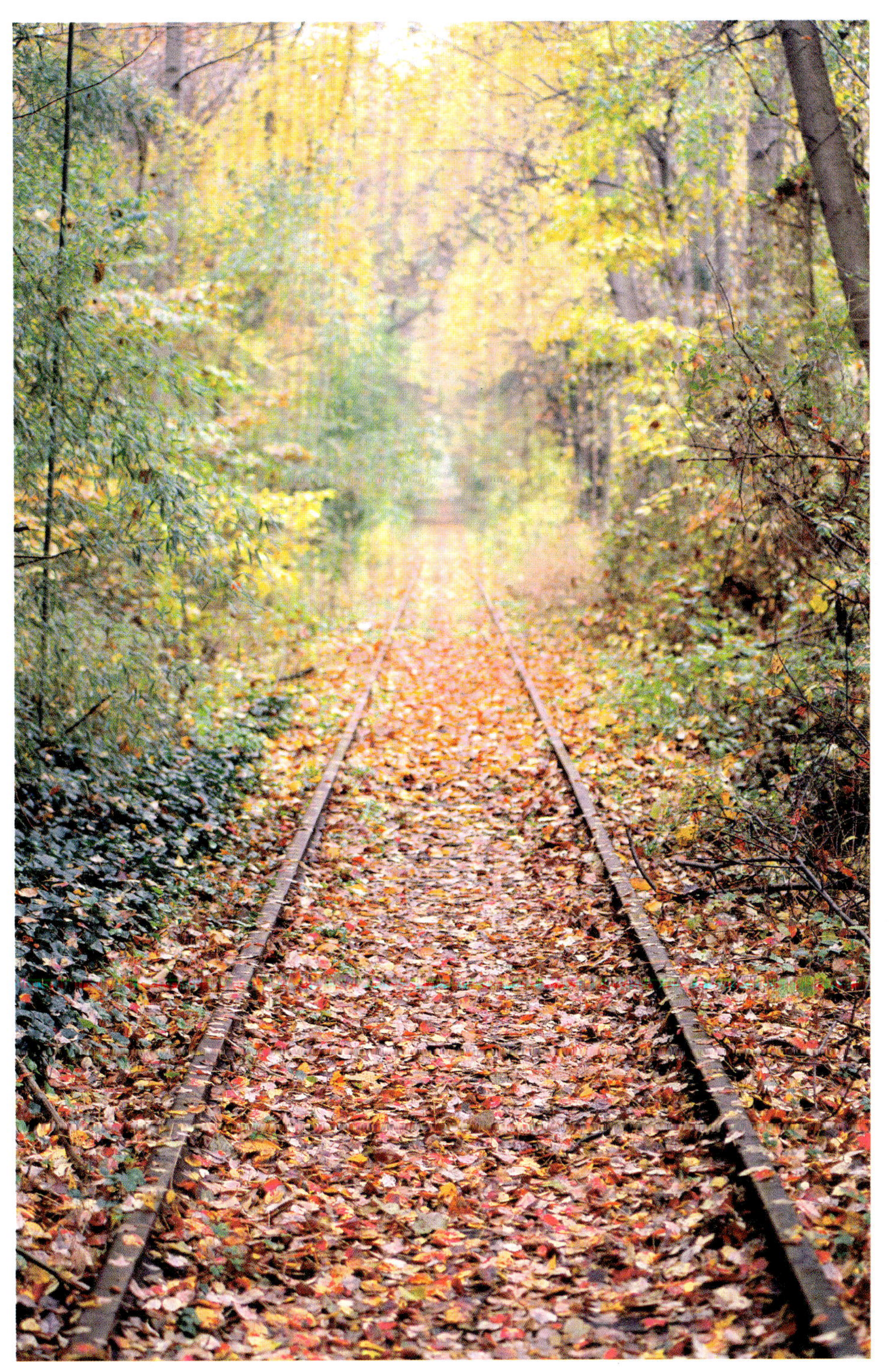

Sleeping Bear Press
310 North Main Street
P.O. Box 20
Chelsea, MI 48118
www.sleepingbearpress.com

Printed and bound in China.

10 9 8 7 6 5 4 3 2 1

Library of Congress Cataloging-in-Publication Data
Gottlieb, Steven, 1946-
Abandoned America / Author/photographer, Steve Gottlieb.
p. cm.
ISBN 1-58536-105-4
1. Photography, Artistic. 2. Gottlieb, Steven, 1946-
3. United States-Civilization-Pictorial works.
4. United States-Social life and customs-Pictorial works.
5. United States-Description and travel. I. Title.
TR655 .G68 2002
779'.9973—dc21
2002007343

For fine art prints and stock usage of images: steve@gottliebphoto.com
The photographer is grateful to Kodak Professional for its support.

Into my very first photo album — I can remember pasting a picture of the remnants of a broken-down New Jersey gristmill next to shots of my family, my friends, and my pet duck, Seymour. I was 13 years old. That old mill has long since crumbled to dust, its foundation

barely visible through underbrush and trees. And the 35mm camera I used back then—the one with the primitive screw-in lens—has long since been replaced by an extensive array of professional equipment. But over these many years my fervor for photographing abandoned objects like that old mill has continued... and intensified. From one end of the country to the other, I've exposed hundreds of rolls of film capturing the varied faces of what I call "Abandoned America." My favorite images are found between these covers.

There was never a commercial motivation behind photographing abandoned subjects—portraits and architecture are my specialties. My "abandoned" slides were stored in a three-ring binder marked "Personal Work" which sat undisturbed except when I opened it to add new photos. Five years ago an advertising agency art director was in my studio and stumbled across that binder. "These are wonderful images," he said simply. "Why don't you do a whole book of pictures like these?" He even suggested the title *Abandoned America*. The notion of creating a book, so obvious in hindsight, had never occurred to me. I was captivated. I decided that between commercial assignments—they are creatively challenging but rarely offer the absolute freedom to please only oneself—I would expand my previously random efforts by photographing all kinds of abandoned objects all over the United States.

Why, you might wonder, was I so fascinated with things abandoned. Why not, for example, photograph *new* houses, *new* factories, *new* cars? As I wandered about taking these pictures, I avoided pondering my motivation. Self-consciousness can interfere with the creative process; don't jinx the visual with the cerebral. But in choosing the photos and writing the captions

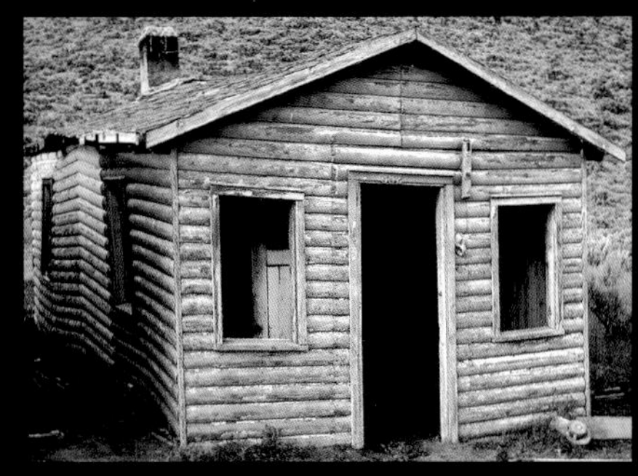

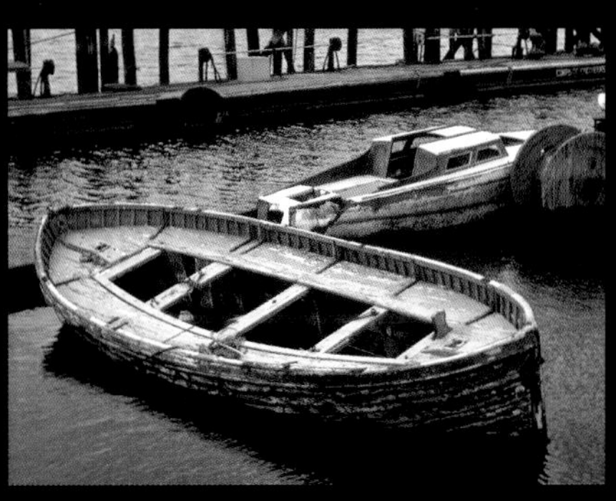

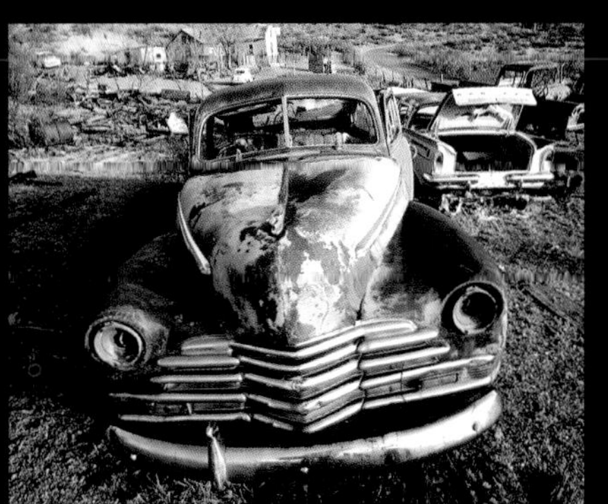

for this book, my underlying motives emerged.

One motivation is that each abandoned object serves as a magic carpet transporting me to a different historical time and place. I imagine myself parked at the drive-in theater in Pittsfield, Massachusetts, circa 1966, with my right arm around my sweetheart. In a paper mill I feel the heavy chemical fumes burning my face. The broken waterwheel on the parched Colorado farm needs my attention. Sitting in the engineer's seat of the caboose, I watch a 1940s landscape fly across the tiny window.

In my time travel I feel the shadowy presence of the people who were there once upon a time: a man slapping grease on coal mining gears in Appalachia; a child fetching water inside a Virginia springhouse; a ferryboat captain and his passengers chugging to Staten Island; a family singing around a 1910 upright piano on a North Carolina Sunday evening.

My journey has not just been a nostalgic adventure into our nation's past but across its magnificent geography as well. I traveled from Maine to California, from the Canadian border to the Mexican, through big cities, small towns and rustic countryside, and across every climate and season. The map of the United States served as my treasure map, but instead of seeking treasure buried beneath a large, black "X," my treasures were found wherever I discovered forlorn objects that kindled my emotions.

As in any treasure hunt worthy of the name, the journey has been a long one, and rarely smooth. Interesting, evocative, photogenic subject matter is not all that common. Many objects have lost their character through decay, many others through renovation. Some of the most wonderful material is hidden away in remote and often impossible locations, and I rarely had the benefit of either a local guide or four-wheel drive. Furthermore, many wonderful old houses and factories have been tightly boarded up or fenced off. On top of these problems, my odyssey included an astonishing number of wrong turns, dead ends, and other assorted snafus. Not surprisingly, many a day yielded not a single good photograph. (Should I do a sequel to this book, I'd be grateful to any reader who suggests a worthy subject...especially if its location is indicated on a *detailed* map!) Despite these problems, to the dedicated and persevering sleuth excellent material can be found everywhere—except Vermont, whose tidy residents made finding worthy subjects beyond my considerable patience. Of course when a successful photograph is taken, the frustrations and disappointments that preceded it become inconsequential.

Beyond the dual pleasures of time travel and treasure hunting another, perhaps even more powerful, motivation beckoned.

There is a part of my soul—the part that feels alone, mortal, and conscious of time's relentless passing—that feels an emotional link with abandoned objects, things whose time has come and very soon will be gone. I identify with the decrepit cabin, the rusted bridge, the empty church, the pickup truck being buried under natural growth...creations of utility and beauty that are now isolated, unused, unsung, vanishing. ("Find your pain," someone once said, "and there you will find your work.") With my camera I seek to take these once-useful, now-fleeting things and give them a measure of permanence by recording them on film. It's as if I'm saying to these vanishing objects: "I know who you are, where you've been, where you're going. I cherish and celebrate your existence. To the extent it is within my creative power, I want my images to bestow upon you (and perhaps myself) a flicker of immortality."

★ ★ ★

I want to express appreciation to the exceptional people who helped bring *Abandoned America* to life: art director Mike Travis, who had the original idea for this book; my son Jason, whose astute visual judgment and sophisticated computer skills were invaluable in preparing these pictures for publication; legendary graphic designer Lou Dorfsman, who kept an encouraging eye on my book design efforts; Howard Millard and Efrat Zalishnick, discerning editors of pictures, and Elizabeth Boleman-Herring and Regina Skyer, discerning editors of words; Yustin Wallrapp, a wise counselor; Elise Caputo, photographer's agent par excellence; Delia and Bill Gottlieb, lovers of photography and ever-supportive parents; my sister Barbara, a font of sound advice; my assistants on the road—most especially my son Brian—who were exceptional companions; Kodak Professional's Audrey Jonckheer for her support; and Heather Hughes and Jennifer Lundahl of Sleeping Bear Press, enthusiastic, gracious, and guiding hands.

Finally, profound thanks go to the dozens upon dozens of Americans I've met all across our wonderful country—the junk dealers and general store proprietors, the county clerks and café waitresses, the farmers and the firemen, the moms and their kids, and everyone else—who lent this treasure hunter a hand, who offered location ideas and access, who forgave me my trespasses and rescued me from my abominable sense of direction, who shared a story and a laugh, and who, above all, made me feel at home wherever I was. In my abandoned America, I never felt abandoned.

Steve Gottlieb

Houses & Barns

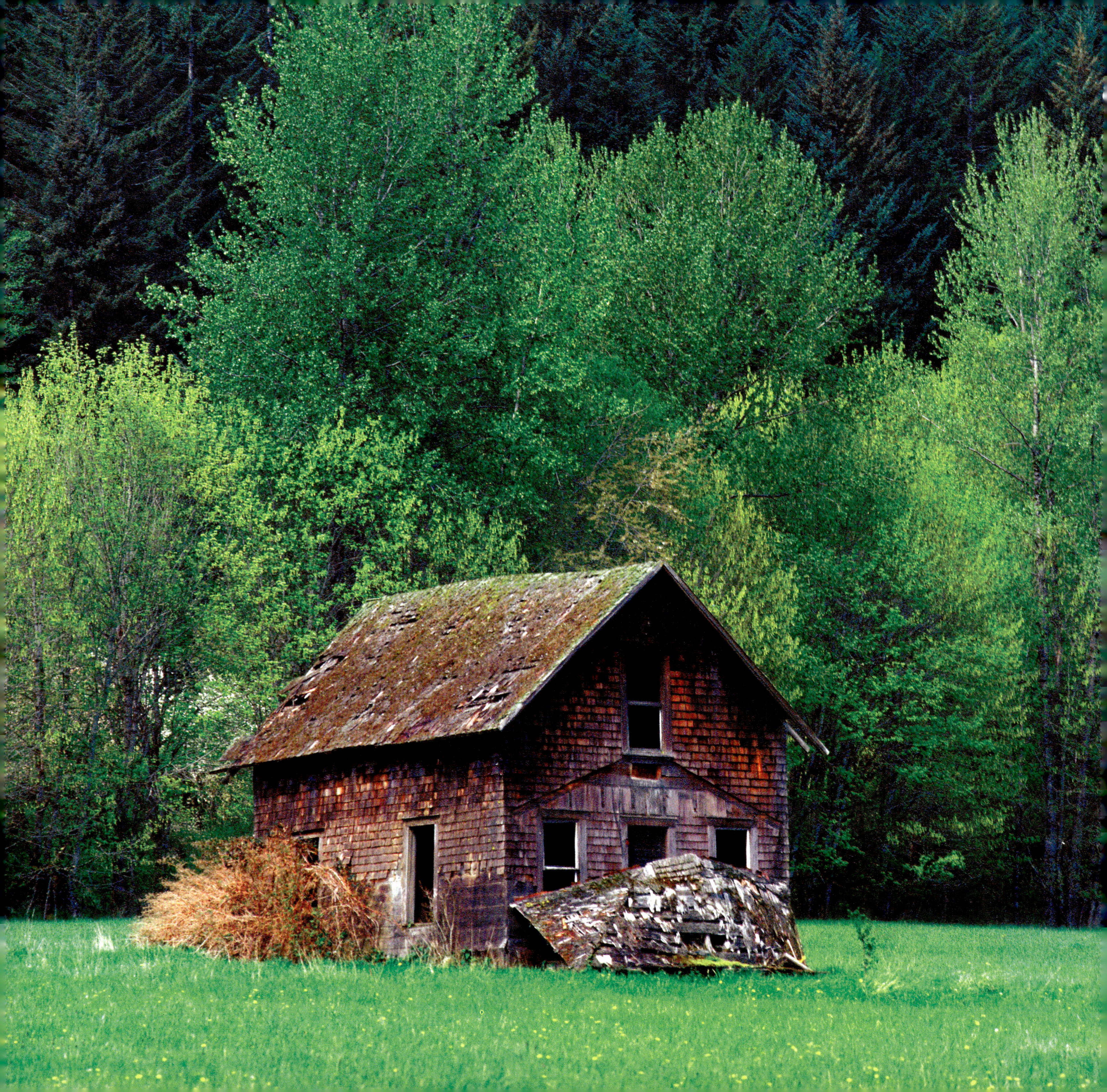

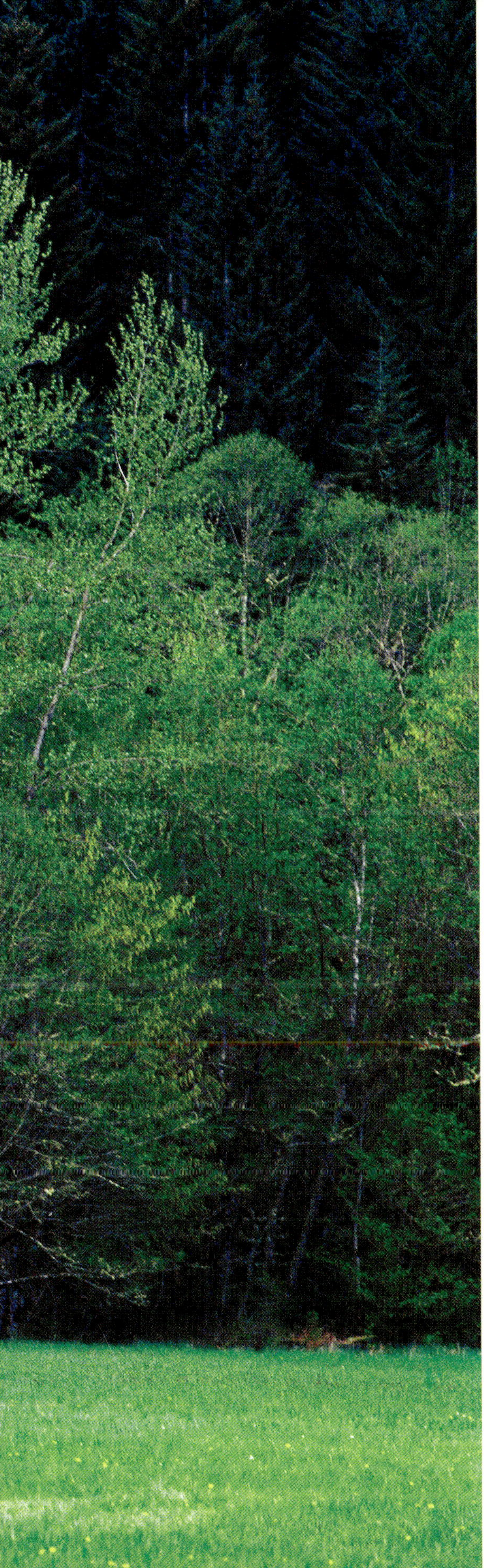

Who once lived there? What were their names? What kind of life did they lead? When did they depart? To where? And why? Every abandoned object poses a mystery whose story line is shaped by the clues left behind...and one's imagination.

Adams County | *Colorado*

The farm seemed like the setting for *The Grapes of Wrath*, John Steinbeck's tale of the Depression-era dust bowl. Summer was still two months away but already the land was parched; it was hard to imagine the wind pump ever drew water.

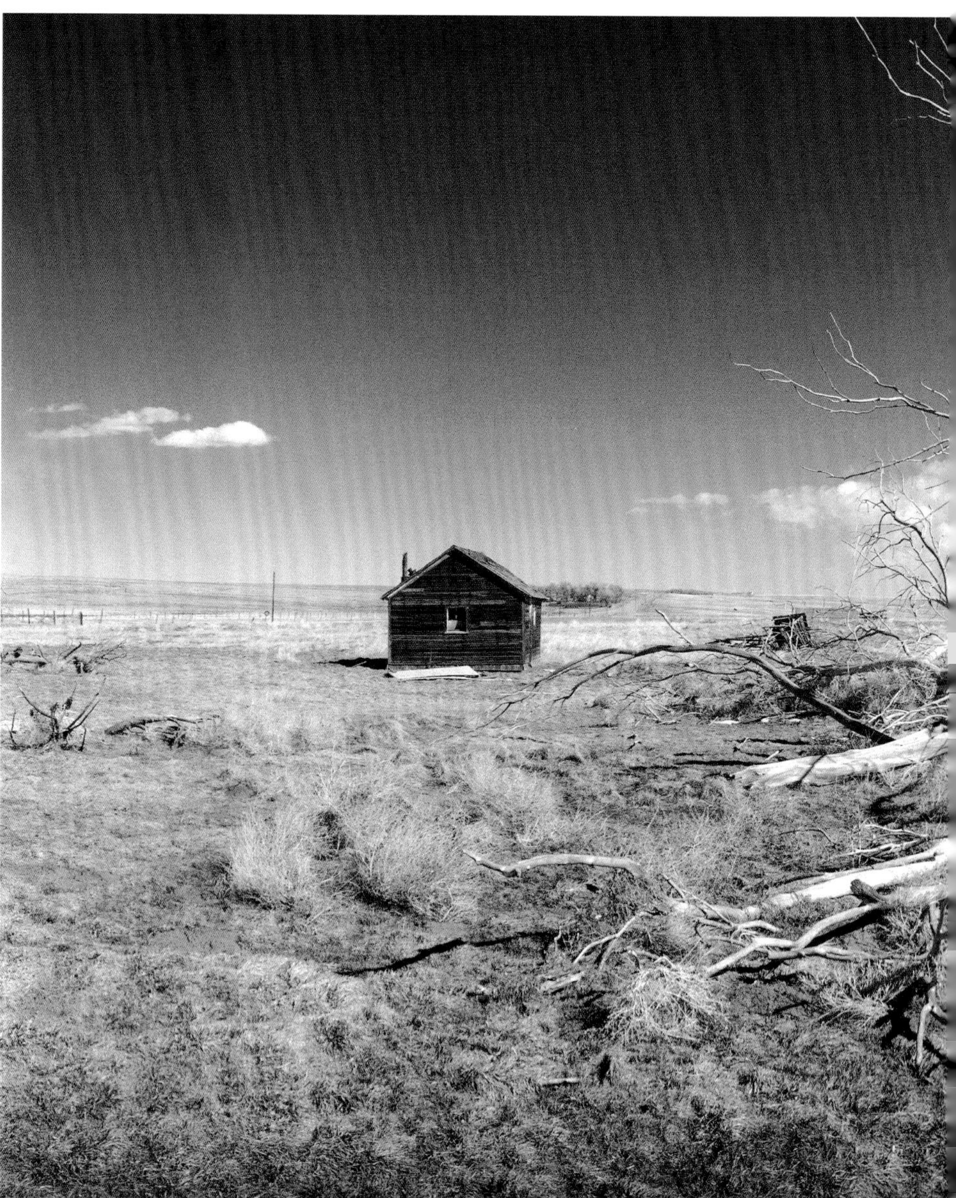

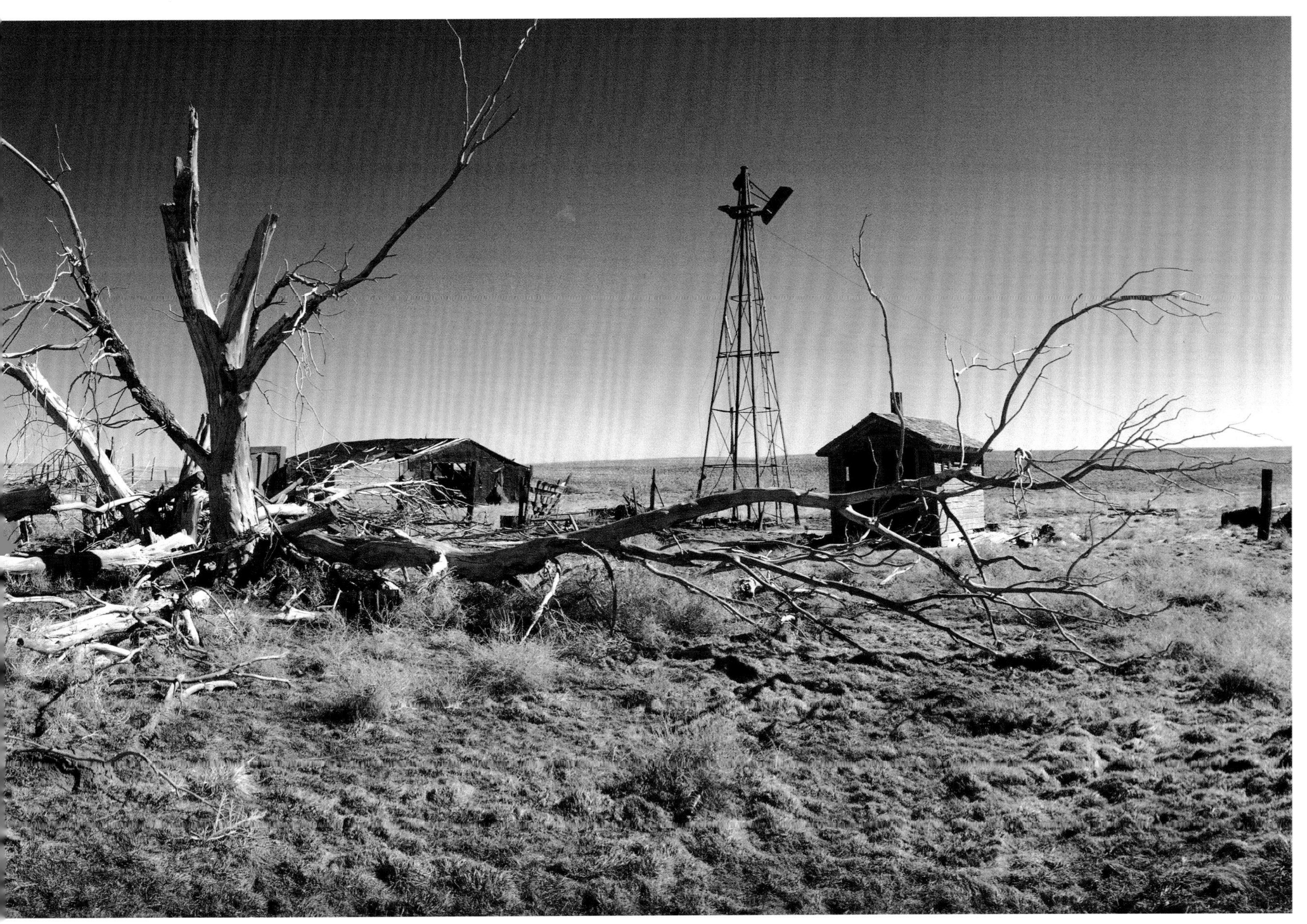

16

Grundy | *Virginia*

In the hills and hollows where Virginia, West Virginia, and Kentucky are nestled together, little villages cluster tightly around steepled churches and babbling brooks, and most coal mines have run their course. It is an exquisitely beautiful land that time—and prosperity—forgot.

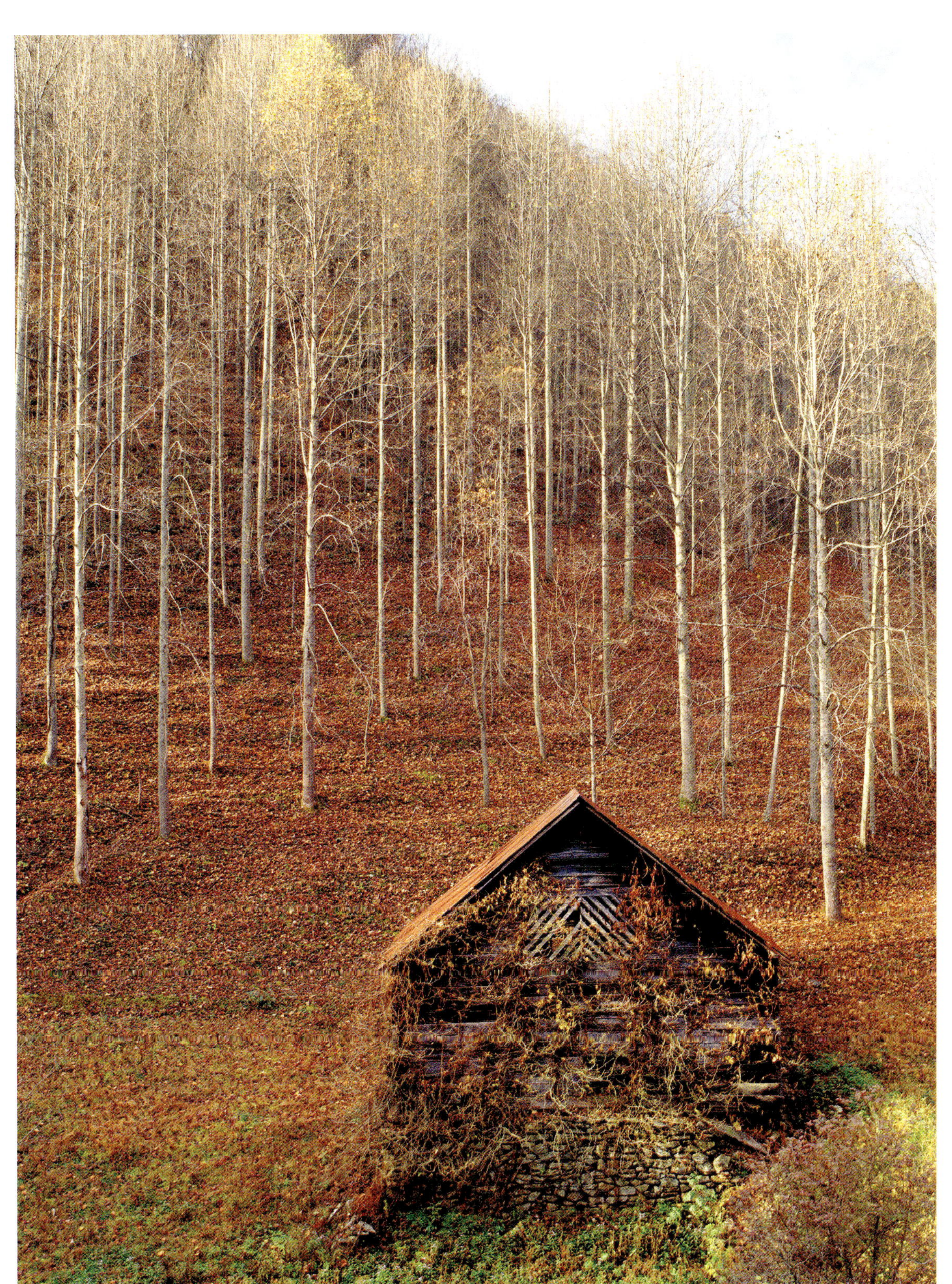

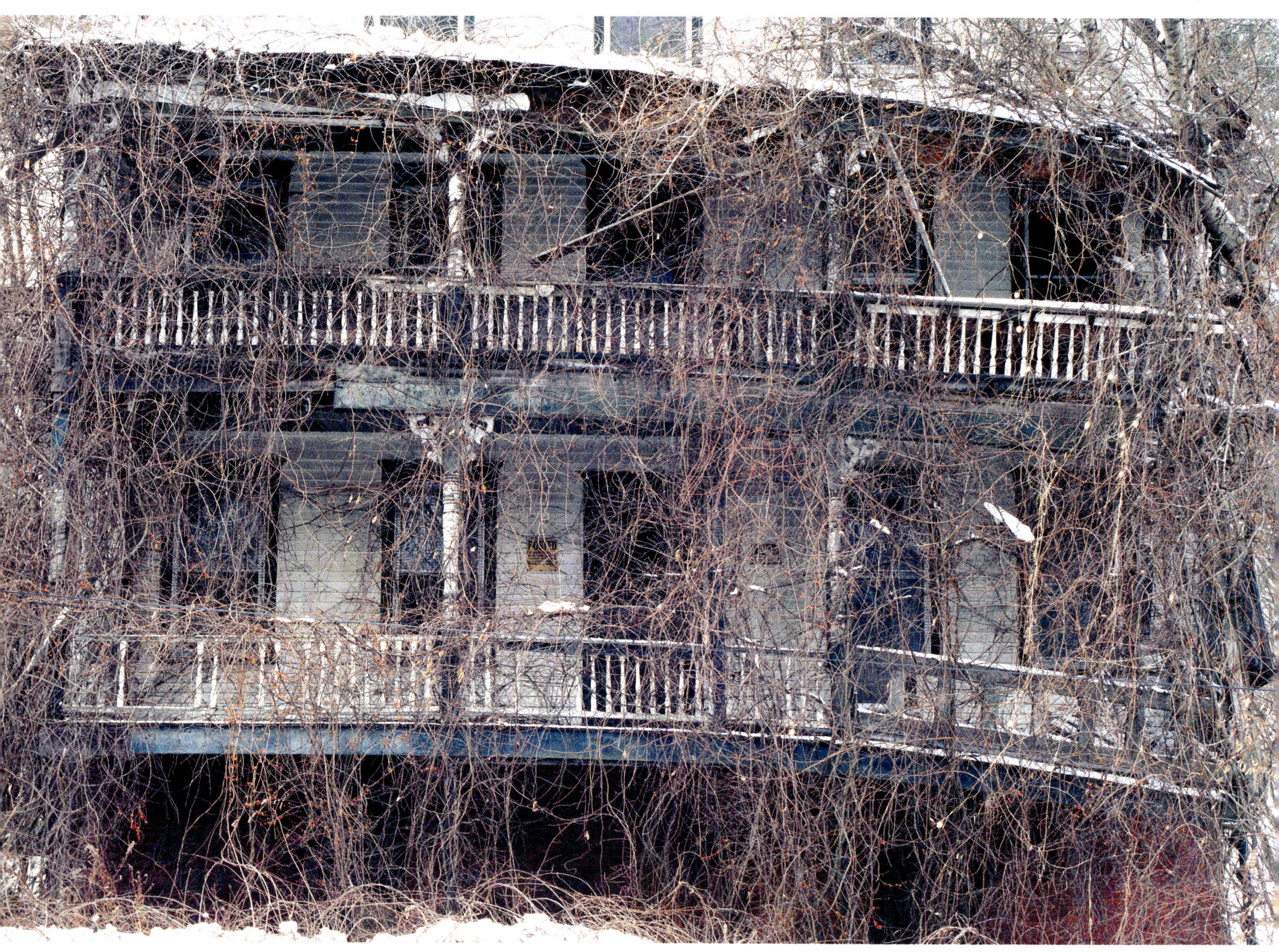

Every state has an abundance of abandoned objects. Except Vermont. After three days of fruitless searching across that state I gave up. And then, just as I was leaving, I spotted this house sitting squarely on the state line with Massachusetts. I've sought to encompass as many states as possible, and so I hereby declare this location to be...Vermont.

Hamilton County | *Kansas*

To a photographer, weathered barn wood with rusty hinges is a hackneyed but still irresistible subject—all the more when a 1927 Henney motor car is stored inside.

"This thing used to be a hearse," the elderly owner told me, "but my father turned it into a pickup truck. There weren't many folks livin' 'round here back then...guess there wasn't much call for a hearse."

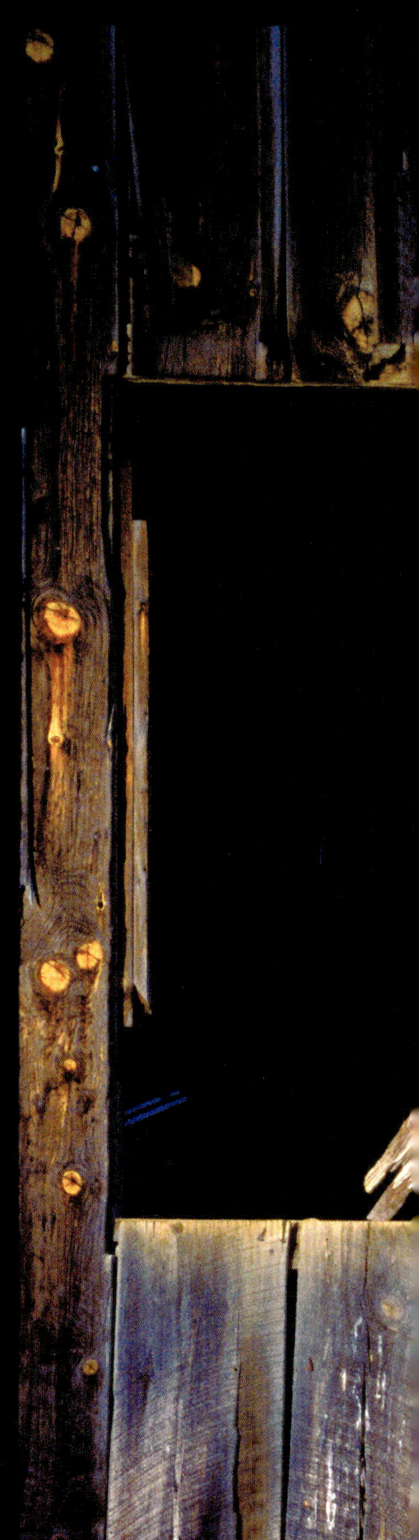

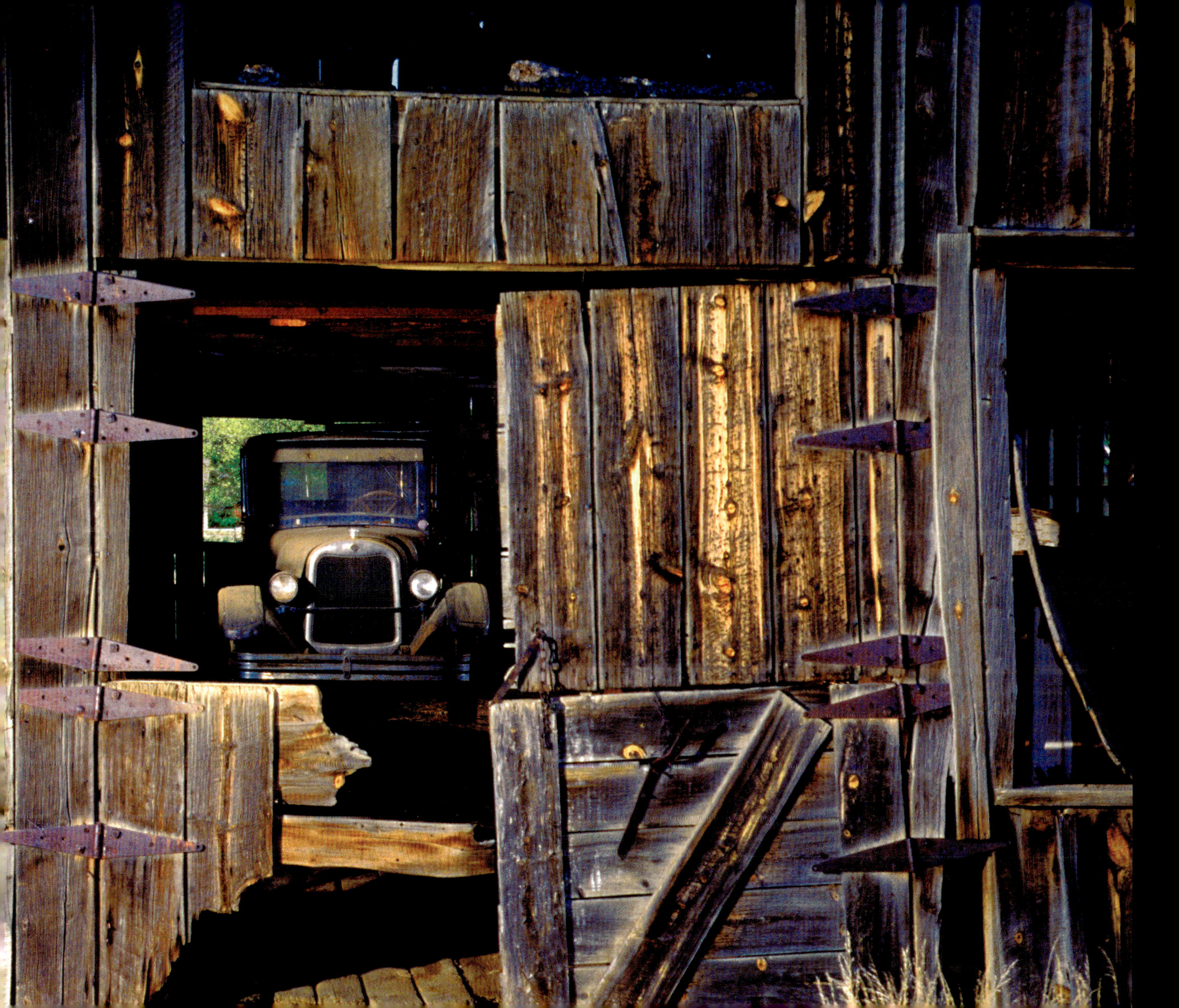

CONNELLY SPRINGS | *North Carolina*

Vernon's farm ceased to function when he became too disabled to work. He sat inside his house, quietly surrounded by teetering barns and equipment sheds built by his father and grandfather. These antiquated structures stood like oversized family gravestones, virtually untouched, except by his cat.

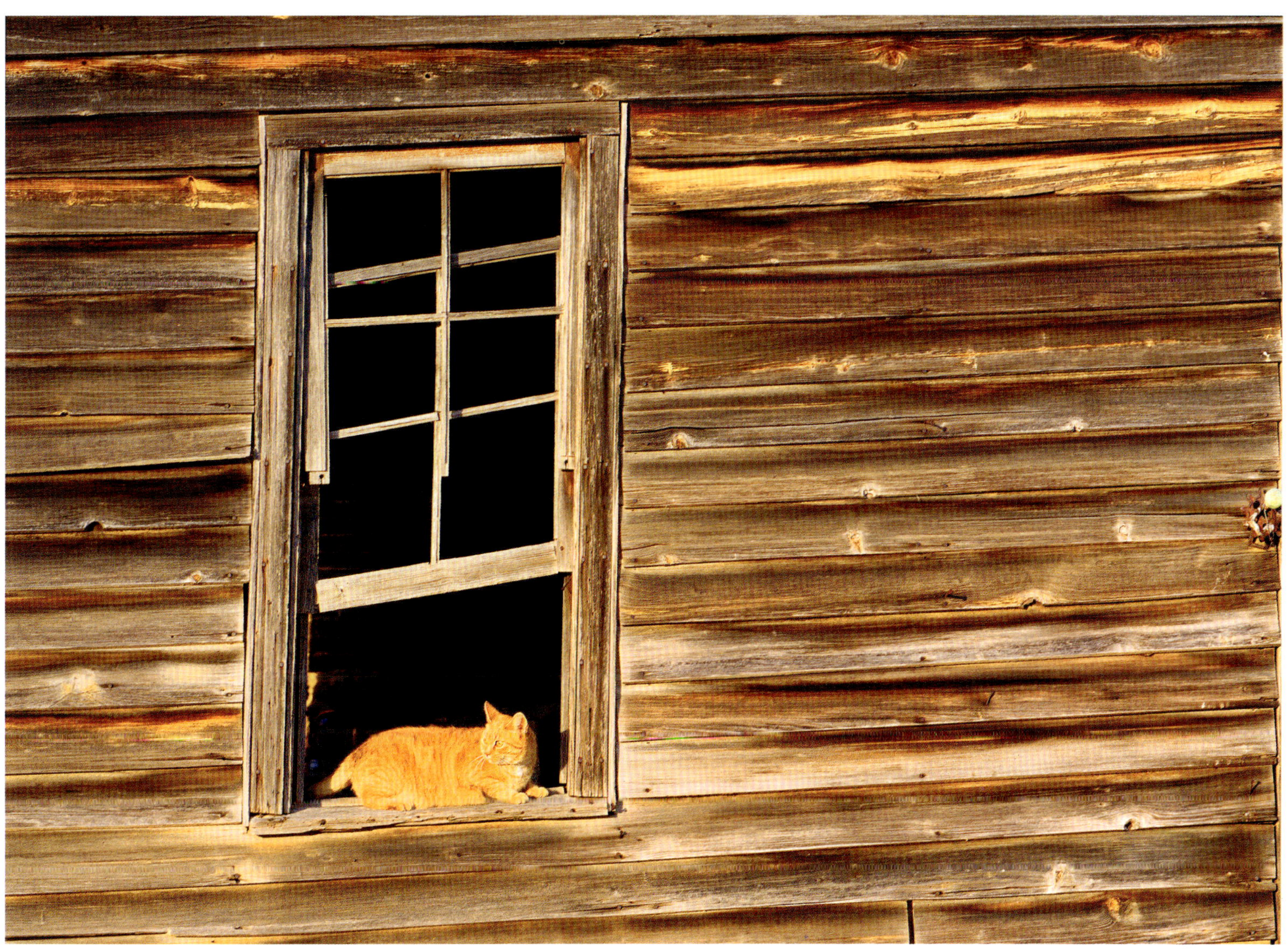

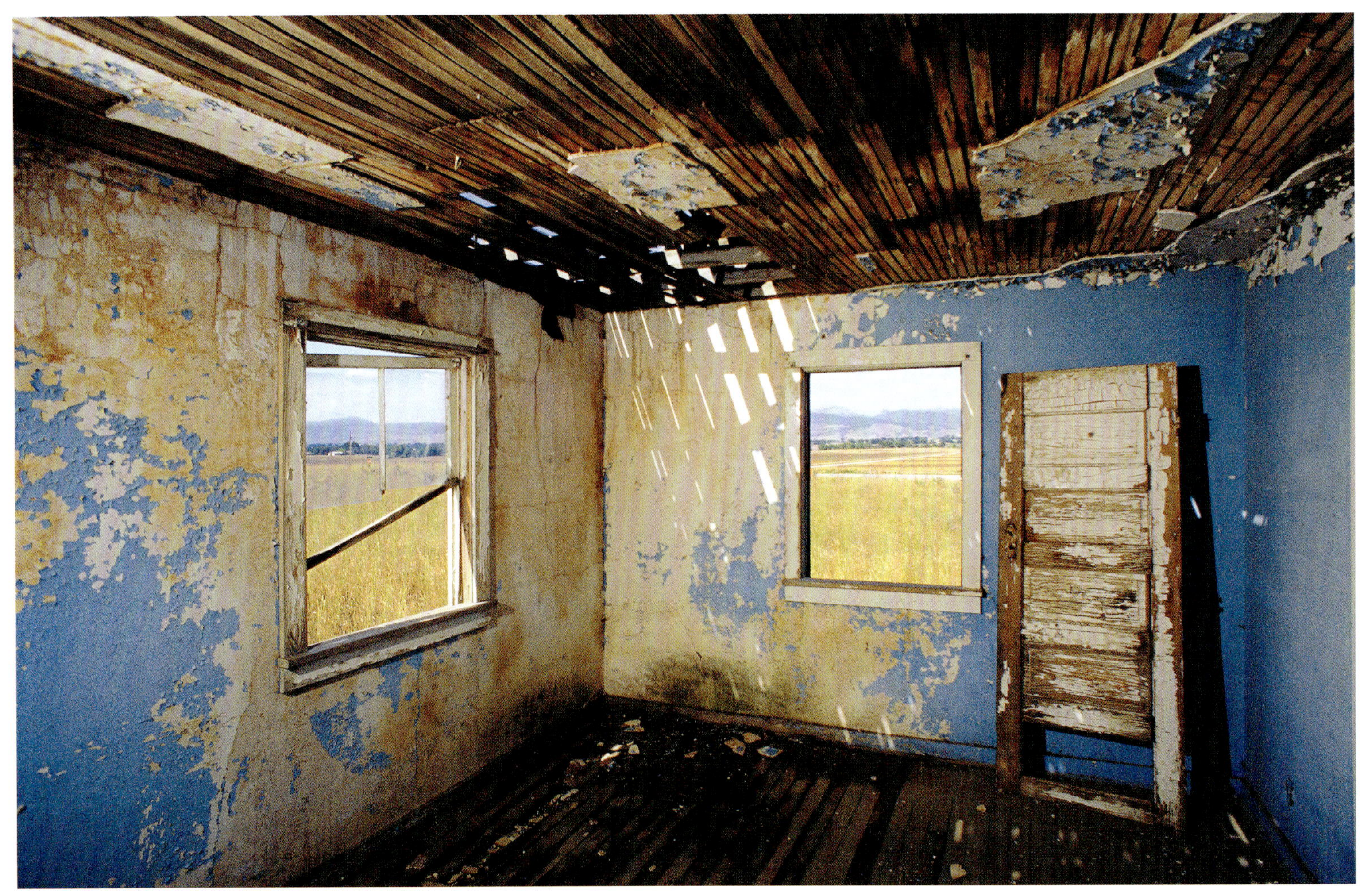

Boulder County | *Colorado*

In this humble shack with the world-class view I searched for clues to the lives that once lived inside. As is often (and mysteriously) the case, everything had been removed—not a bedspring, or faded newspaper, or broken doll, or half-eaten jar of peanut butter—as if someone had attempted to expunge evidence of a crime.

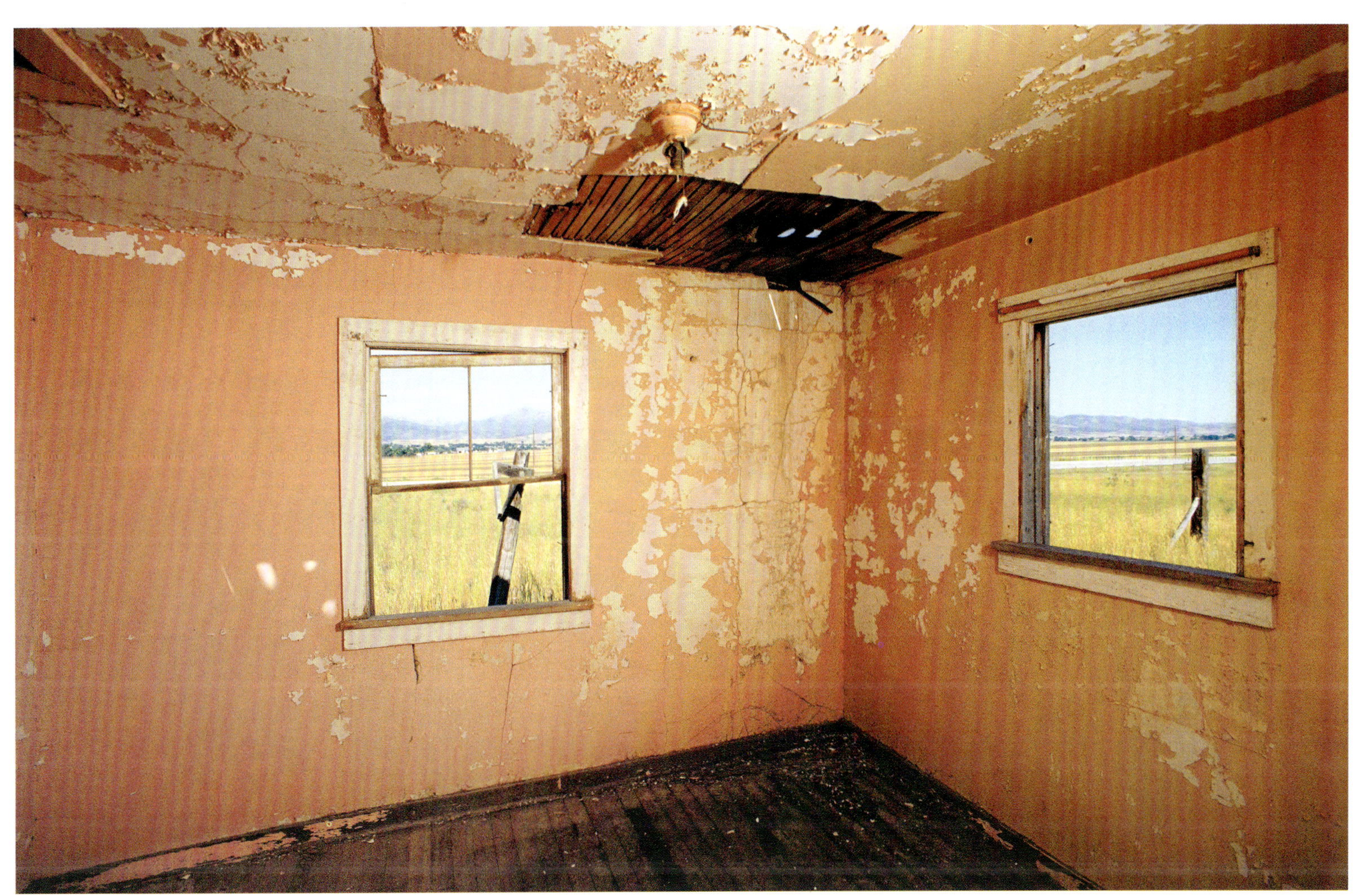

TRIDELPHIA | *West Virginia*

This foyer was scorched by heat but escaped the flames that left much of the house a charred ruin.

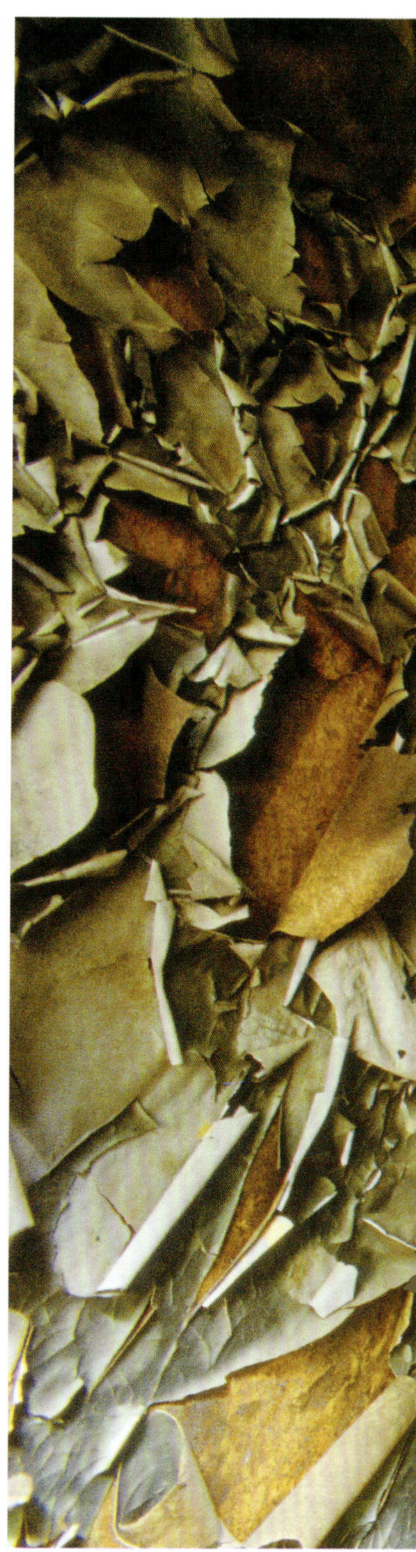

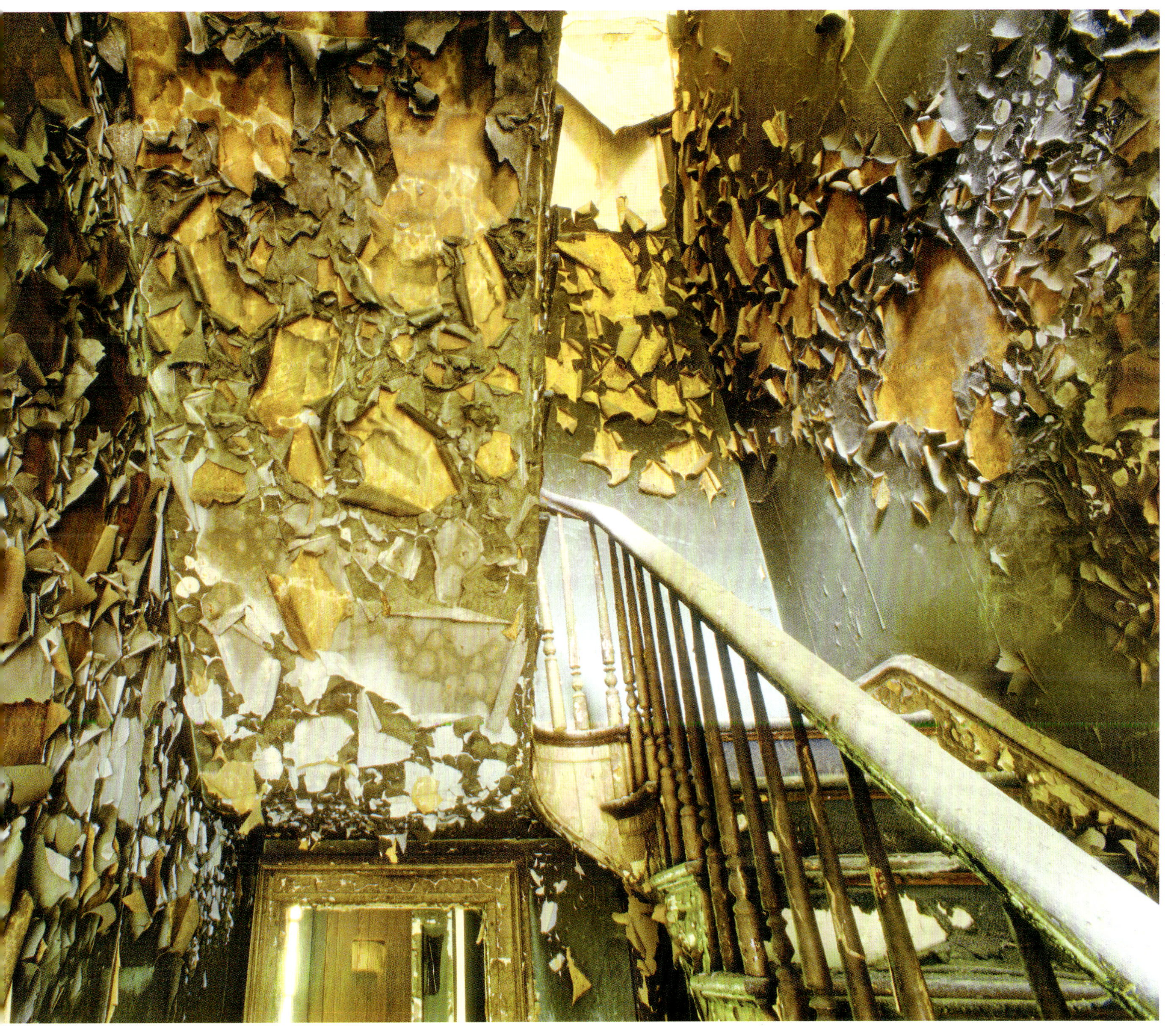

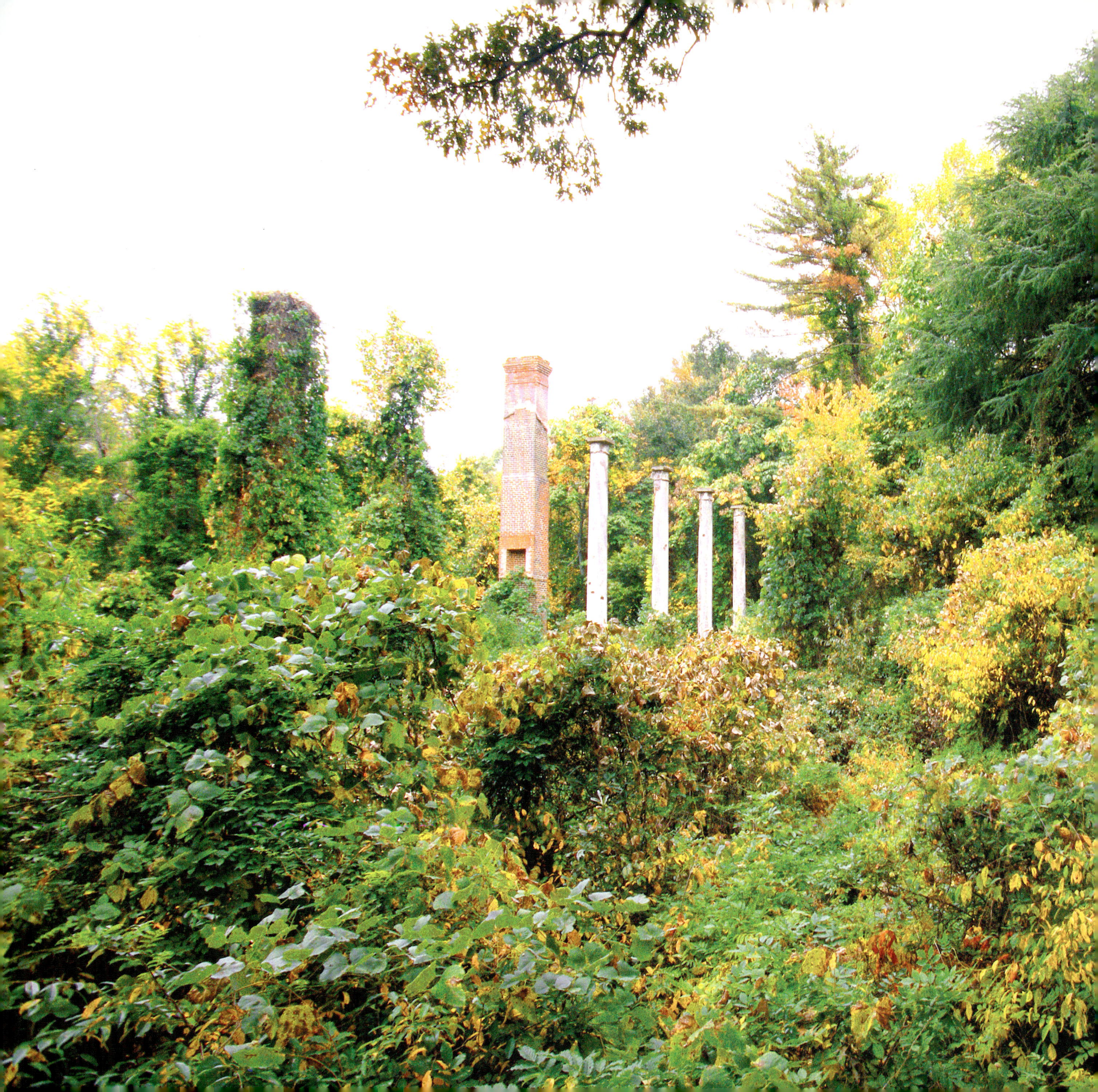

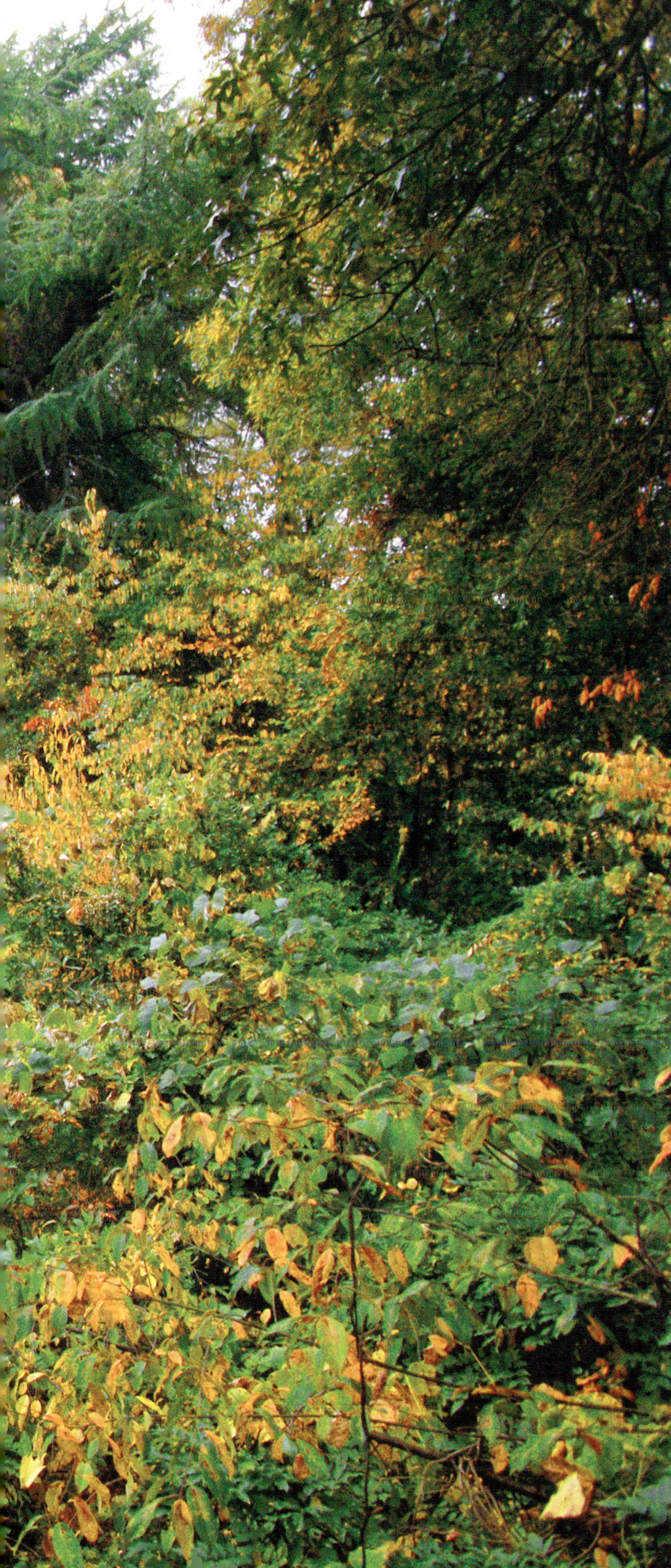

"If you walk into those woods," said the white-haired gentleman gesturing with his hand, "you'll find what's left of a pre-Civil War plantation house where I played when I was a kid, back in the 1920s. If you hack your way under the brush near an ivy-covered chimney you might uncover...

Pendleton | *South Carolina*

...the old slave quarters; you'll see the bars

that kept the slaves locked in at night."

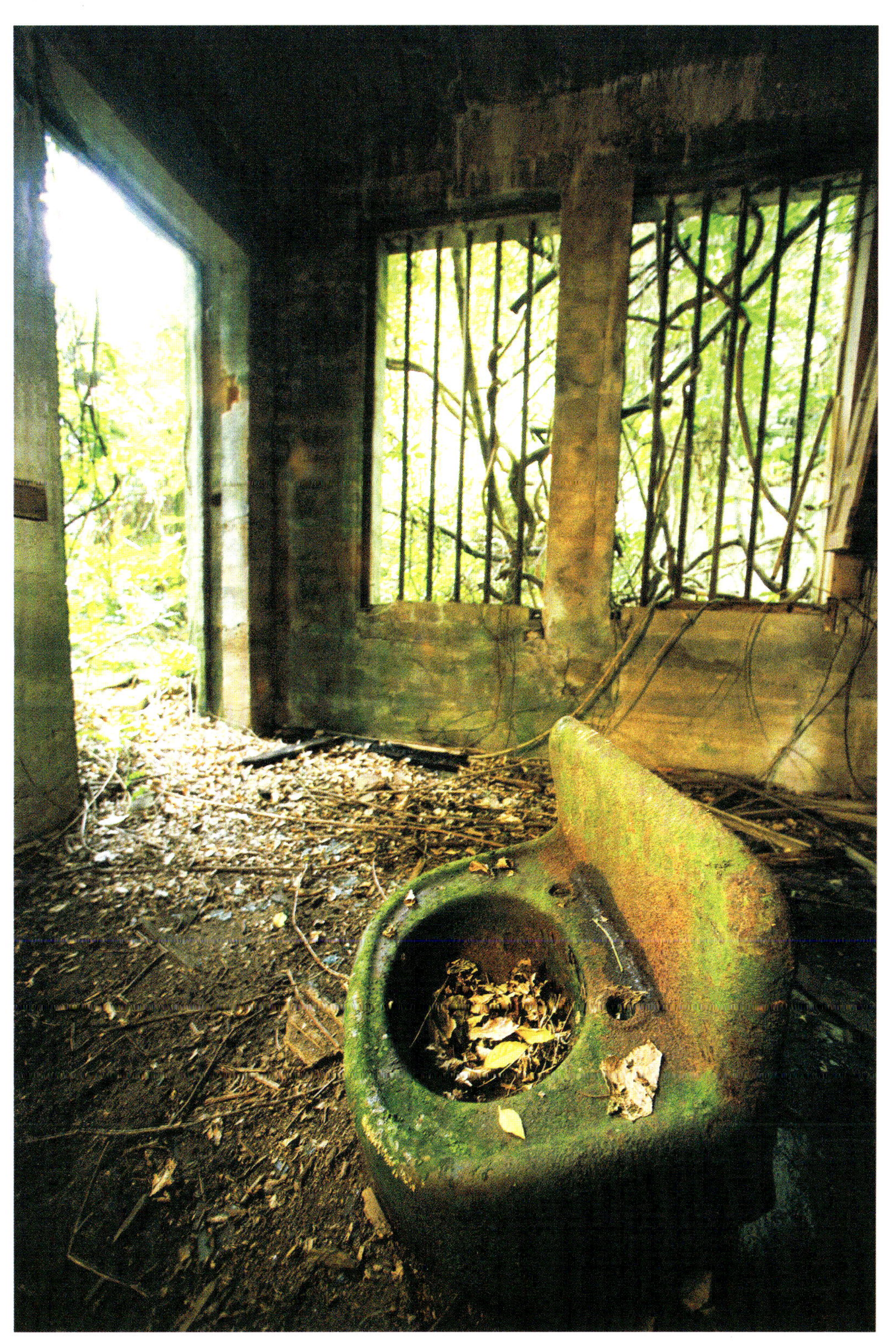

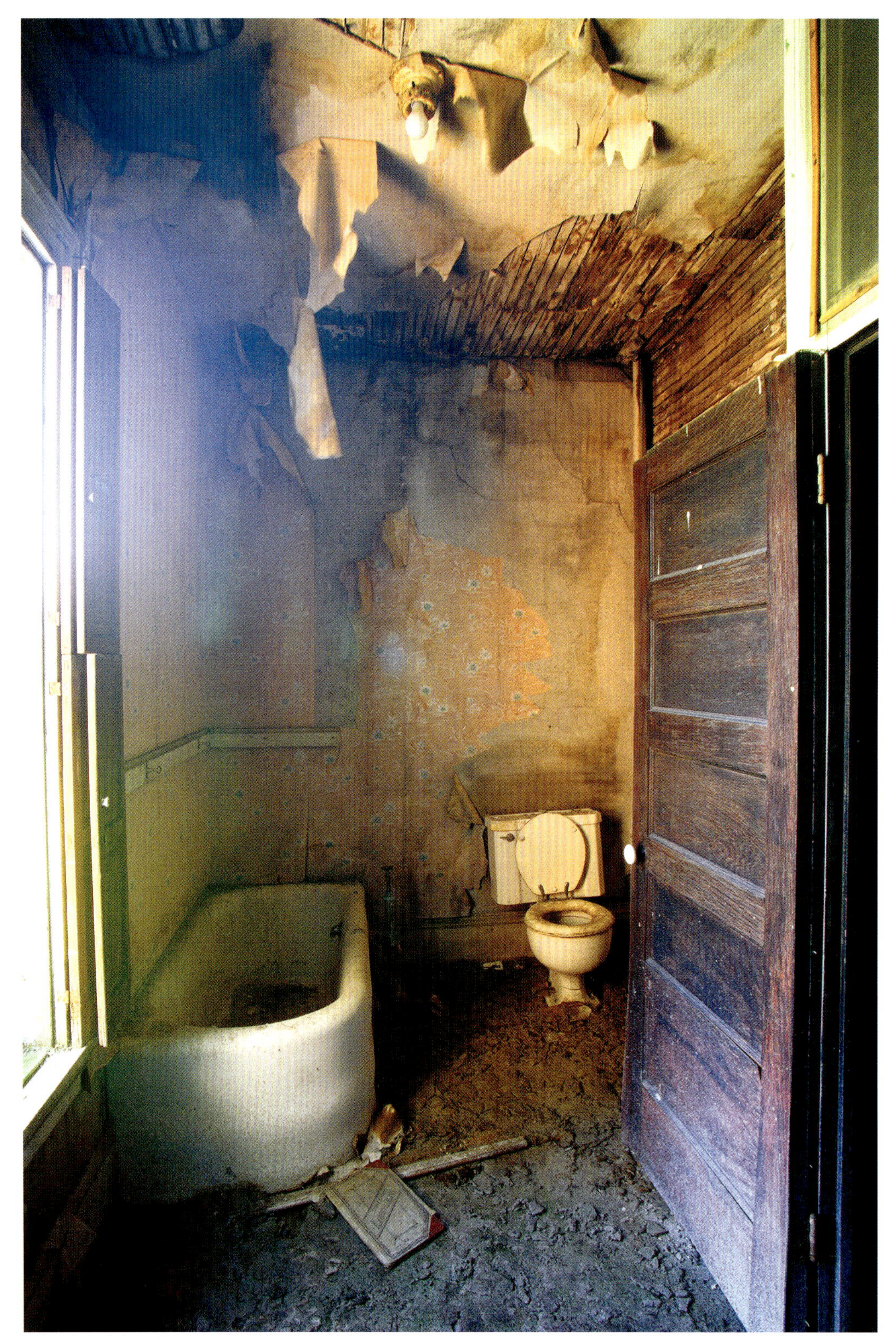

This ordinary toilet and bathtub, rising out of the coagulated dust of decades, were located in a majestic house with wide hallways, sweeping staircases, ornate banisters, and spacious rooms. One could lounge in the tub while soaking up a breathtaking view of the Allegheny Mountains.

34

BODIE | *California*

In a remote reach of the Sierra Nevada Mountains lies the lovingly preserved ghost town of Bodie. In 1876, during the height of the mining boom when Bodie had 2,000 residents, it boasted 56 saloons and gambling joints and one killing a day.

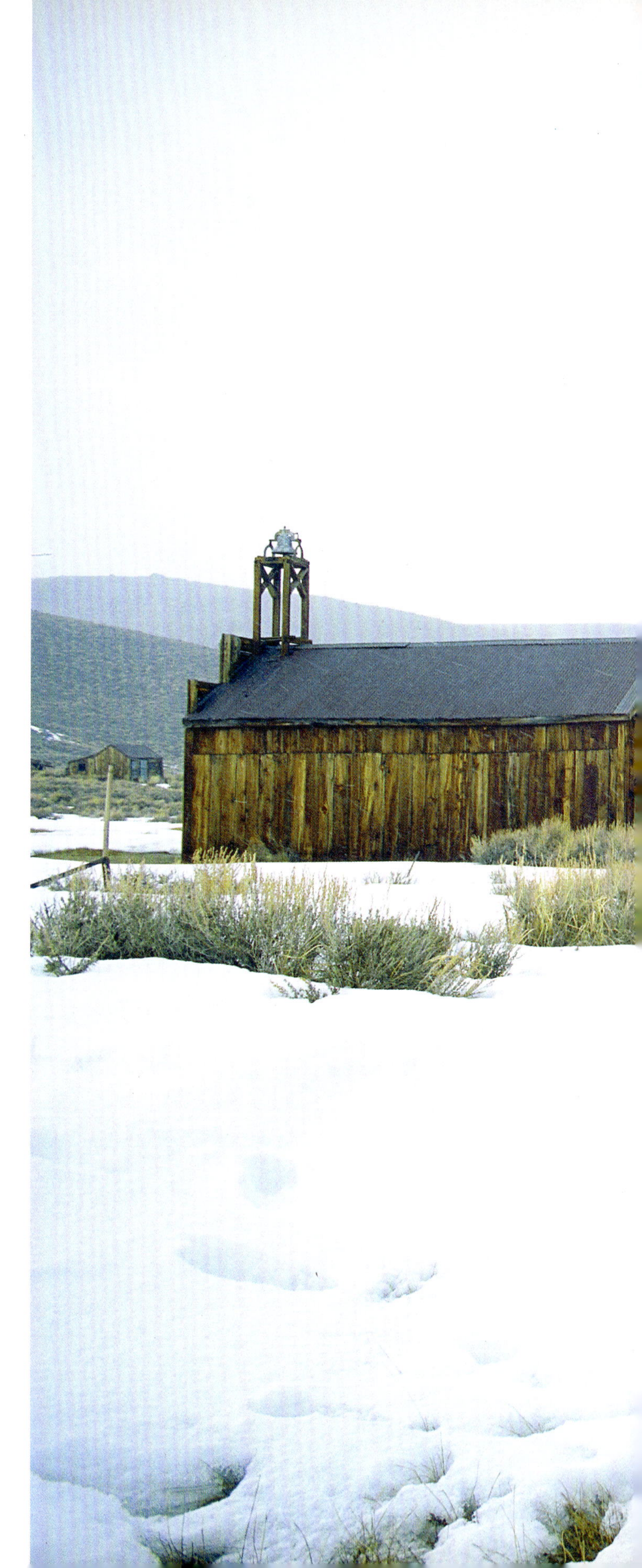

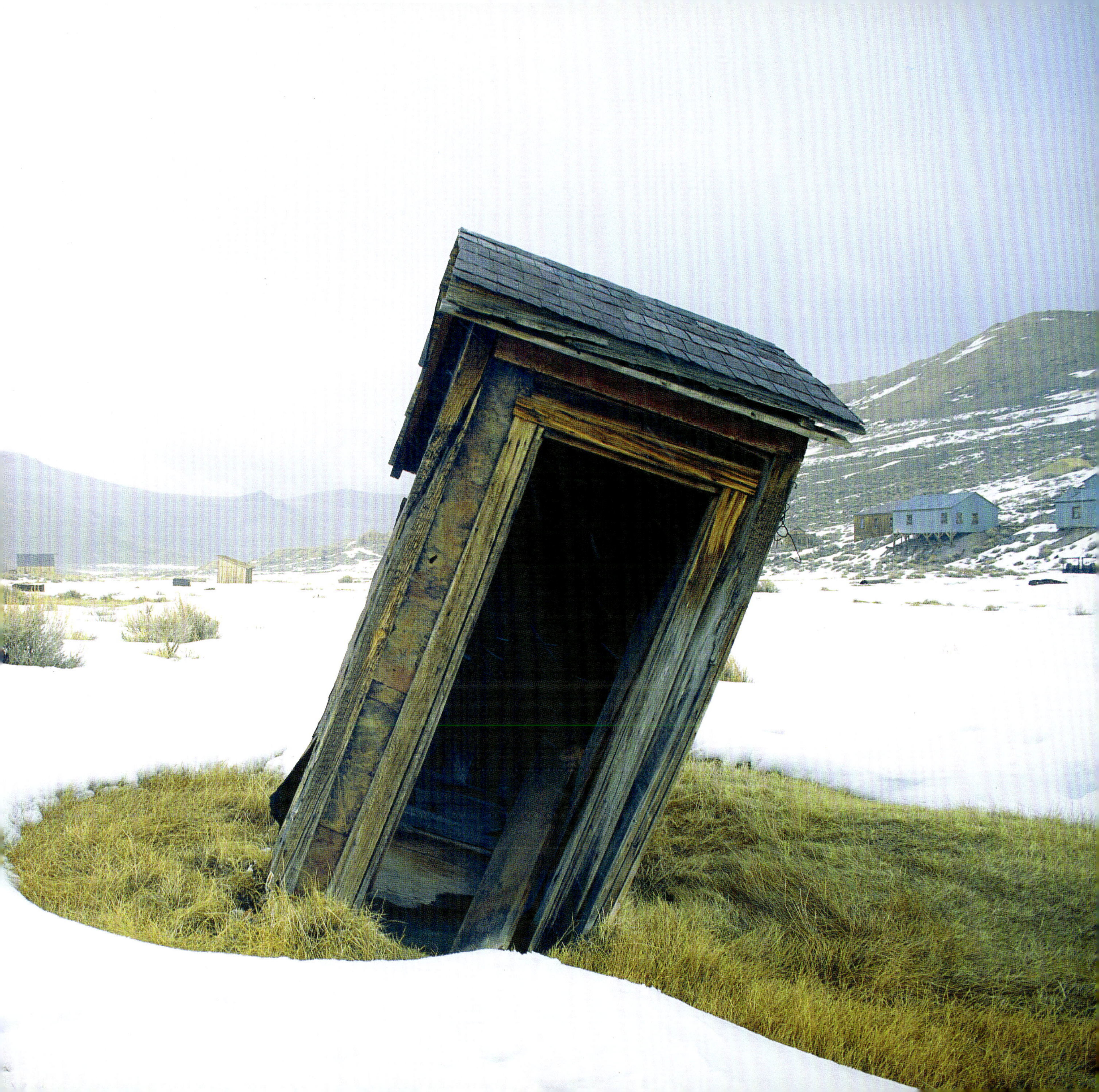

SILVER PLUME | *Colorado*

Then: eggs frying, a pie in the oven, biscuits in the designated "warming closet," and heat from the wood stove filling the cozy mountain house. *Now:* broken chairs, a handleless saw, torn wallpaper, and snow blown in through unhinged doors and shattered windows.

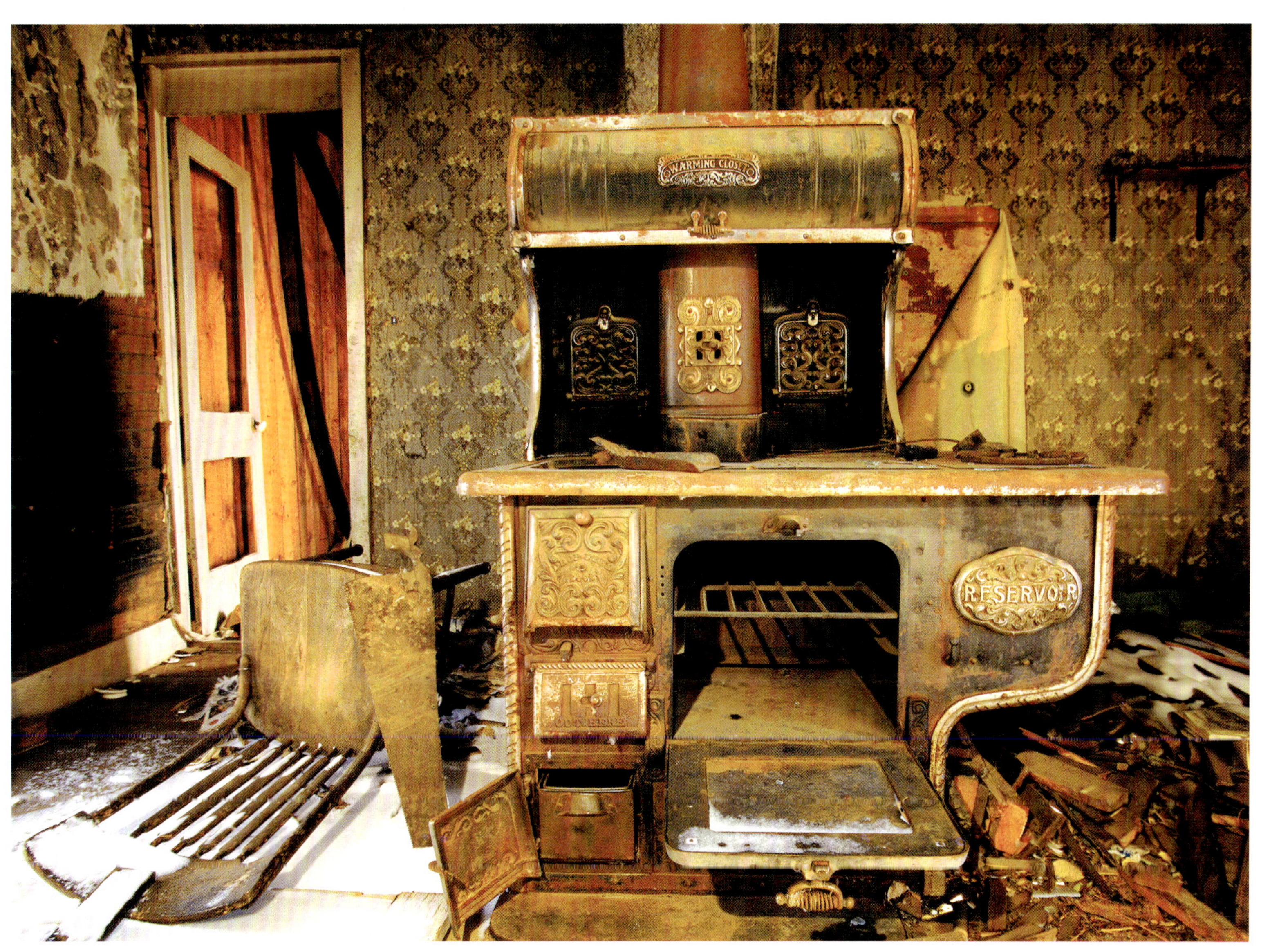
WARMING CLOSET
RESERVOIR

PACKWOOD | *Washington*

Through the moldy, cobwebbed windows of this gingerbread house I could see someone's belongings, long abandoned. The rusted lock could have been snapped with a light kick, and I was tempted, but a board and a branch had been propped against the door to reinforce the lock's message to "Keep Out."

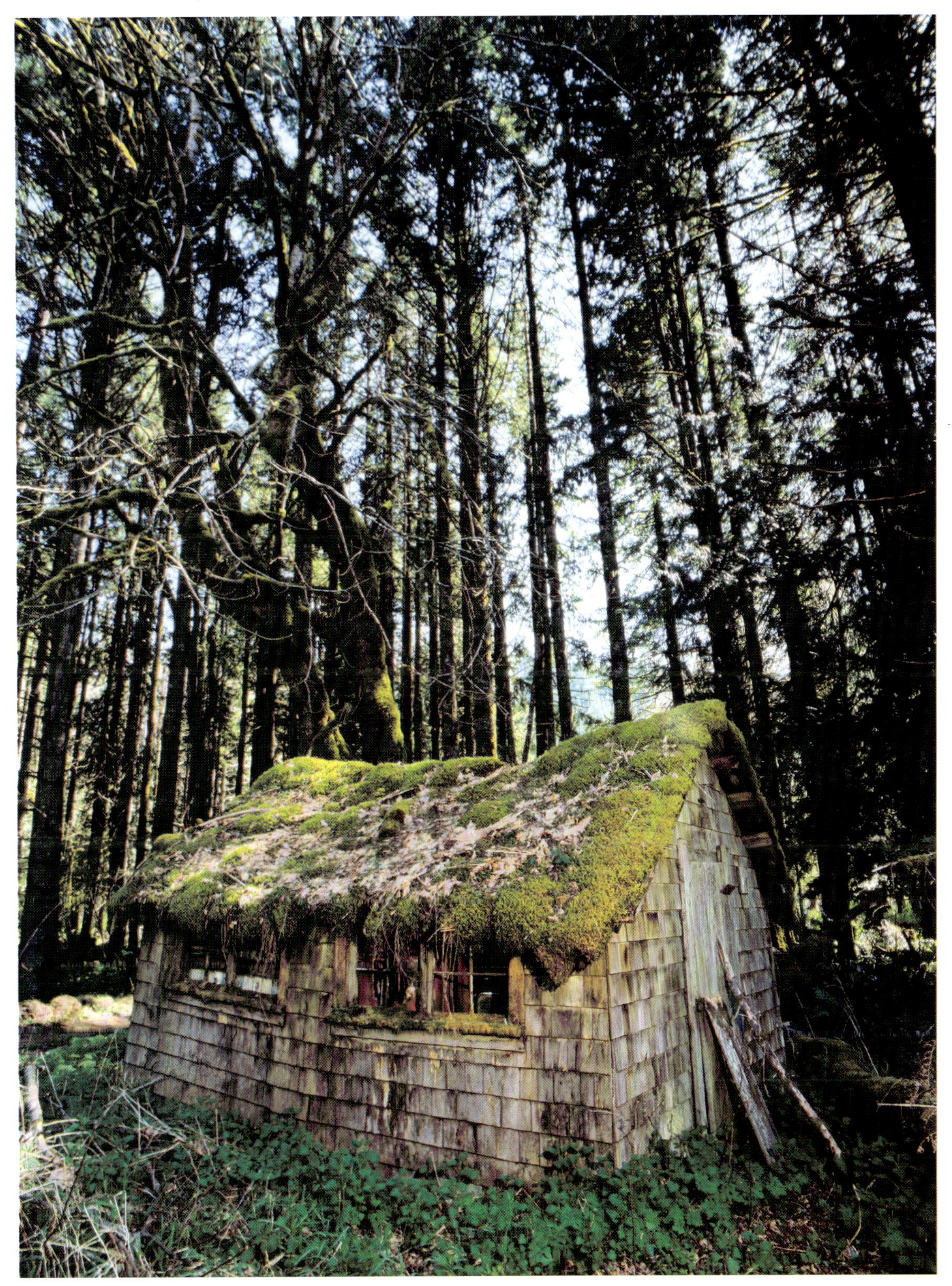

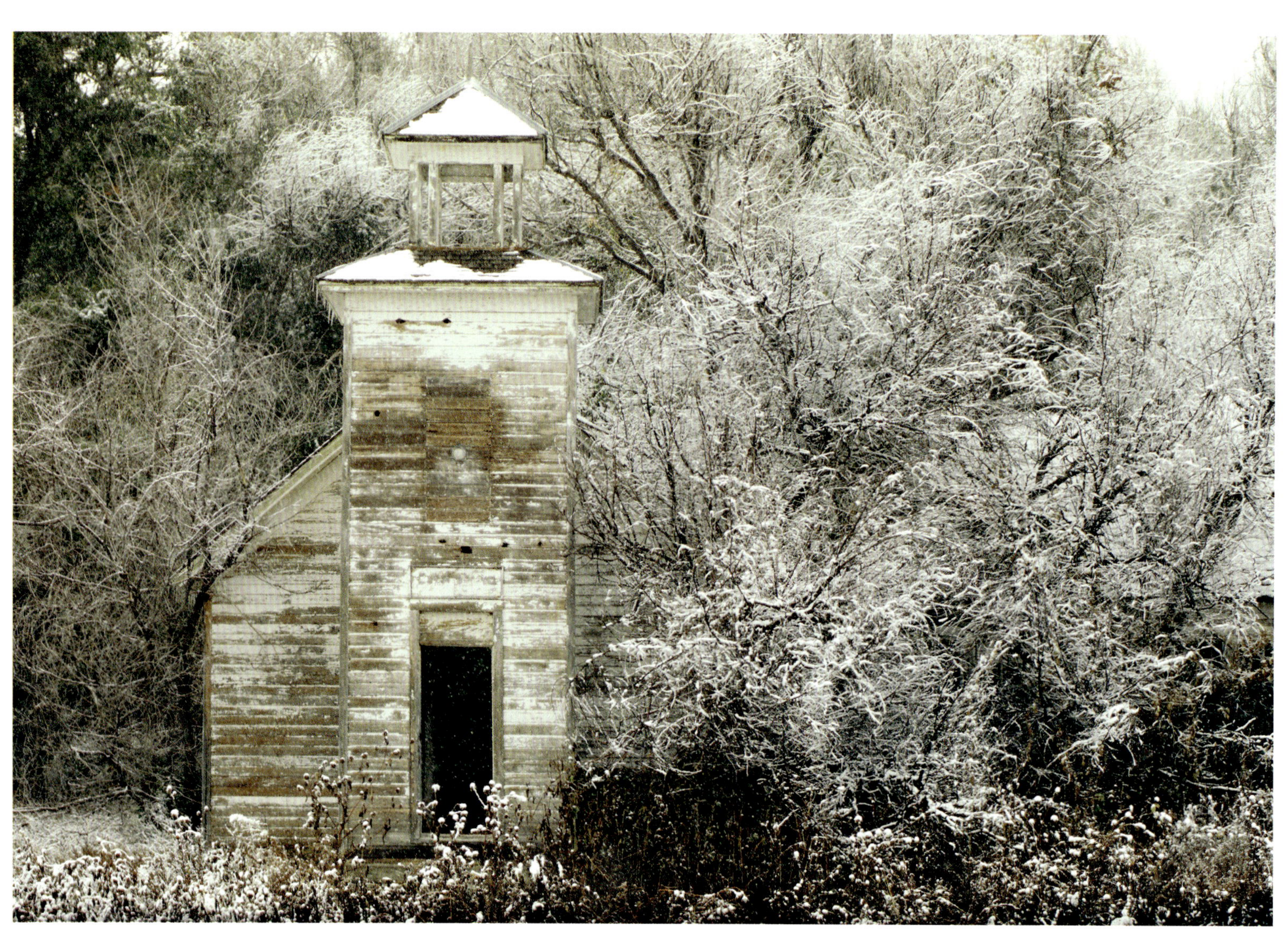

Had it been a house of worship or a schoolhouse? Would I find evidence inside of children or parishioners? The front door was invitingly open, but it was so bitterly cold out that I skipped my customary up-close inspection and promptly retreated to the heat of my car.

42

Wupatki National Monument | *Arizona*

An hour after sunset, a full moon lit the brick remains of this Anasazi Indian dwelling. This structure, and others like it throughout the Southwest, are silent but powerful testimonials to the advanced culture of builders that vanished without a trace over 600 years ago.

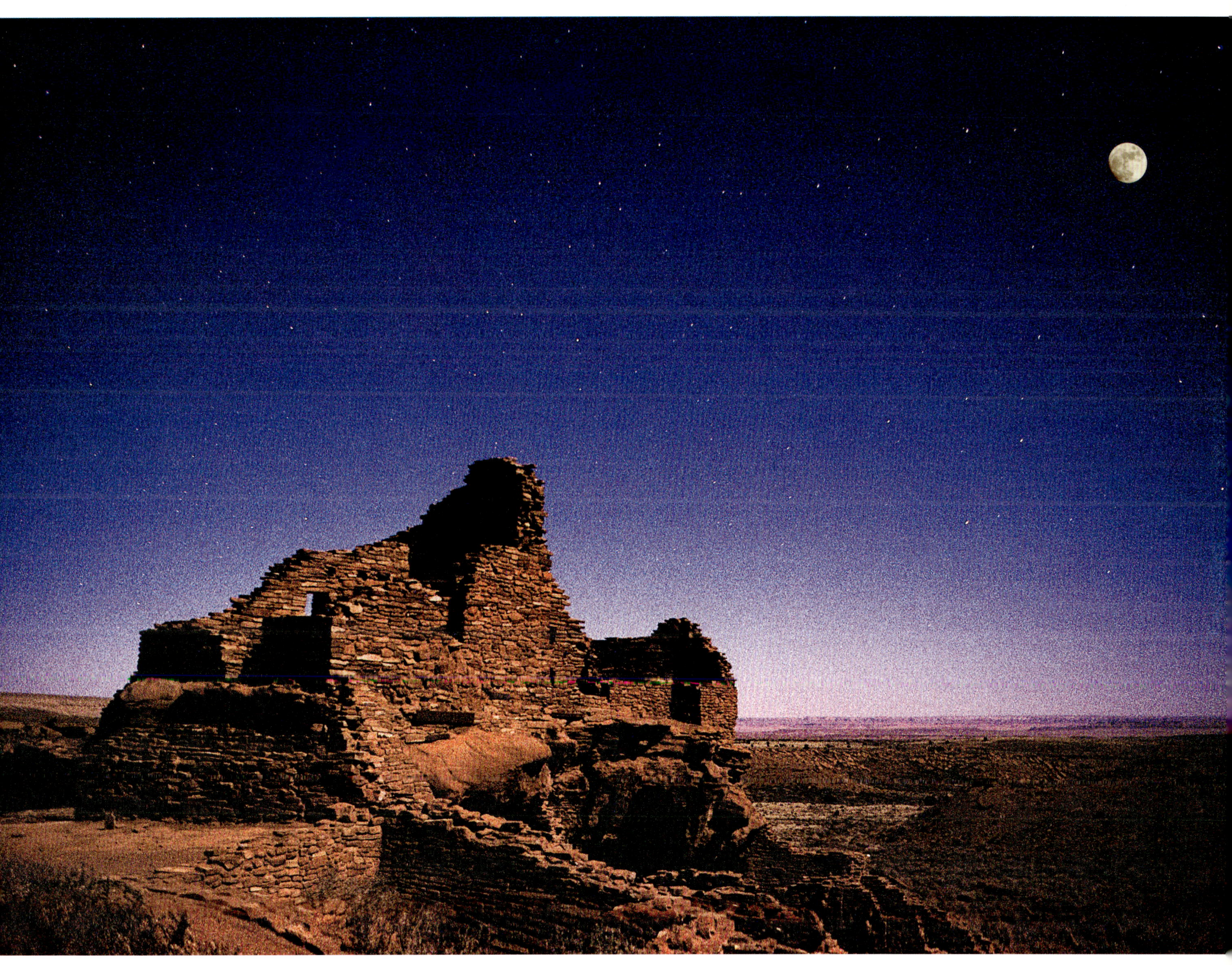

Factories & Equipment

Atlanta | *Georgia*

This view of a cotton mill destroyed by fire bears an eerie resemblance to images taken by Civil War photographer George Barnard. During the last year of the war, Barnard documented the unprecedented devastation resulting from General Sherman's march to the sea, during which the Union Army swept through Atlanta, perhaps passing by this very spot.

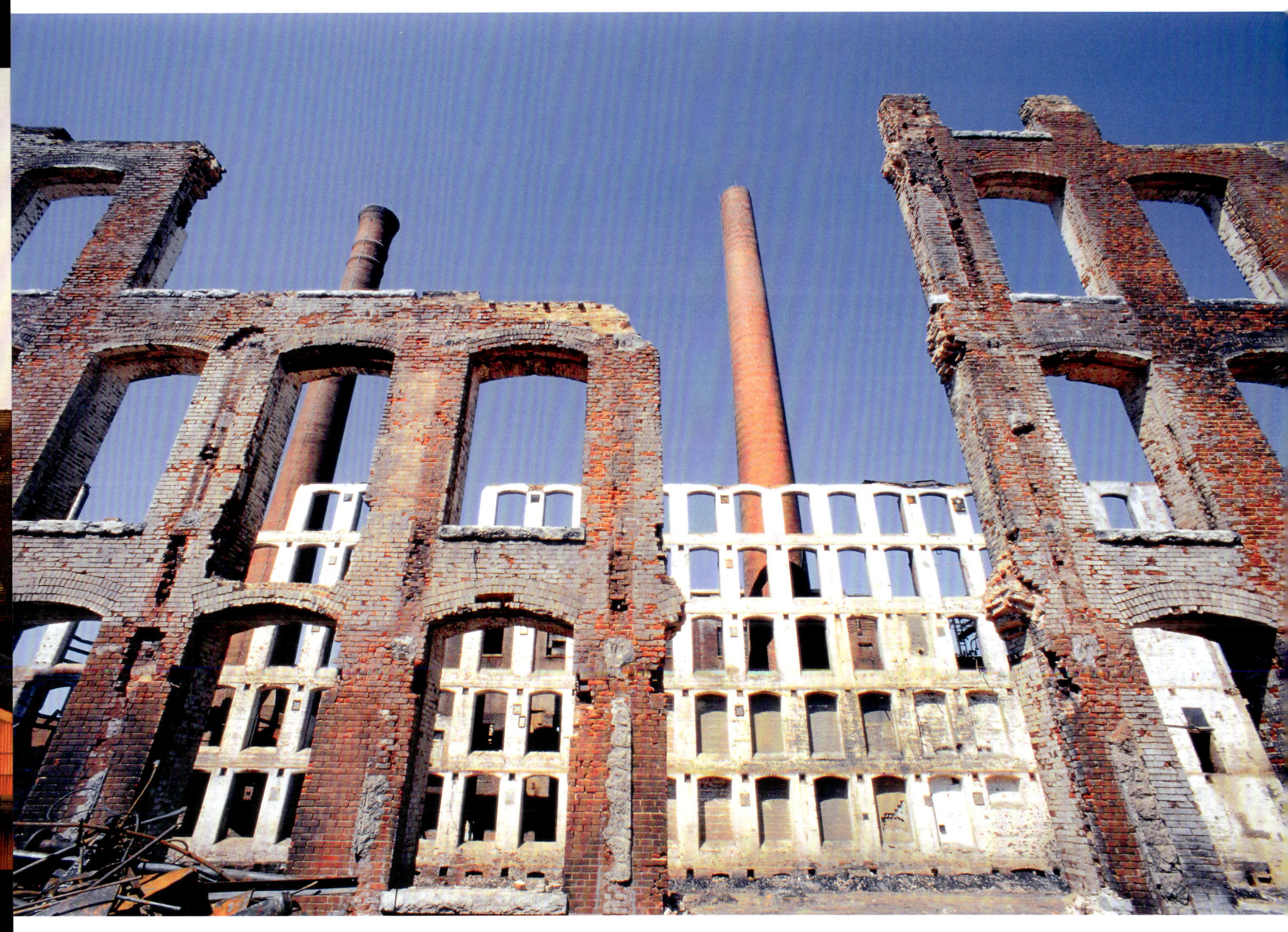

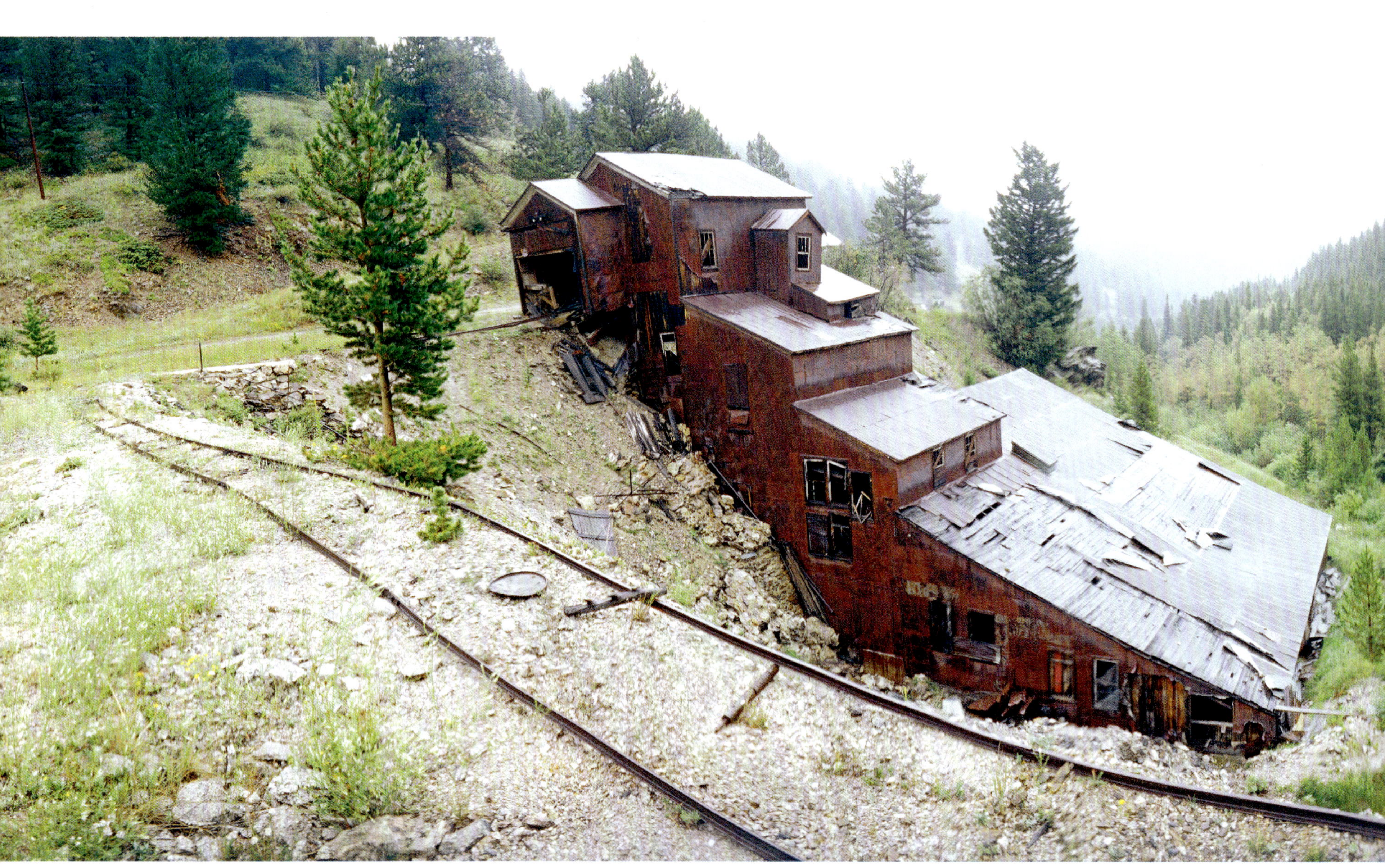

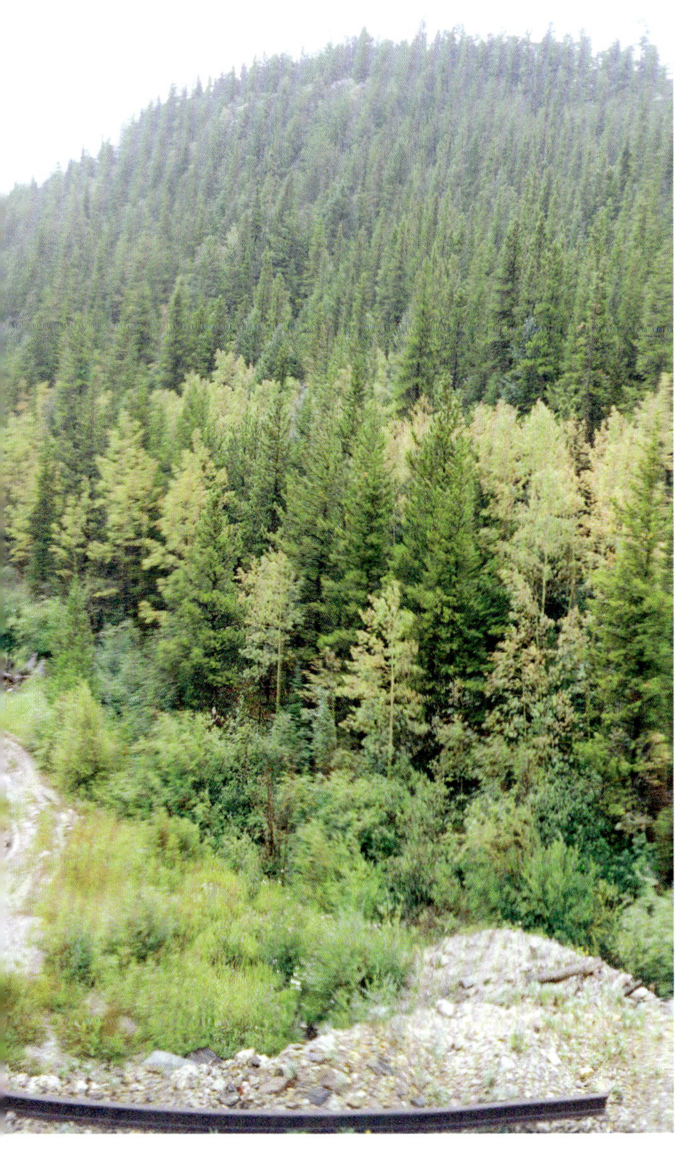

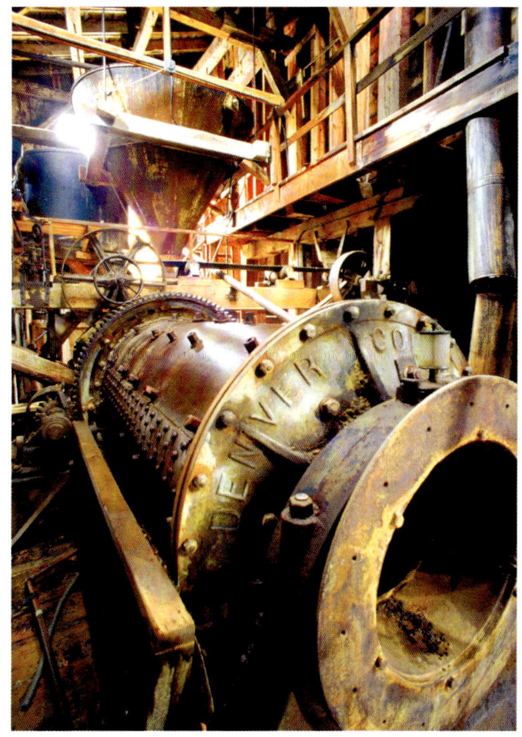

Caribou | *Colorado*

"Between the harsh climate and the invasion of summer residents, the old silver, gold, and tungsten mines and mills in this area have been decimated," complained Dan Martin, who serves as historian and loving caretaker of much of what still remains. "This mill saw action from 1905 to 1945. The huge cylinder pulverized silver ore; the funnel back there...

Caribou | *Colorado*

"...was where chemicals helped extract silver from the ore.

The rust color and texture is the chemical residue from the process."

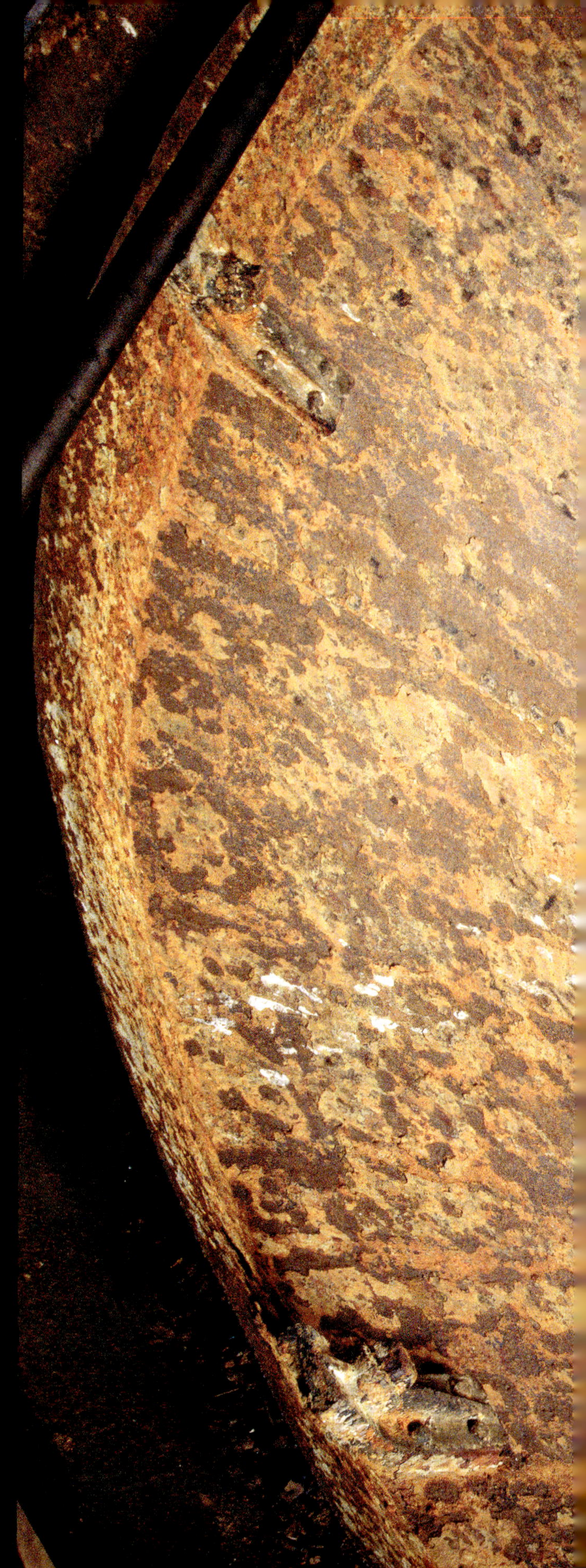

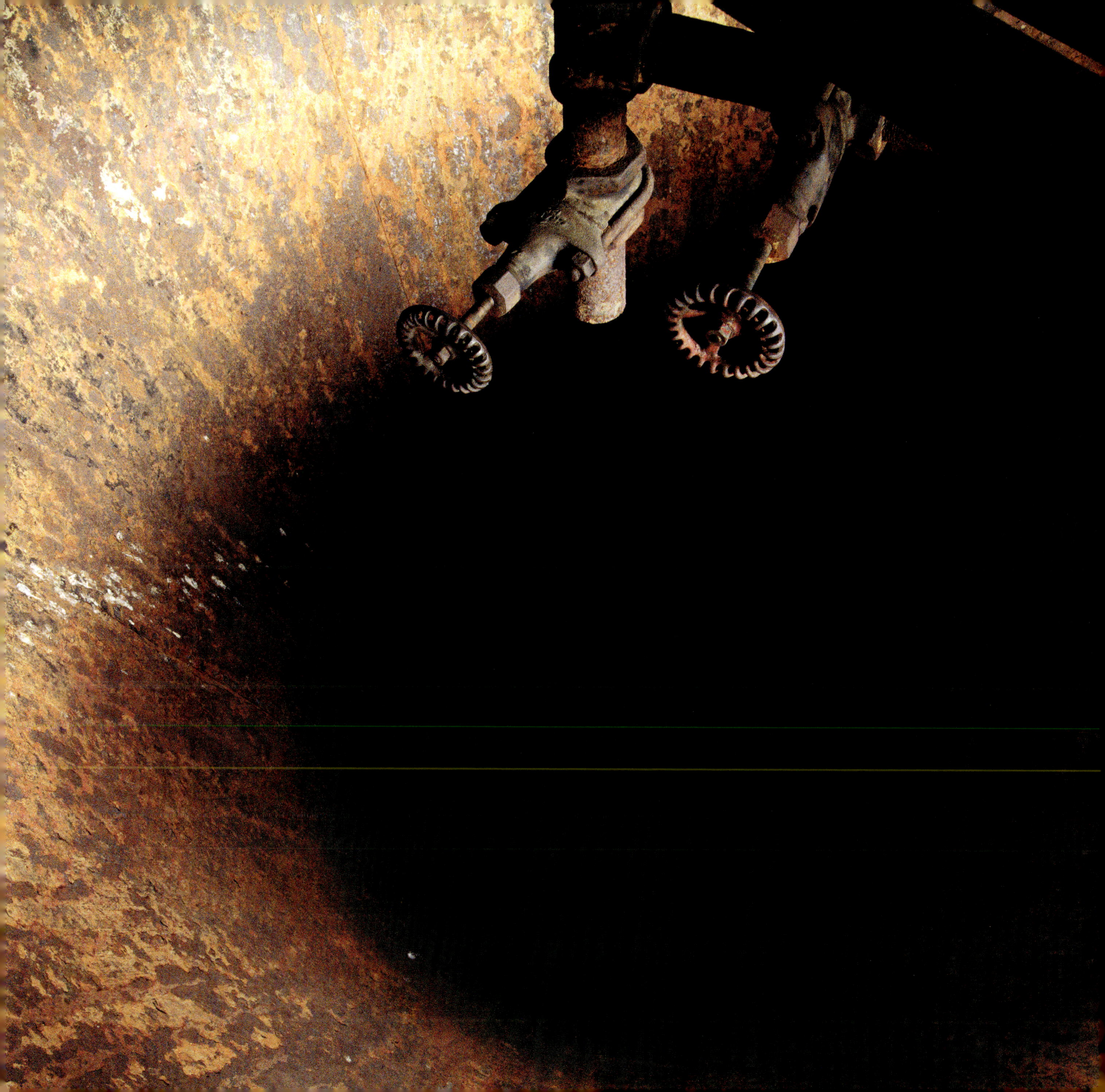

Eight-foot-long grooved cylinders with greased gears at both ends were once used to spin large conveyor belts that transported coal through the mining process.

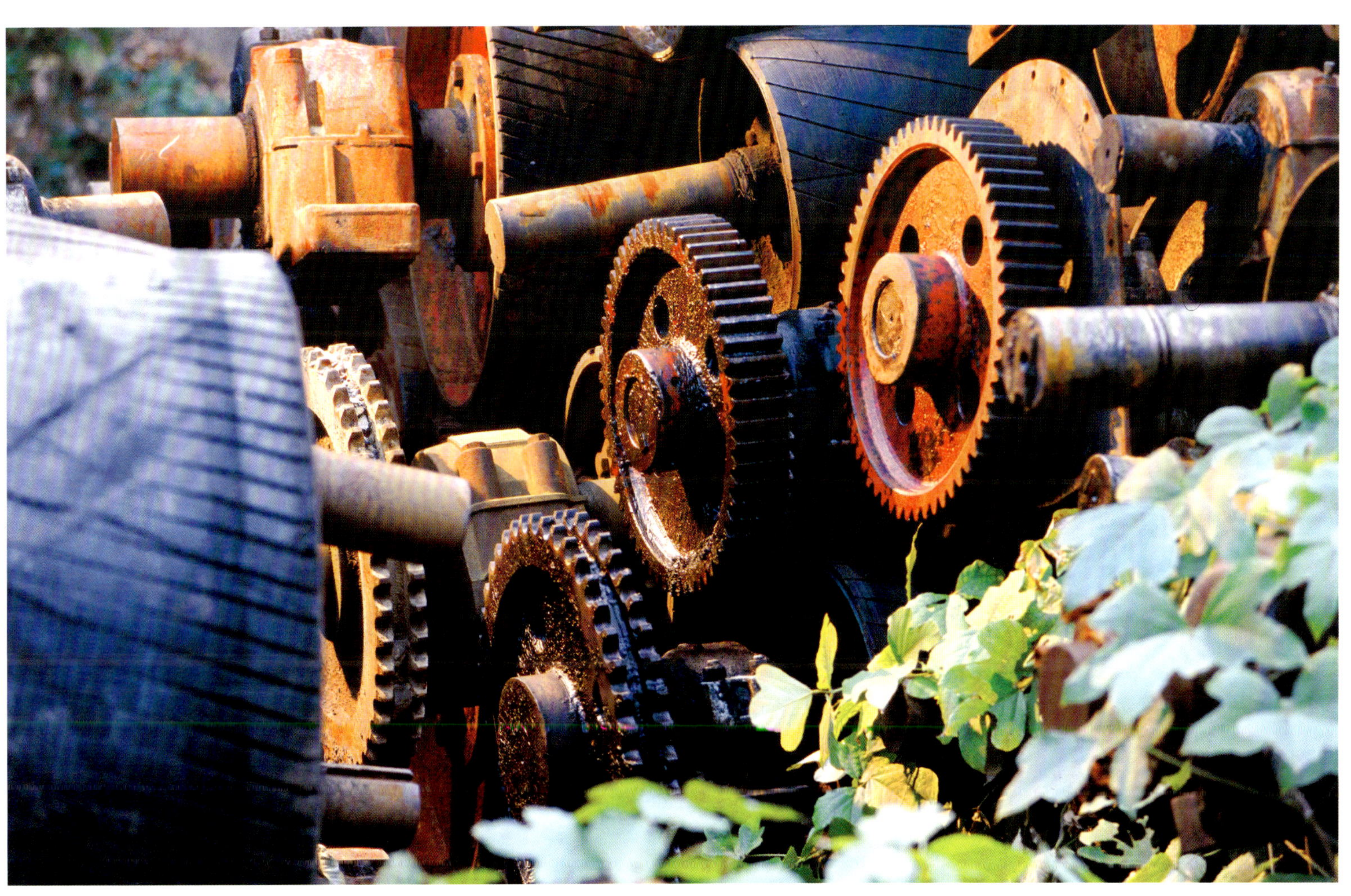

56

Elkhorn City | *Kentucky*

The defunct mines littering Appalachian coal country are colorless places filled with gray and black equipment, except for the gears I found in Virginia (prior page) and this iridescent coal mine shed in eastern Kentucky.

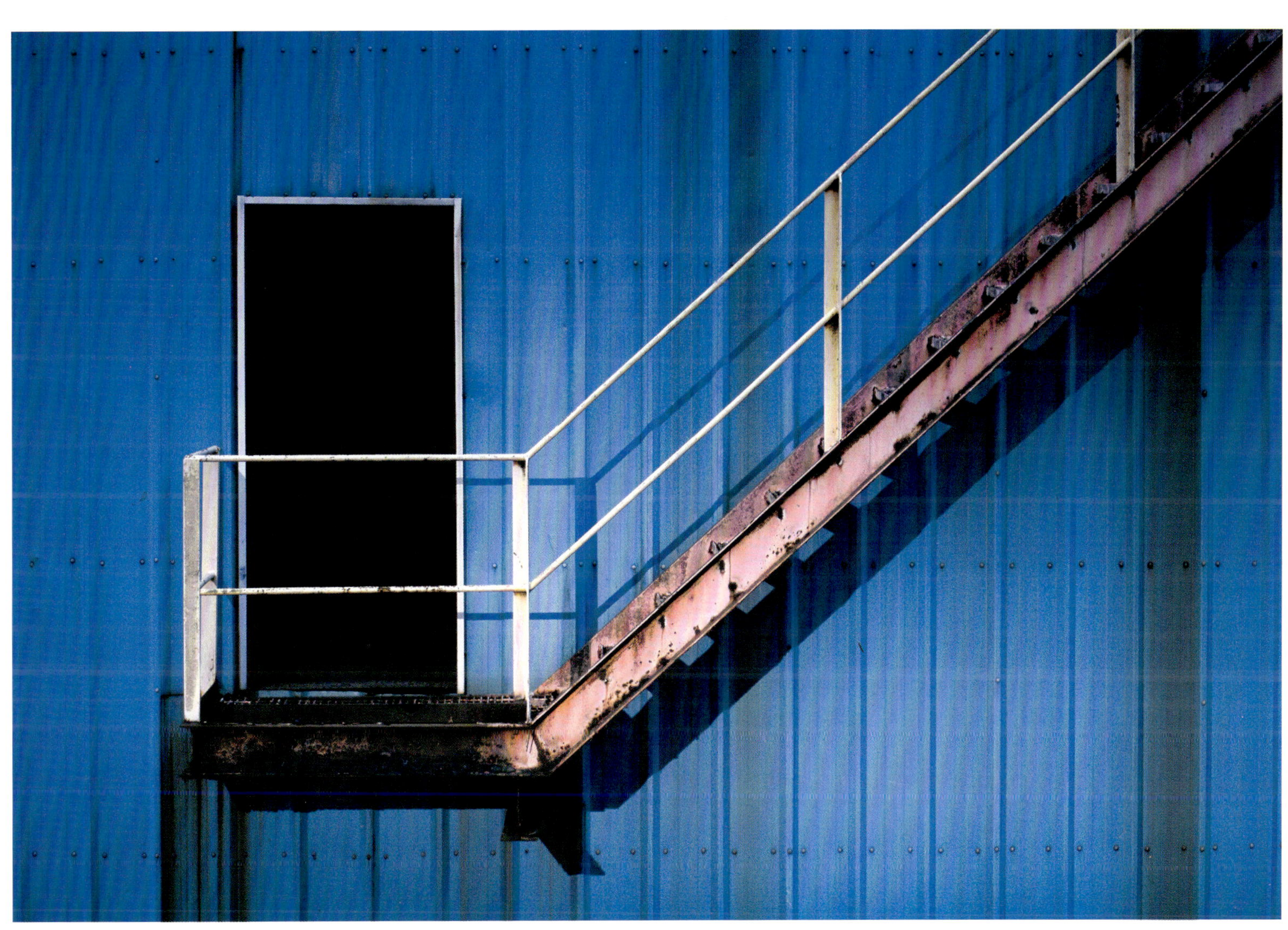

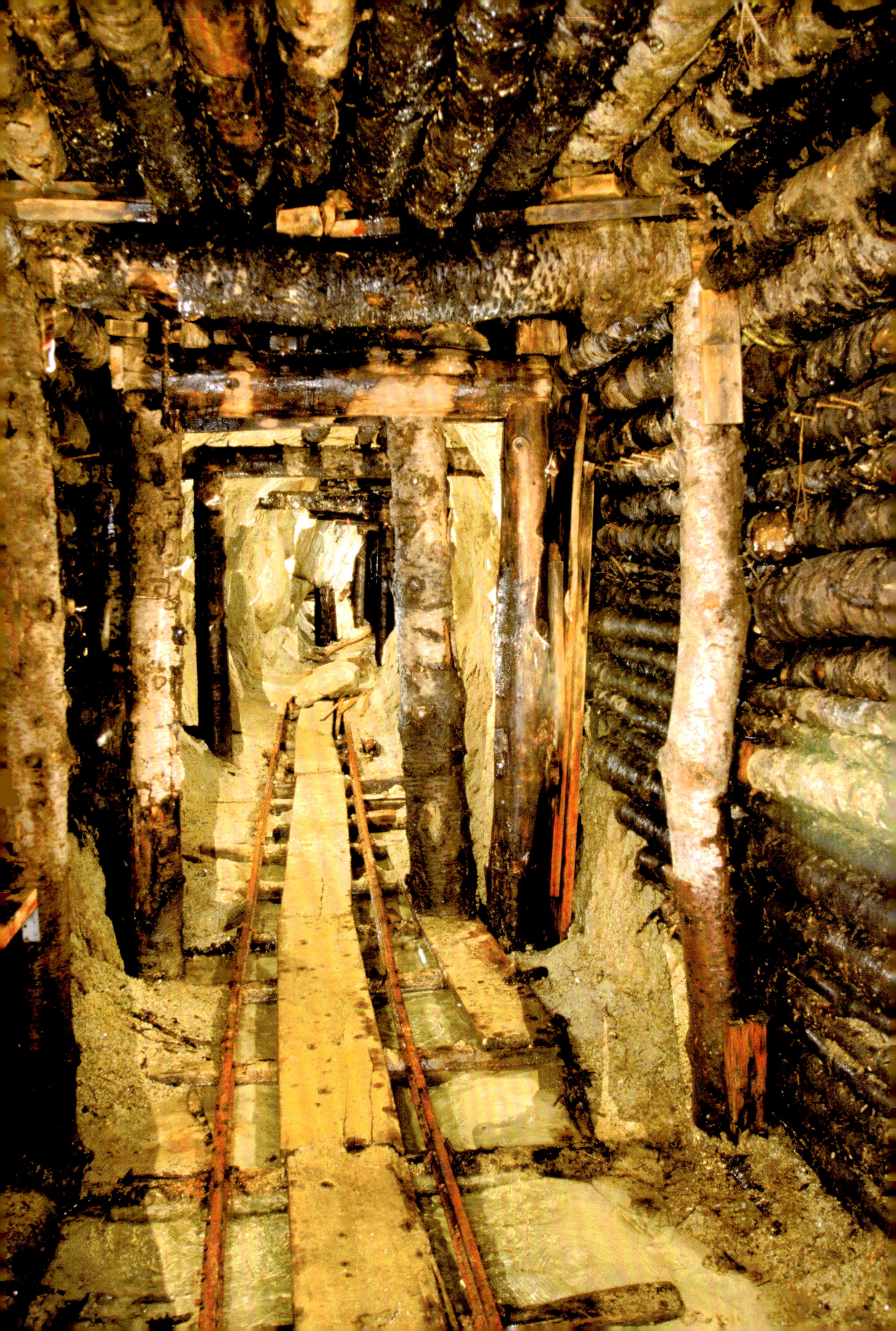

From his cabin 7,618 feet above sea level, a grizzled, one-eyed prospector pointed me to this tapped out mine shaft. "When the price of gold or silver jumps back up," he prophesied, "plenty of these mines will be back in action."

Note: The county name commemorates (in misspelled form) the many Hawaiians who once worked the mines.

Eatonville | *Washington*

This wood drying kiln popped out of the landscape like a rusted space ship in the shape of a badminton birdie. In the background: Mt. Rainier, whose glacial-topped summit is partially exposed by timber clear-cutting.

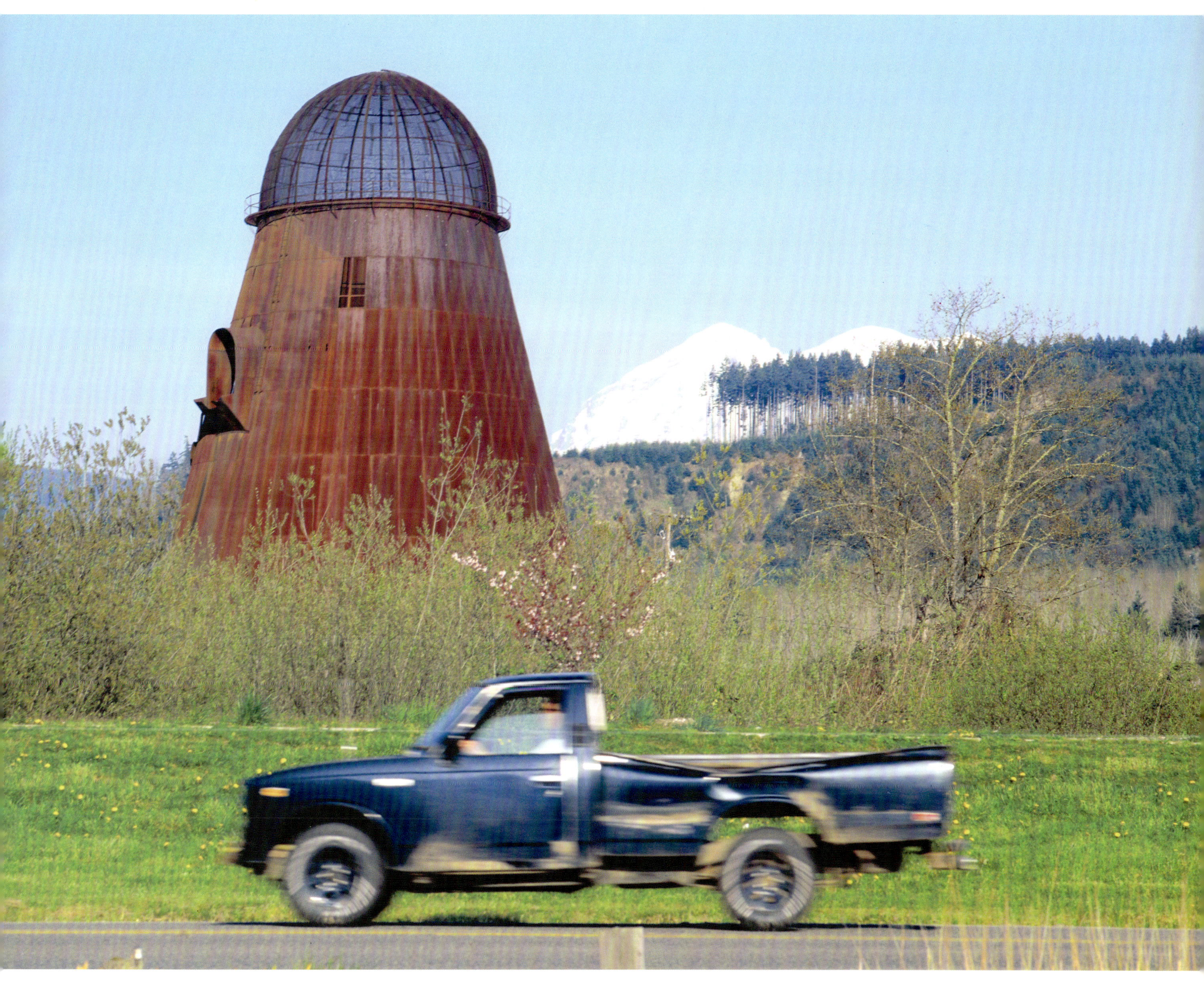

These tools must have plowed through many an acre of Carolina clay to allow planting of cotton, or tobacco, or soybeans, or wheat, or corn, or...

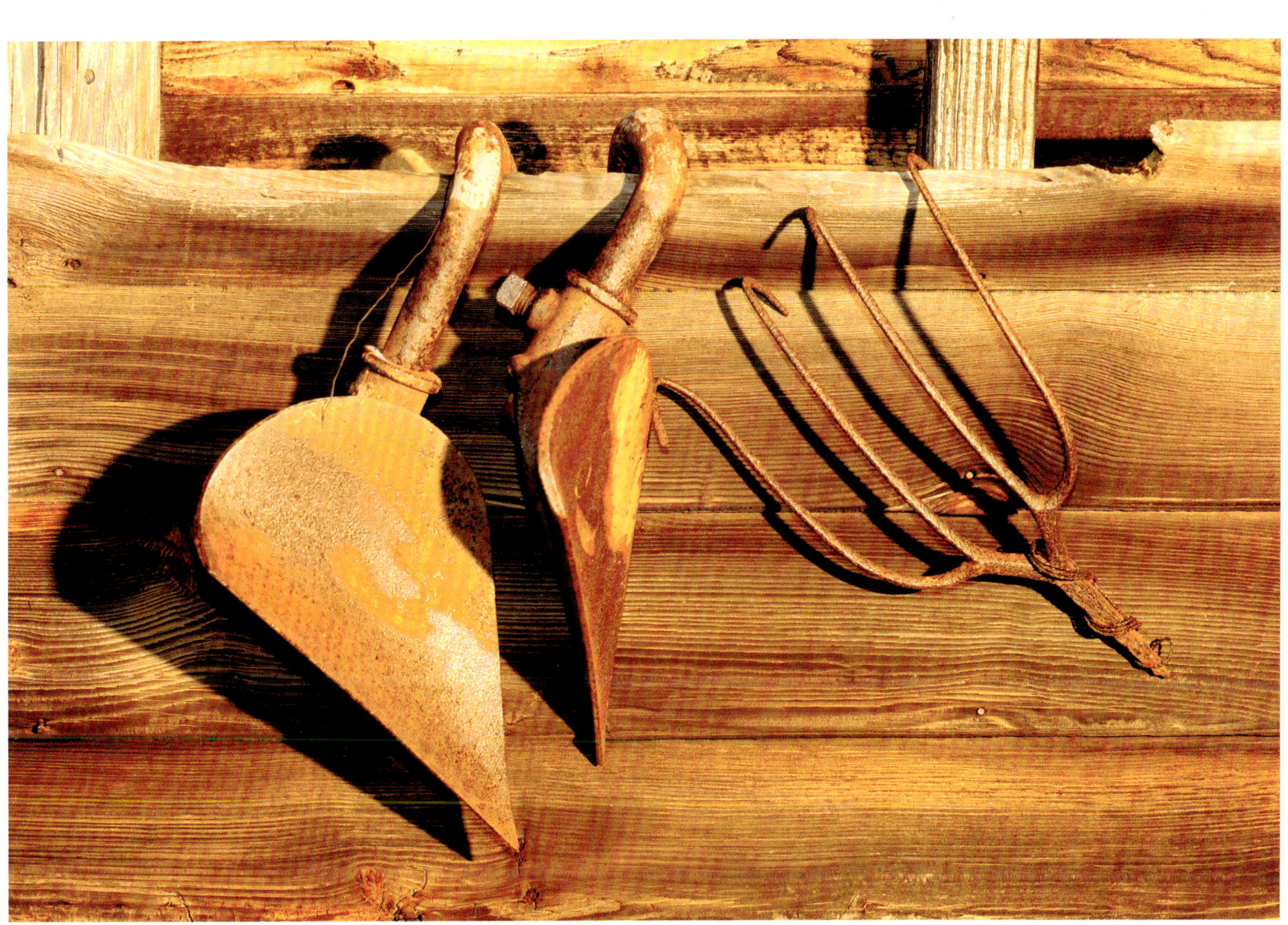

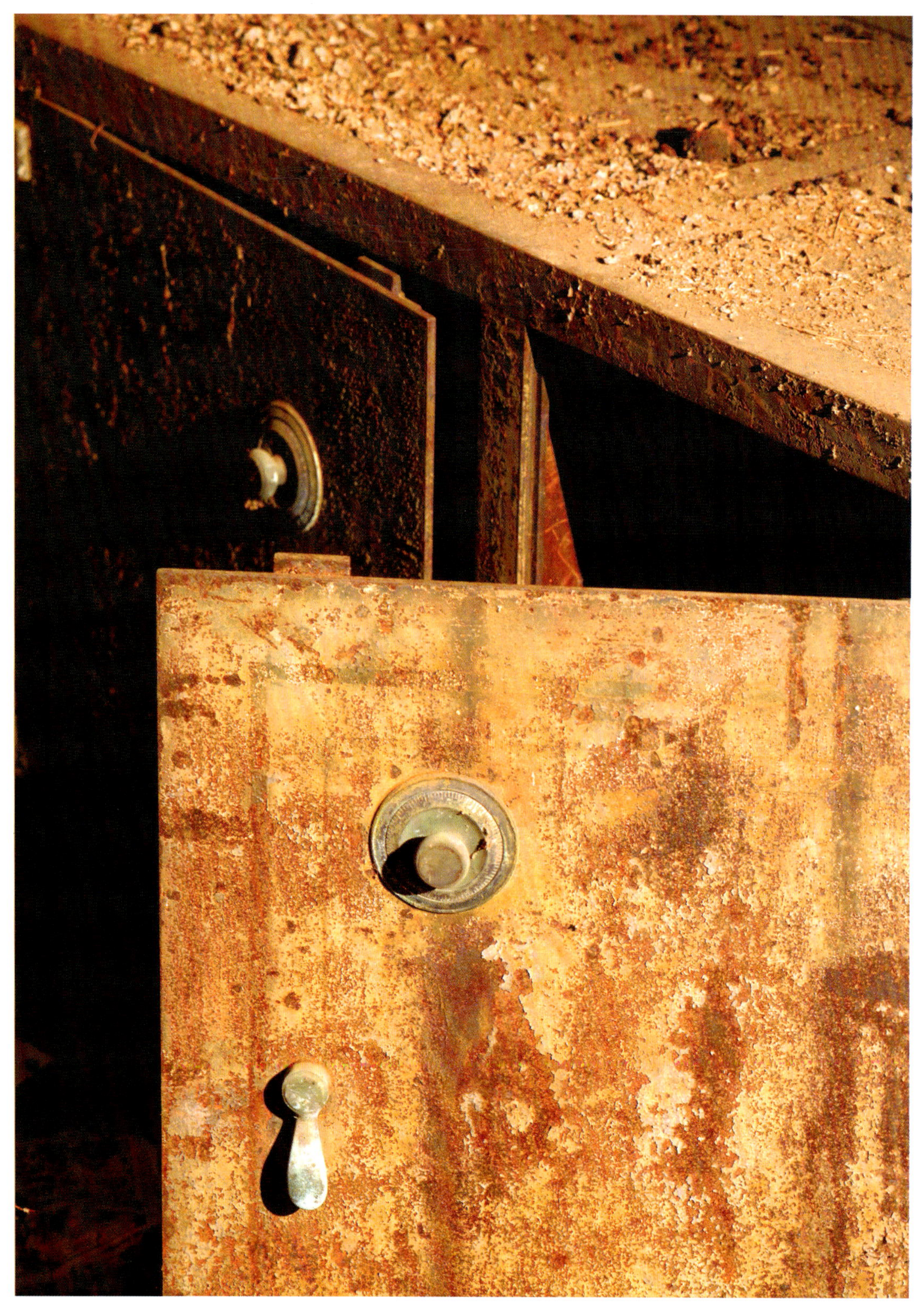

An old barn's hodgepodge inventory: two bicycles with flat tires, three broken window frames, bent plastic lawn chairs, a still-shiny toaster, flaking newspapers, a checkbook ledger (Sussex County Bank, last recorded date 1976) and a rusted two-door, 300 pound steel safe once used for...what?

EASLEY | *South Carolina*

Strewn about the factory were enough buttons to keep seamstresses busy for years pumping the wrought iron pedals of these Singer machines.

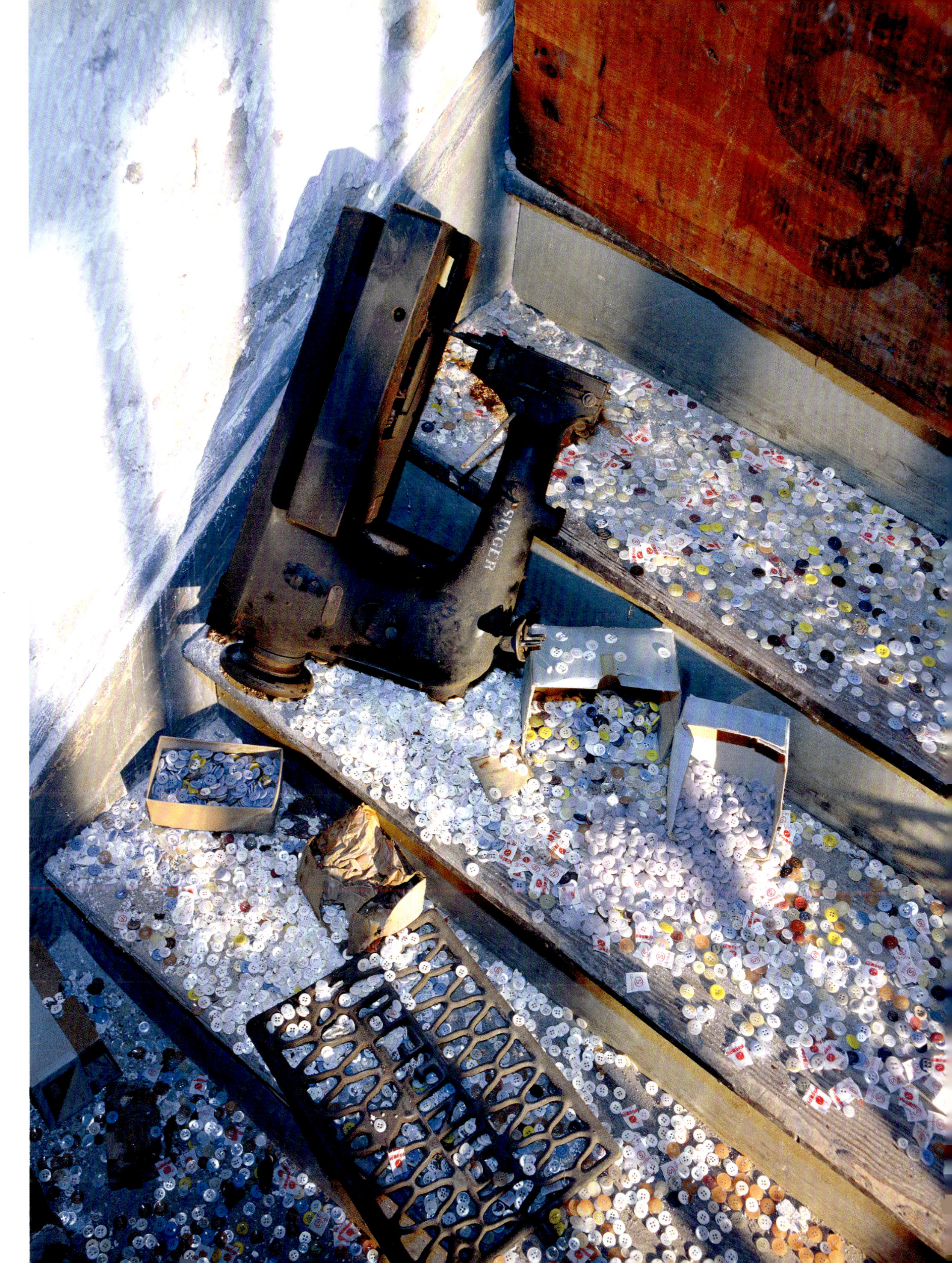
SINGER

Cedar Rapids | *Iowa*

"My father and grandfather stored just about everything in our barn. Old horseshoes and old signs, this crumbling medical bag, that coffee pot large enough for 30 farmhands, and, well, look around, you'll see for yourself."

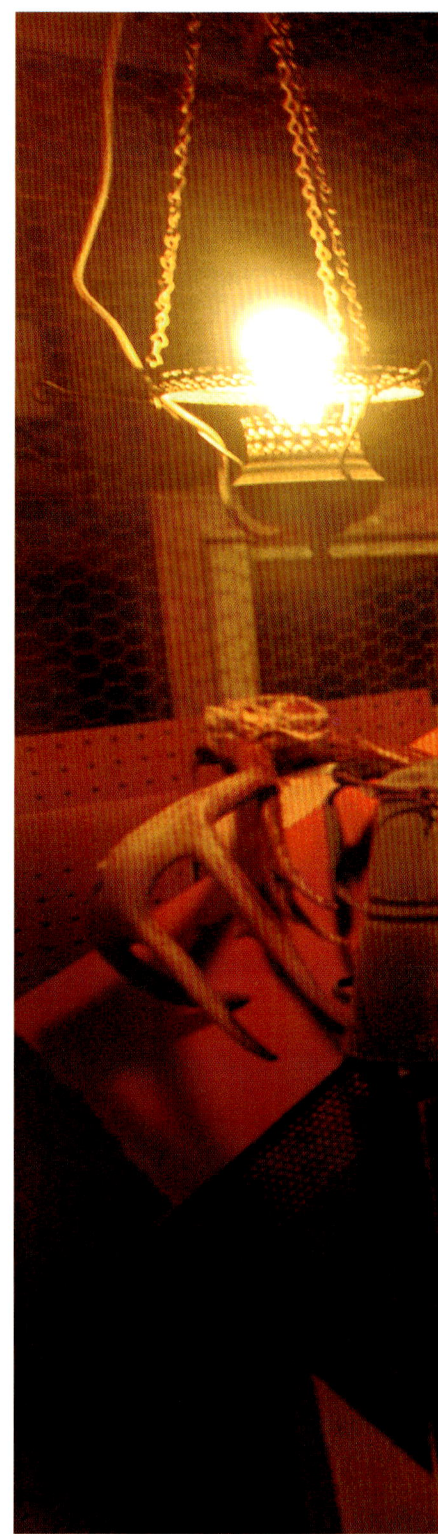

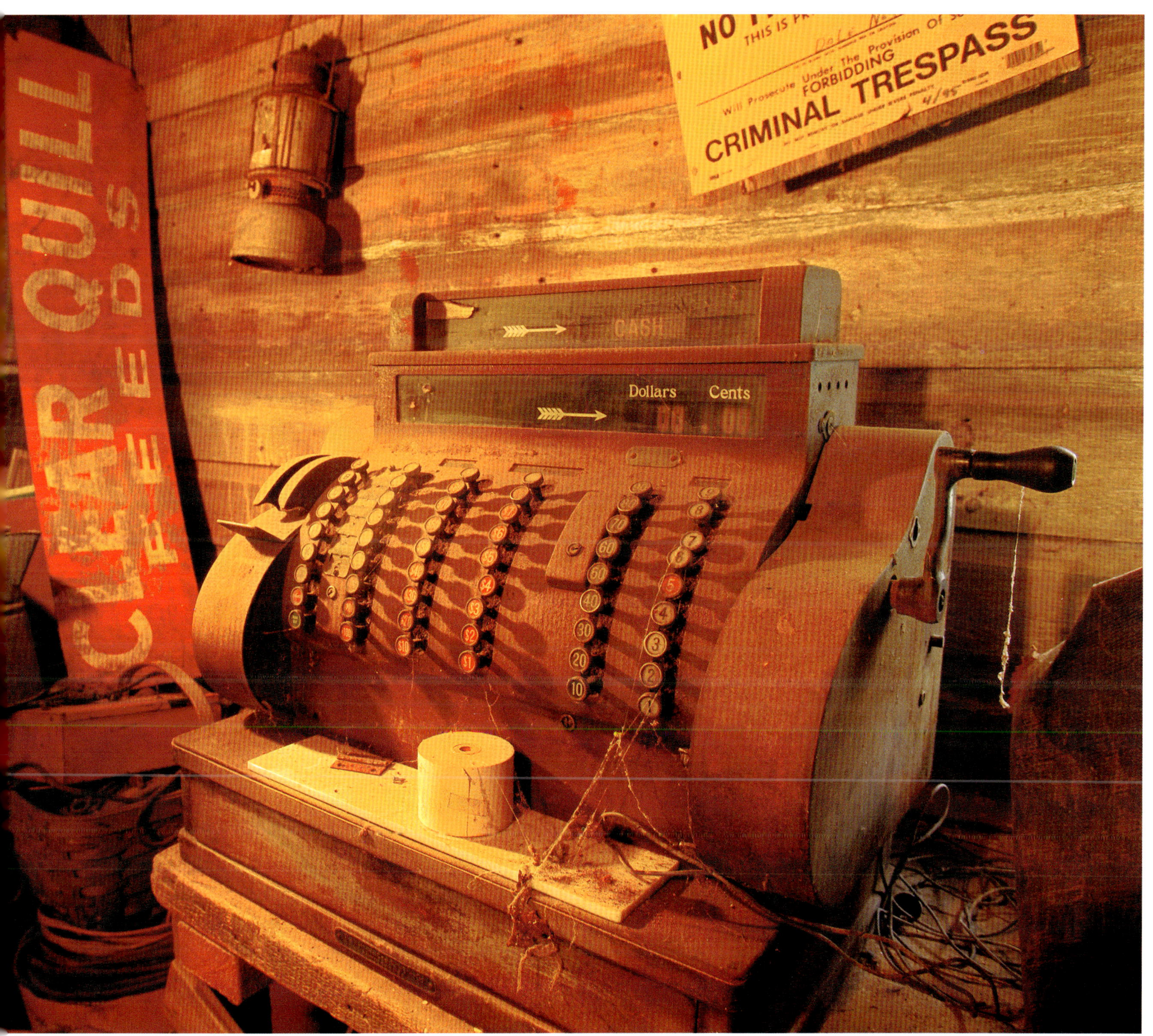

Will Prosecute Under The Provision Of
FORBIDDING
CRIMINAL TRESPASS
CASH
Dollars Cents

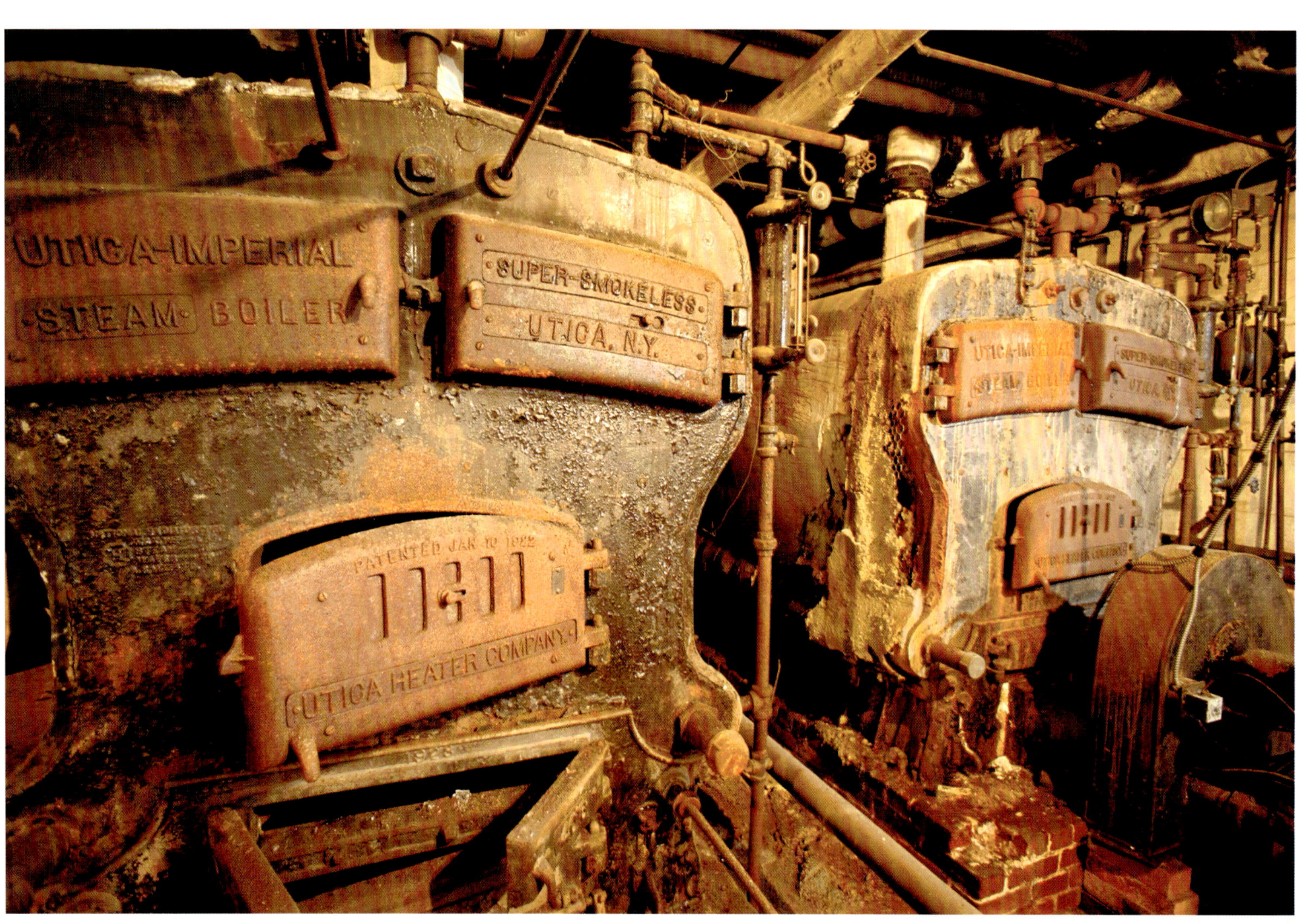

UTICA-IMPERIAL
STEAM BOILER
SUPER-SMOKELESS
UTICA, N.Y.
PATENTED JAN 10 1922
UTICA HEATER COMPANY.

A town in the Appalachian hills was an unlikely location for a stately opera house. Three dark stories below the stage—a *Phantom of the Opera* setting—was a spooky labyrinth of musty rooms with cracked paint, corroding pipes, a few bare 25-watt bulbs, and two coal furnaces, patent date 1922.

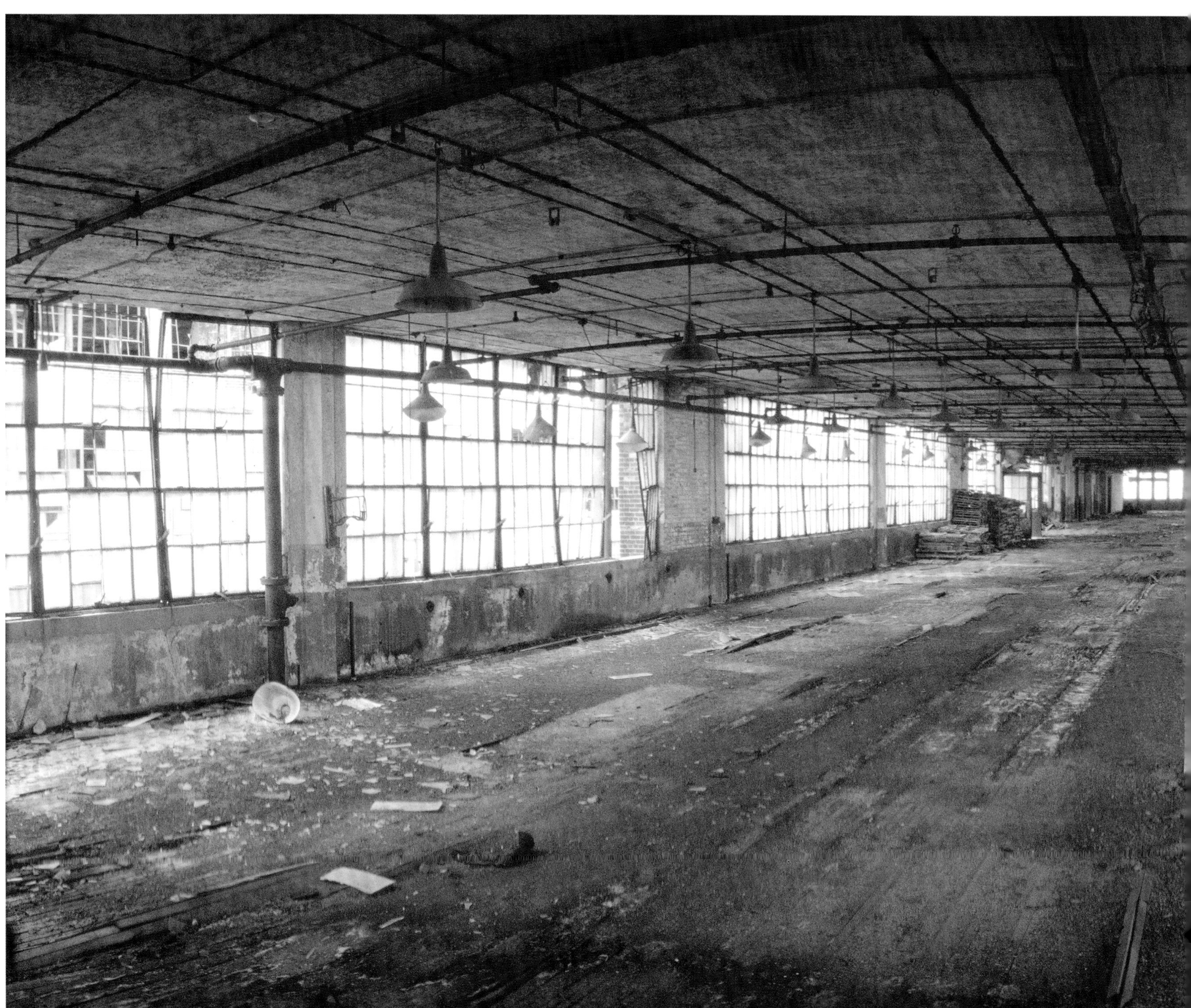

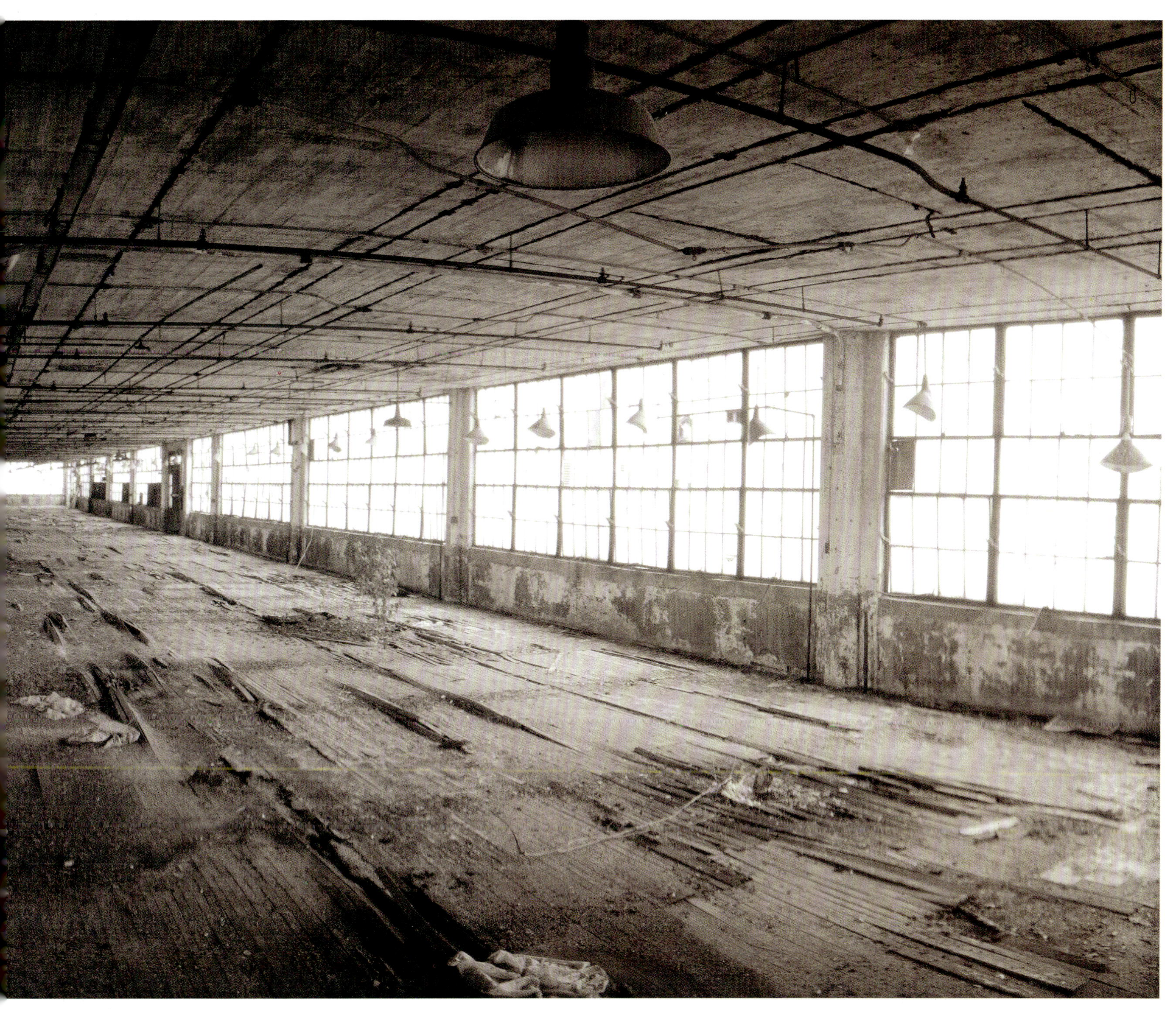

Packard Motors was a major presence in the auto business for decades. Its jaw-droppingly vast production facility—3.5 million square feet spread across 47 acres—was state of the art in industrial design when it was built in 1903. Fifty-three years later, the very last car came off the line.

Vehicles

Photographed in 1990, this pickup truck is by now probably buried under a mound of earth and ivy, but back then nature and man seemed in a state of exquisite equilibrium.

People often ask whether I painted the inscription on the door. For one thing, such inspired irony would not have occurred to me. For another, I don't radically manipulate situations (so I didn't put the bullet hole in the window, either).

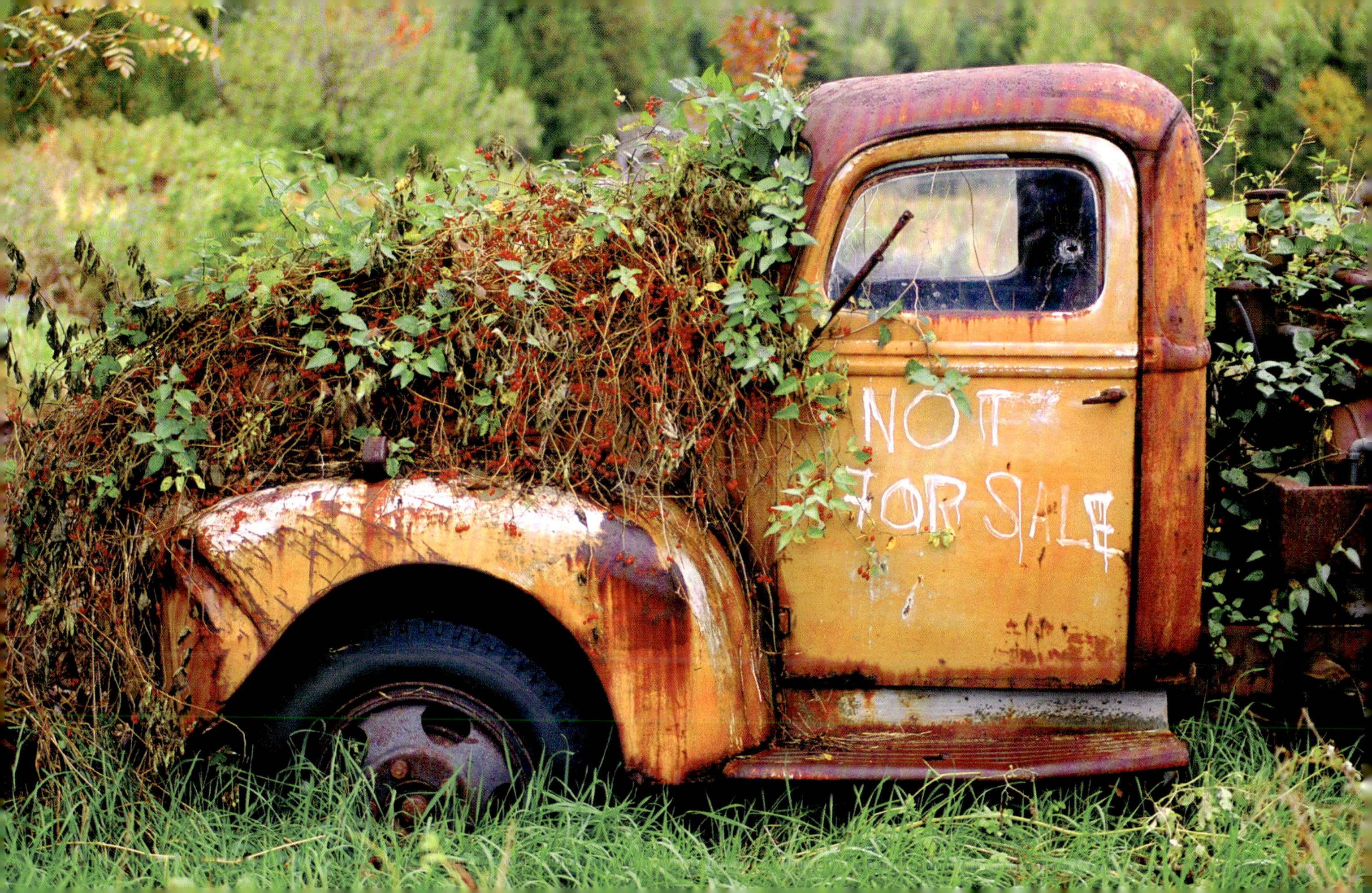
NOT
FOR SALE

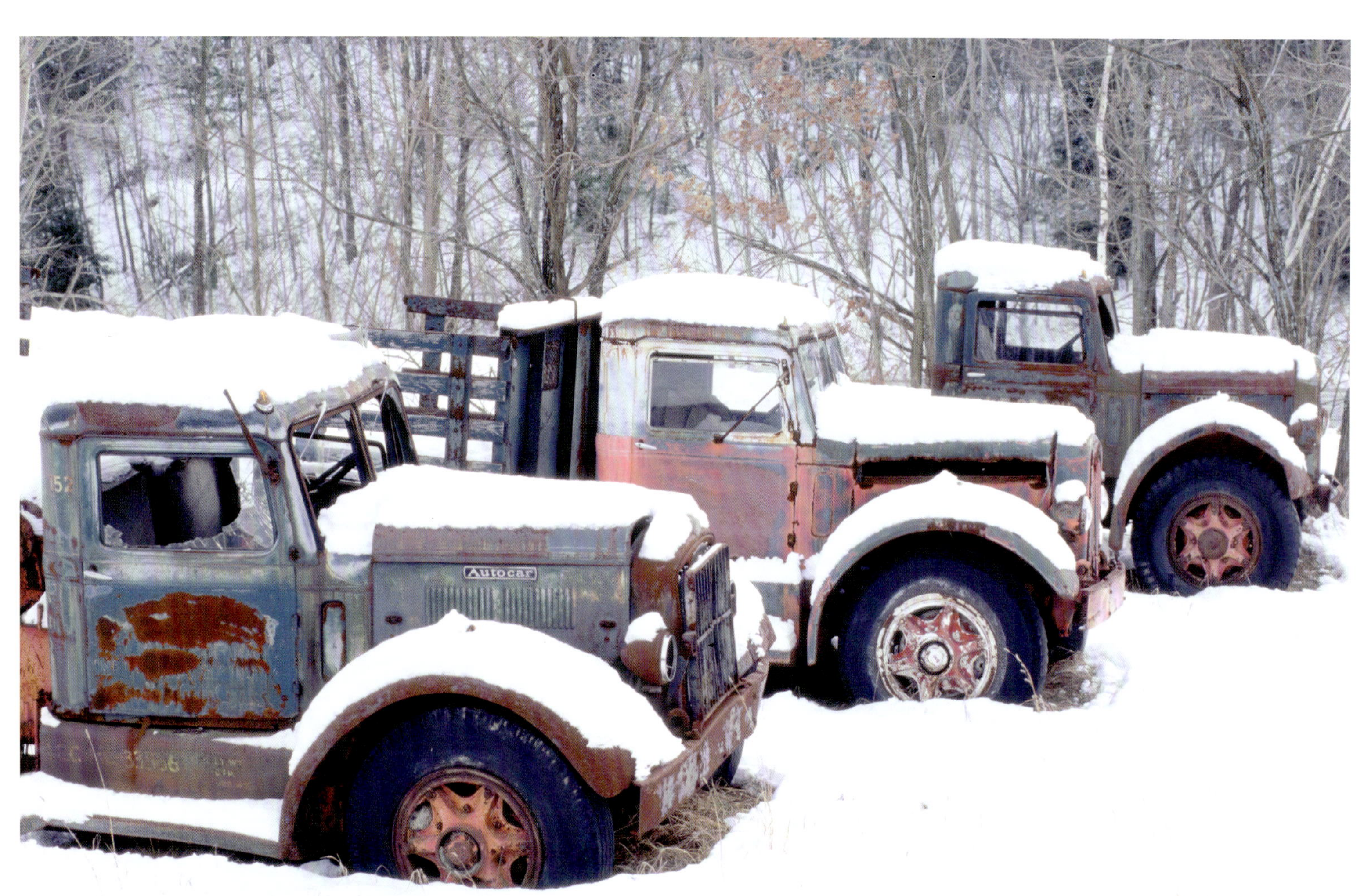
152
Autocar

In the side yard of his house someone arranged a pick-up truck graveyard into a kind of pastel-hued Stonehenge.

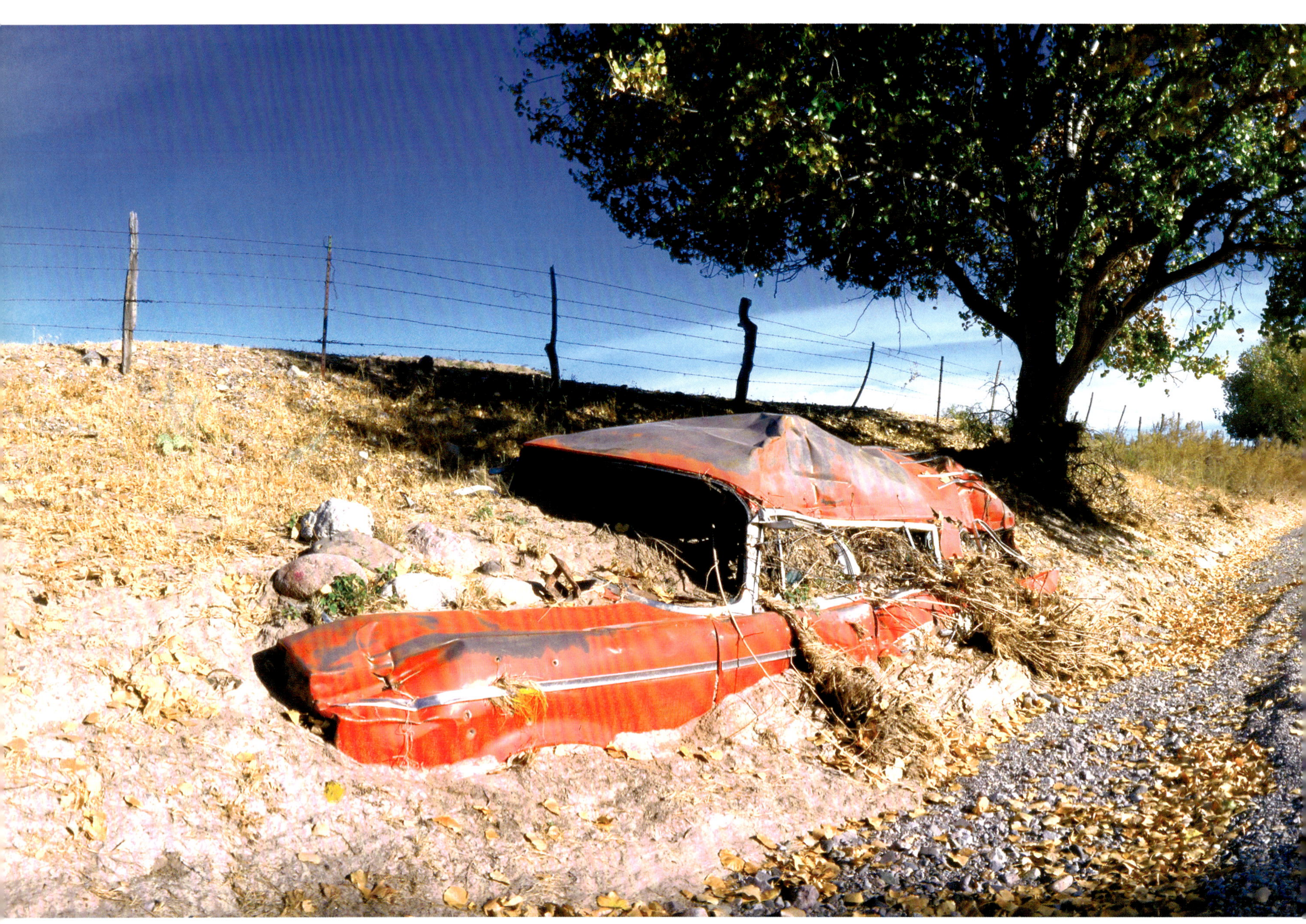

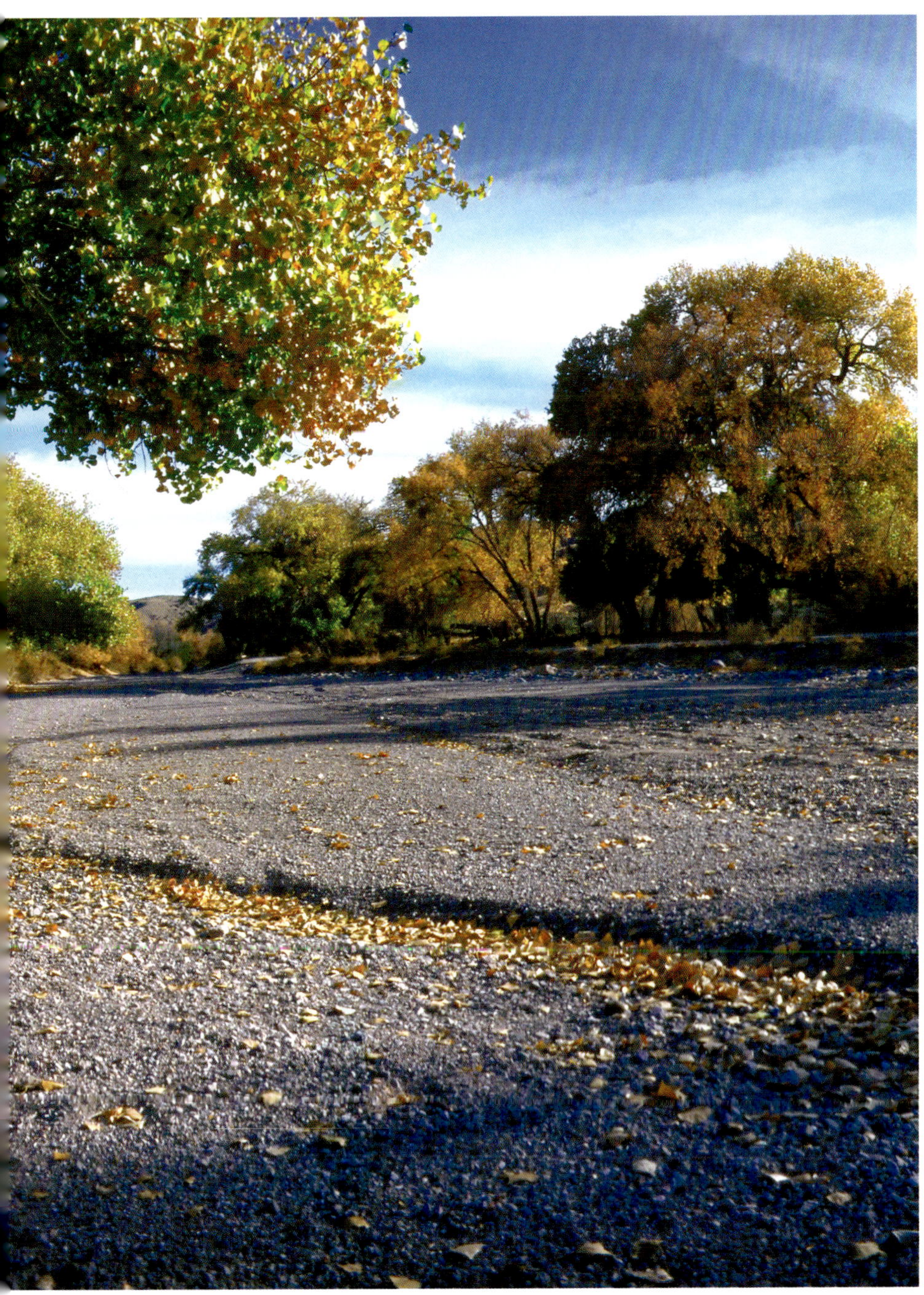

"Listen, Steve. Go north on the interstate about 17 miles, then west on Route 52 for about nine miles. There's a wide unmarked dirt road going off at an angle like so. Take that road—it's in real bad shape, y'know—take it about, I dunno, maybe four miles and you'll see a big 'NO TRESPASSING' sign, but just ignore it...it's a public road...this guy up there put it there to scare people away. Pass that sign and you'll hit a wide riverbed—it's bone dry this time of year—follow that about three miles—and look over on your right. What you'll see stuck in the riverbank is just the kind of thing you're lookin' for, for sure. OK, you got all that, Steve?

"Hey Steve, you got four wheel drive?"

—Owner of antique/junk shop,

Truth or Consequences, New Mexico

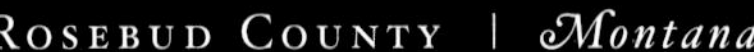

ROSEBUD COUNTY | *Montana*

They're not biodegradable, they're problematic to tow to a junkyard, and they're a handy source of replacement parts. No wonder abandoned automobiles litter the countryside. Still, how did it come to pass that this wreck sat, like a lost orphan, in the middle of a vast field, far from any road?

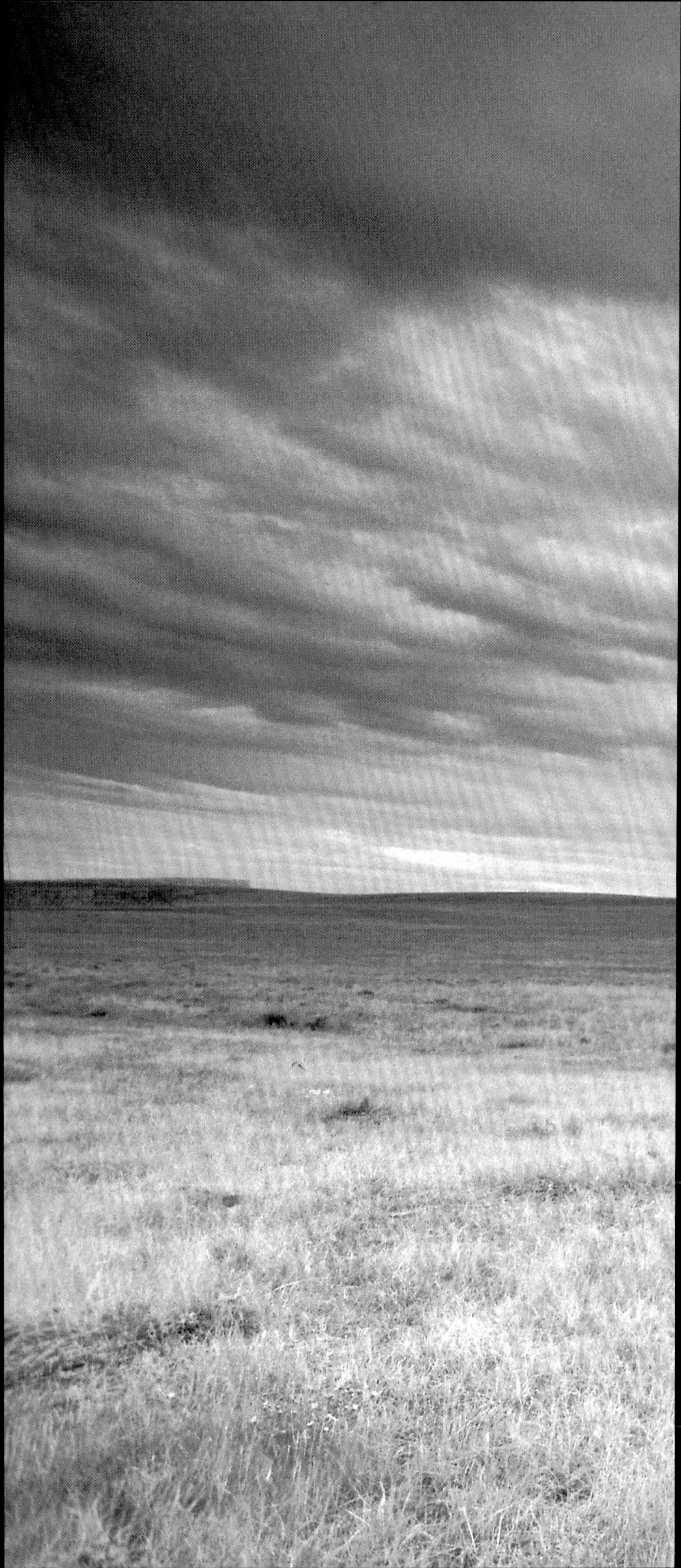

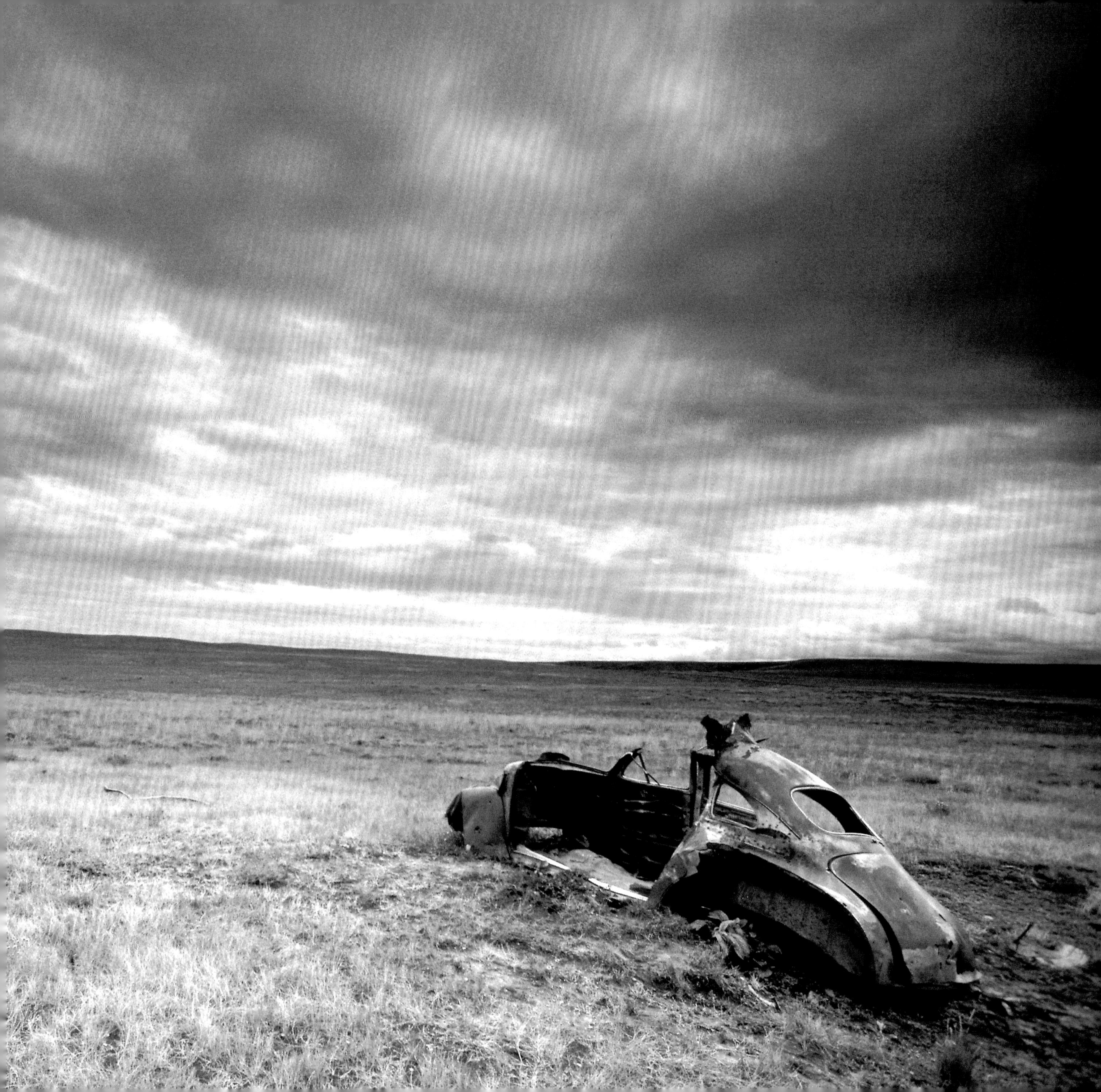

Acoma Indian Reservation | *New Mexico*

A freight train of seemingly infinite length fortuitously drove right across the windshield of this ramshackle pickup, which sat there like a carcass tied to a hitching post.

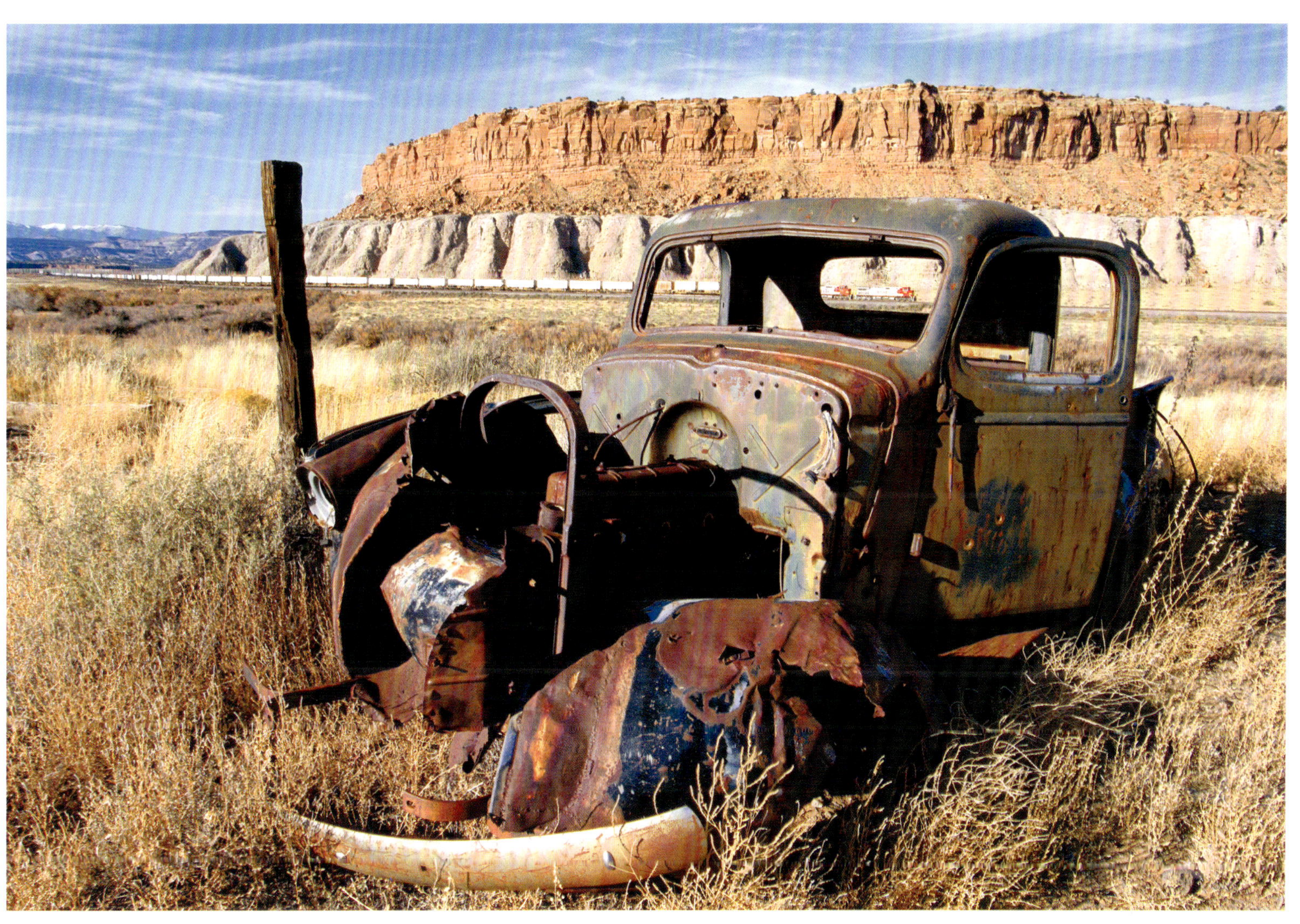

In the movie *Sleeper*, Woody Allen awakens 200 years in the future, comes upon a Volkswagen Beetle, gets inside, and—presto—it starts right up. Given the quality of this 1960s VW's paint finish after decades of exposure to the elements, I imagined I could do the same...if only someone had left the key.

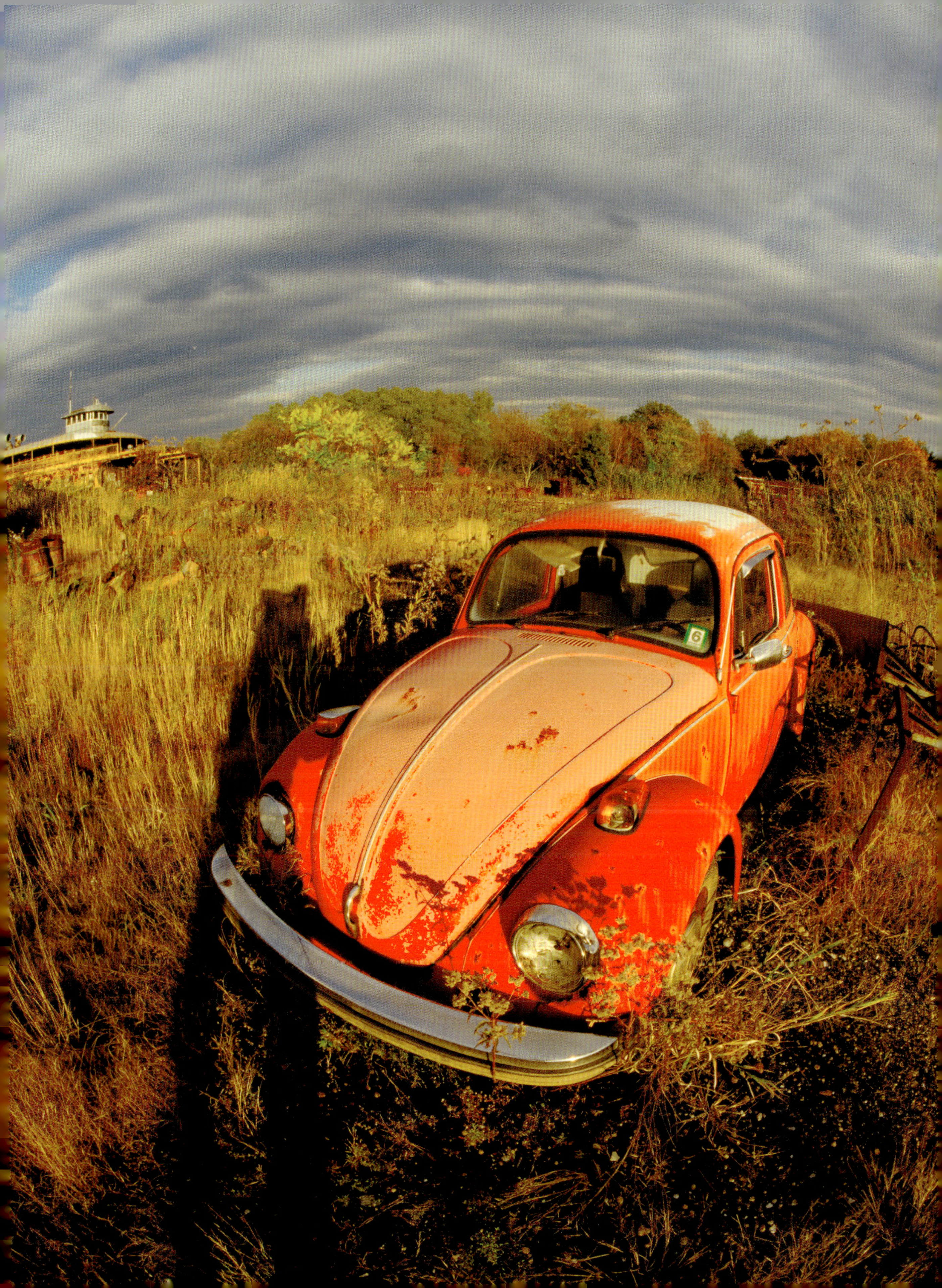

Oregon

"You're welcome to photograph whatever you want," said Sharon who, with her husband Brad, owned the most varied and unusual collection of decayed vehicles I'd ever seen, "but, if you ever publish your 'Abandoned' book, please don't reveal our location...we already get too many tourists and photographers knocking on our door."

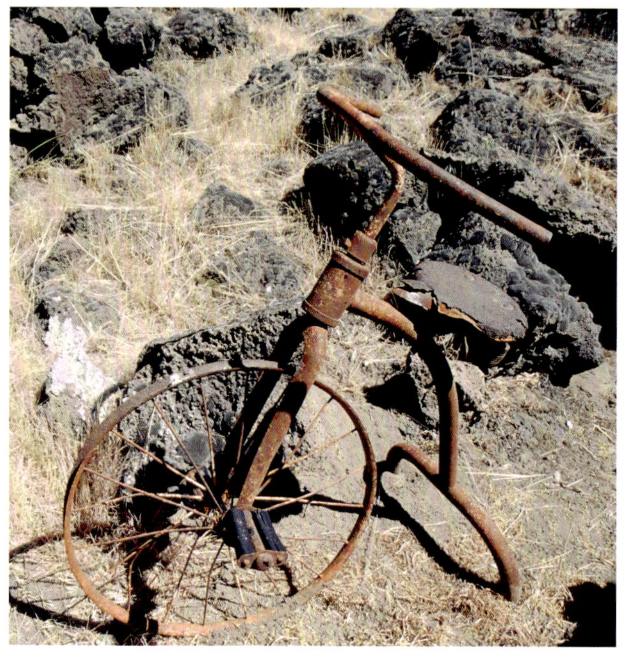

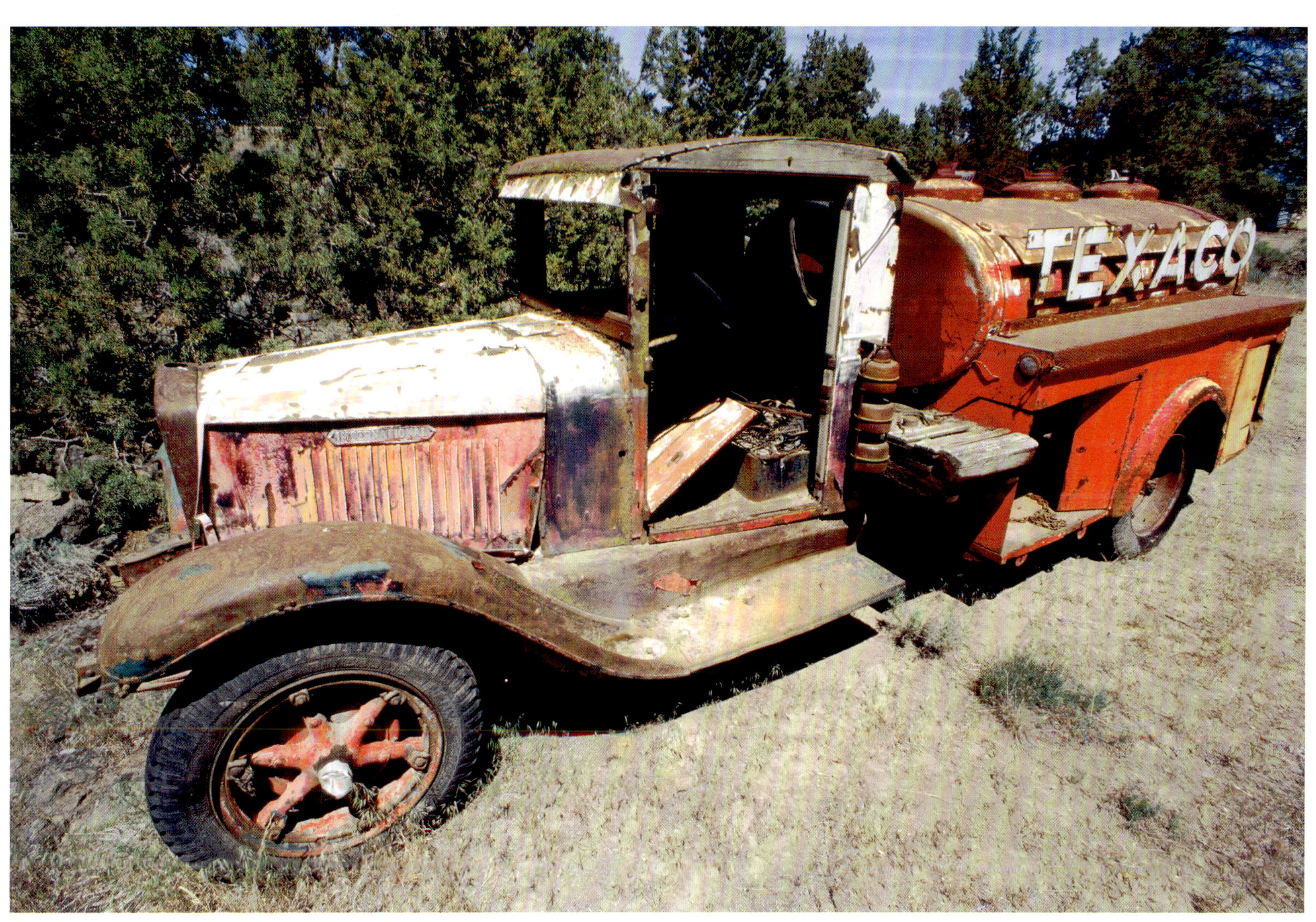
TEXACO

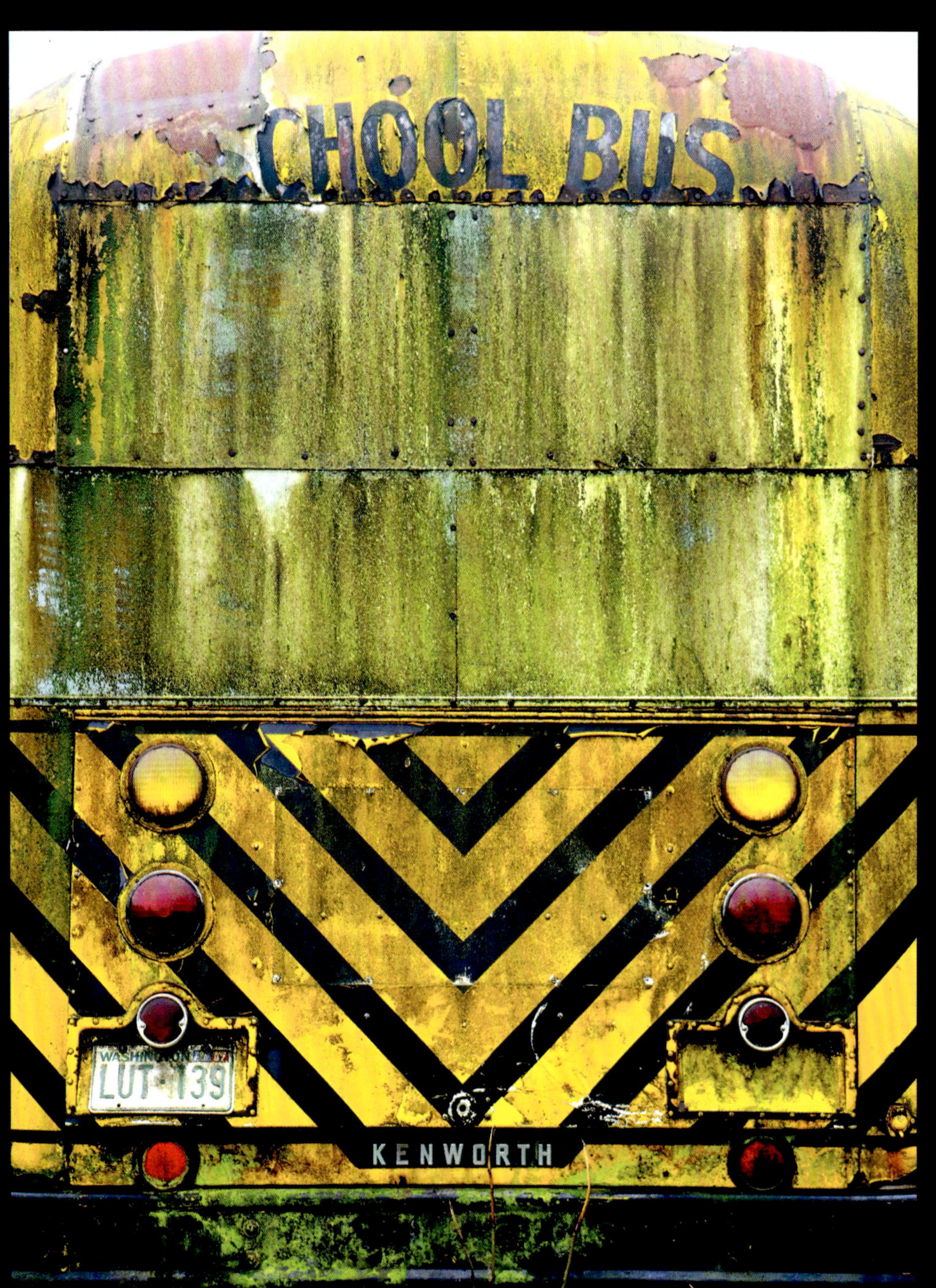
CHOOL BUS
WASHINGTON
LUT 139
KENWORTH

Old school buses are sometimes used for dry storage, especially in the Puget Sound area, the wettest region of the country. The colors and patterns on the rear of this boarded-up bus were, as the surviving letters indicate, totally "chool."

PENNINGTON COUNTY | *South Dakota*

A mere foot or two of added height often provides a much better camera angle. When I'm not using my van—which has both roof rack and ladder—I improvise, standing on fence posts, paint buckets, a stack of rocks or, in this case, an inverted plastic kiddy pool used to water cows (which helped me juxtapose my shadow with the tractor.)

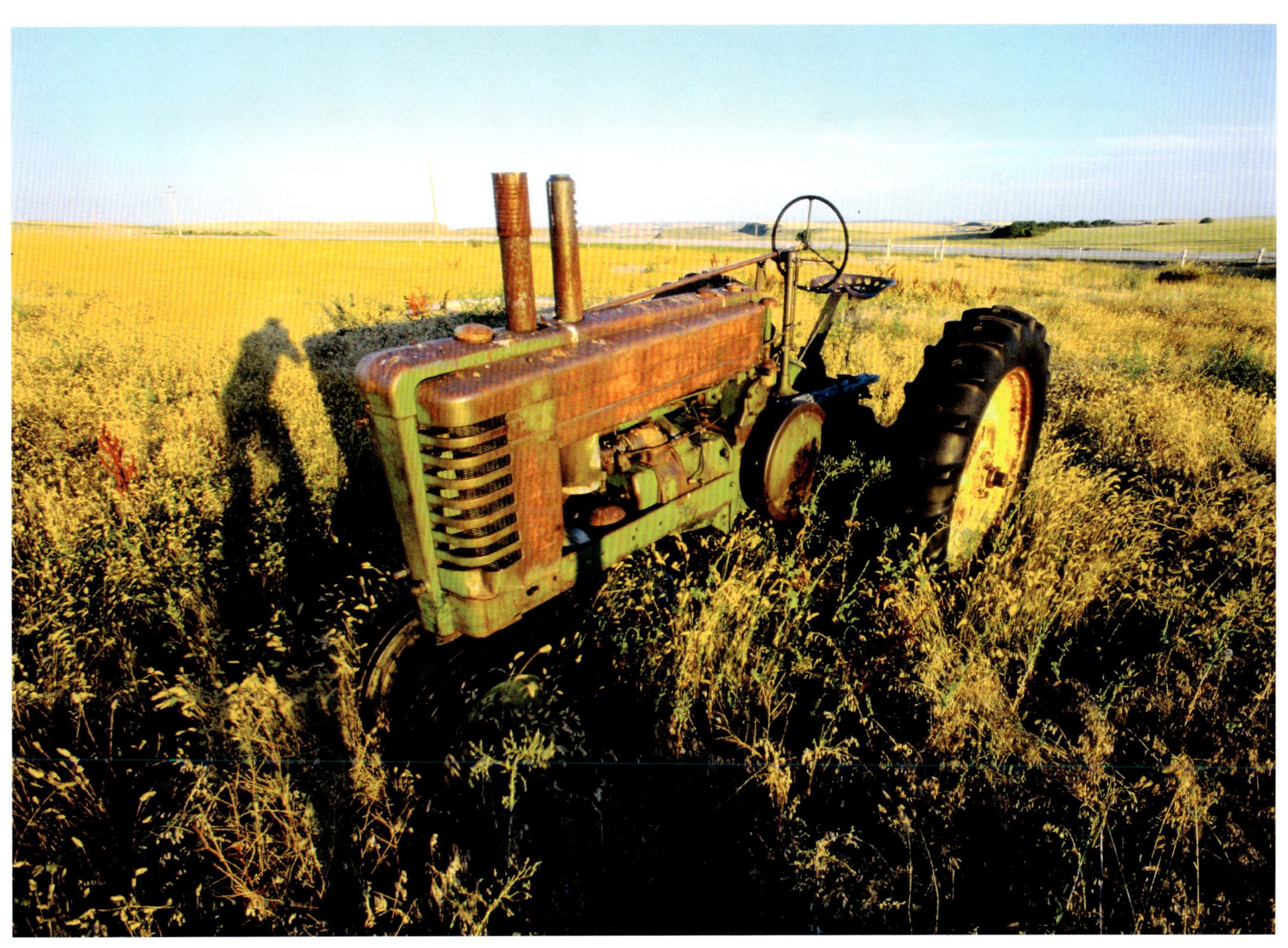

JORDAN VALLEY | *Oregon*

Mike Hanley started to renovate his 1865 stage coach 20 years ago but had to stop—he had a big farm to maintain—and so it lay, stripped of its wooden-spoked wheels, settling into the mud behind his barn.

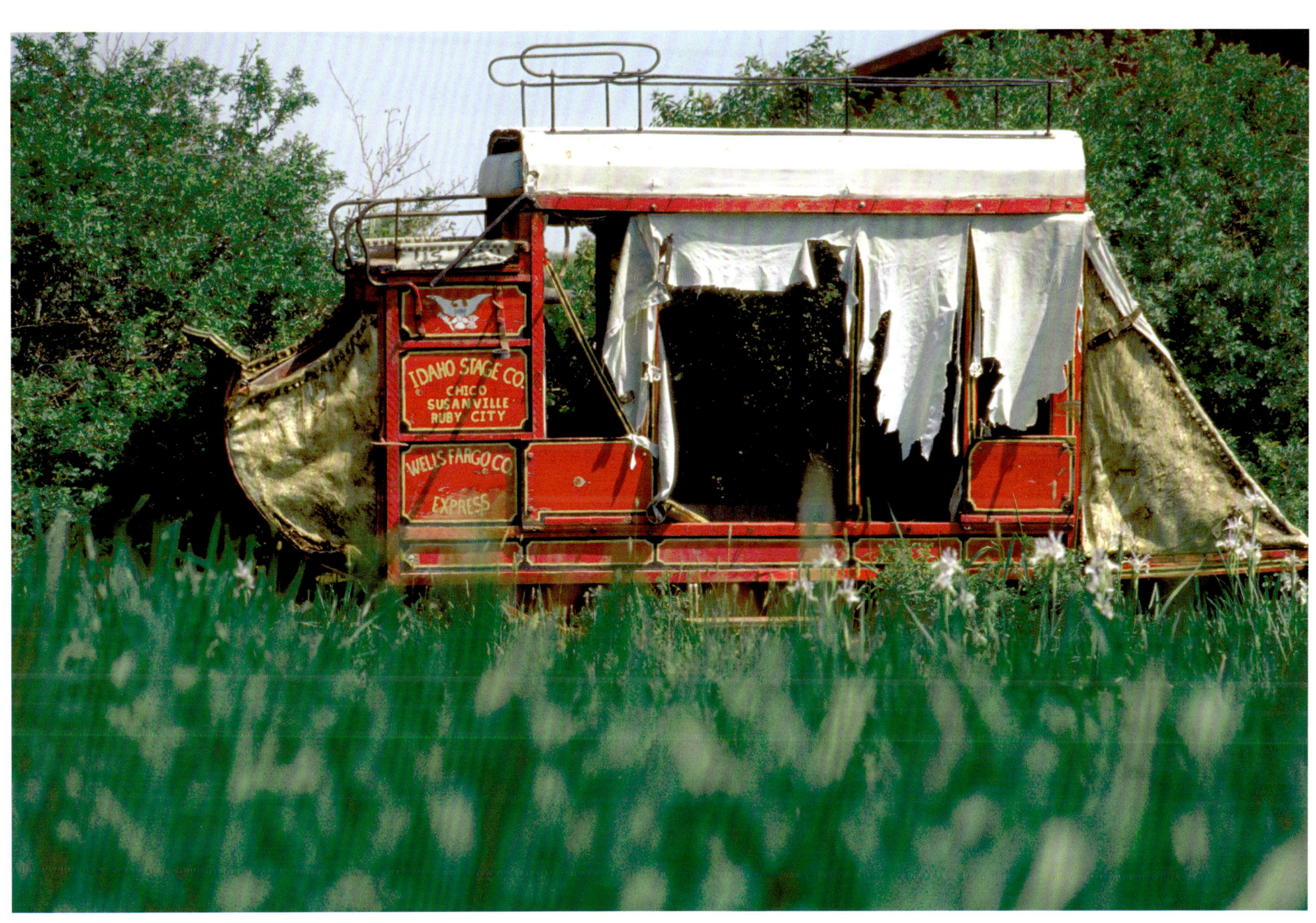
IDAHO STAGE CO.
CHICO
SUSANVILLE
RUBY CITY
WELLS FARGO CO.
EXPRESS

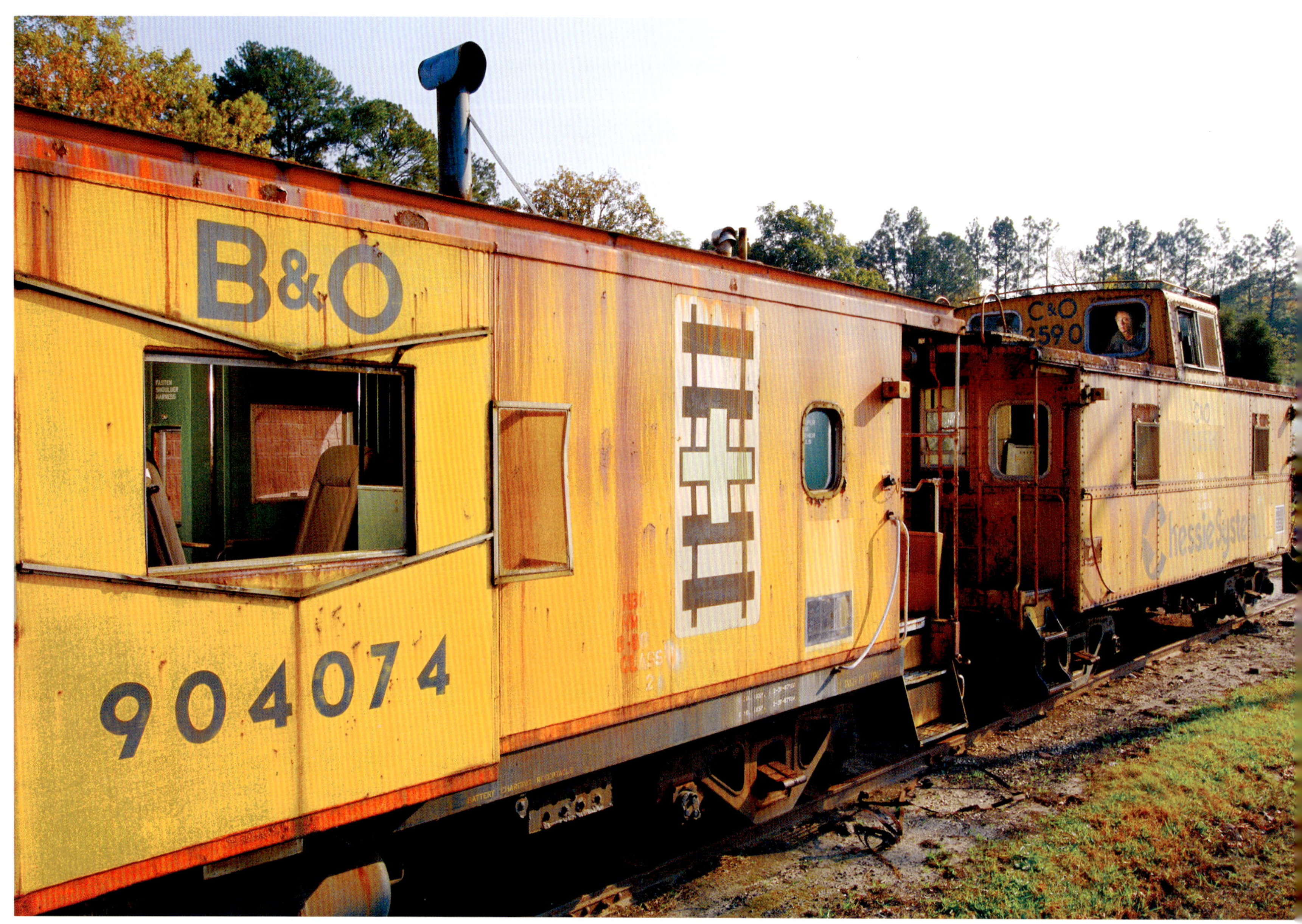
B&O
904074
C&O

Old railroad cars may be abandoned, but only temporarily;
they are coveted objects which are generally set aside,
awaiting the renovator's loving hand.

MONONGAHELA RIVER | *West Virginia*

With its tracks removed and a few of its railroad ties having dropped 60 feet into the river below, this acrophobic photographer traversed the bridge with the confident stride of Oz's Tin Woodsman.

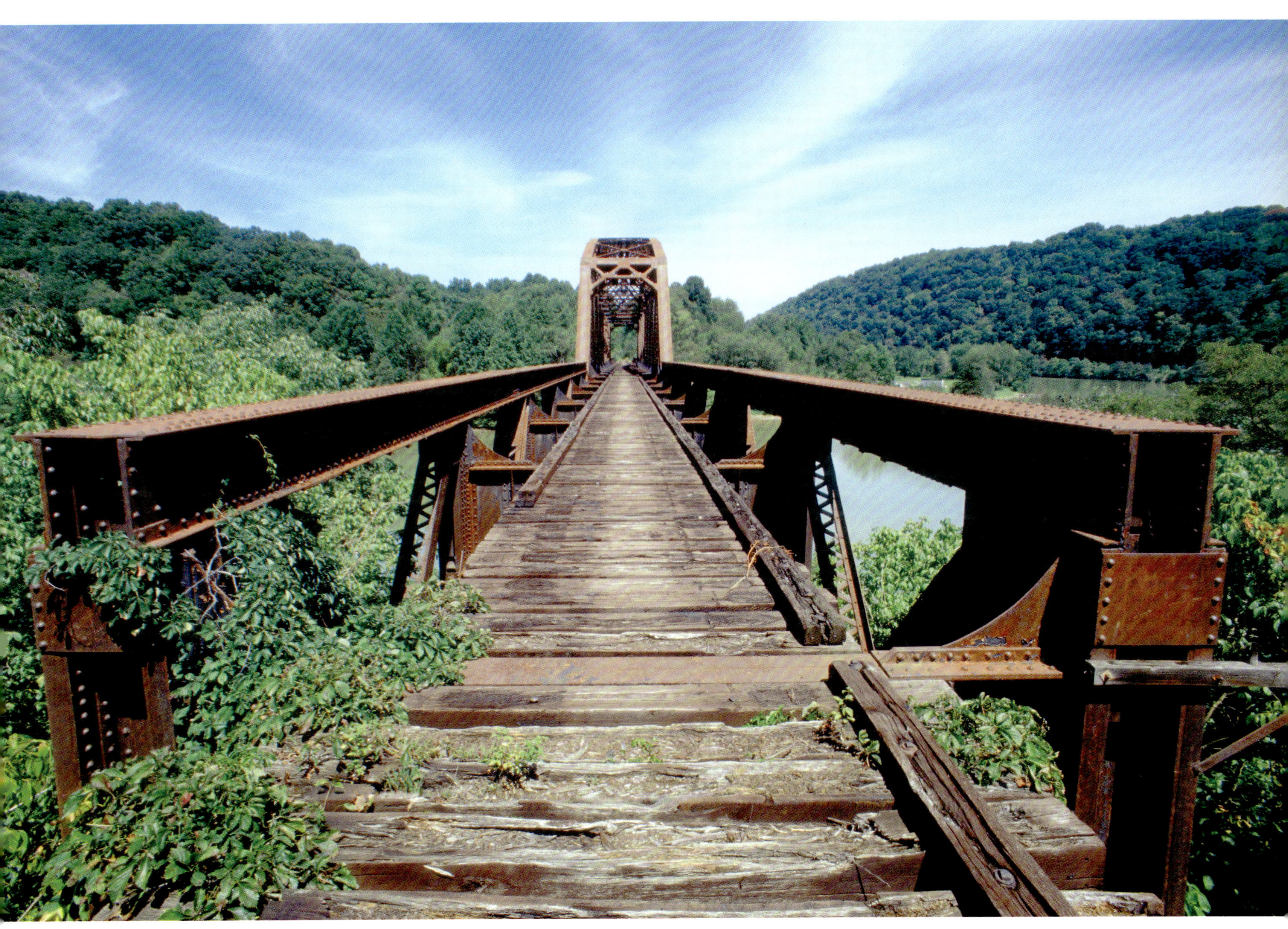

Bellingham | *Washington*

Hidden deep in a forest with no signs of tracks on either side of the river, this wooden trestle bridge stands, like the Venus de Milo, with its arms broken off.

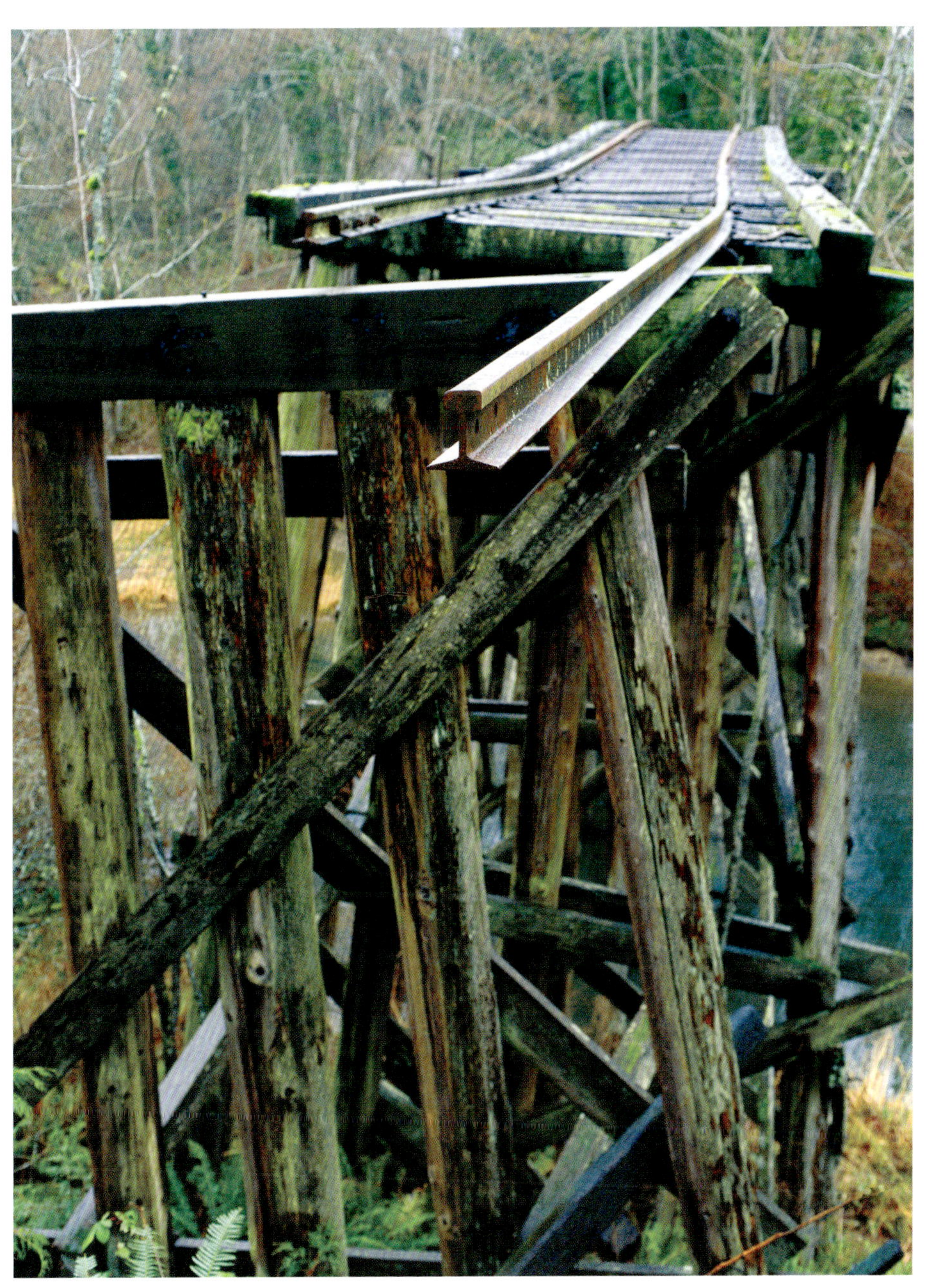

PROVIDENCE | *Rhode Island*

Except for its rusty tracks, this raised drawbridge was in superb condition; I had the unnerving sensation that at any moment it would be lowered and I'd have to jump into the river below to dodge an oncoming train.

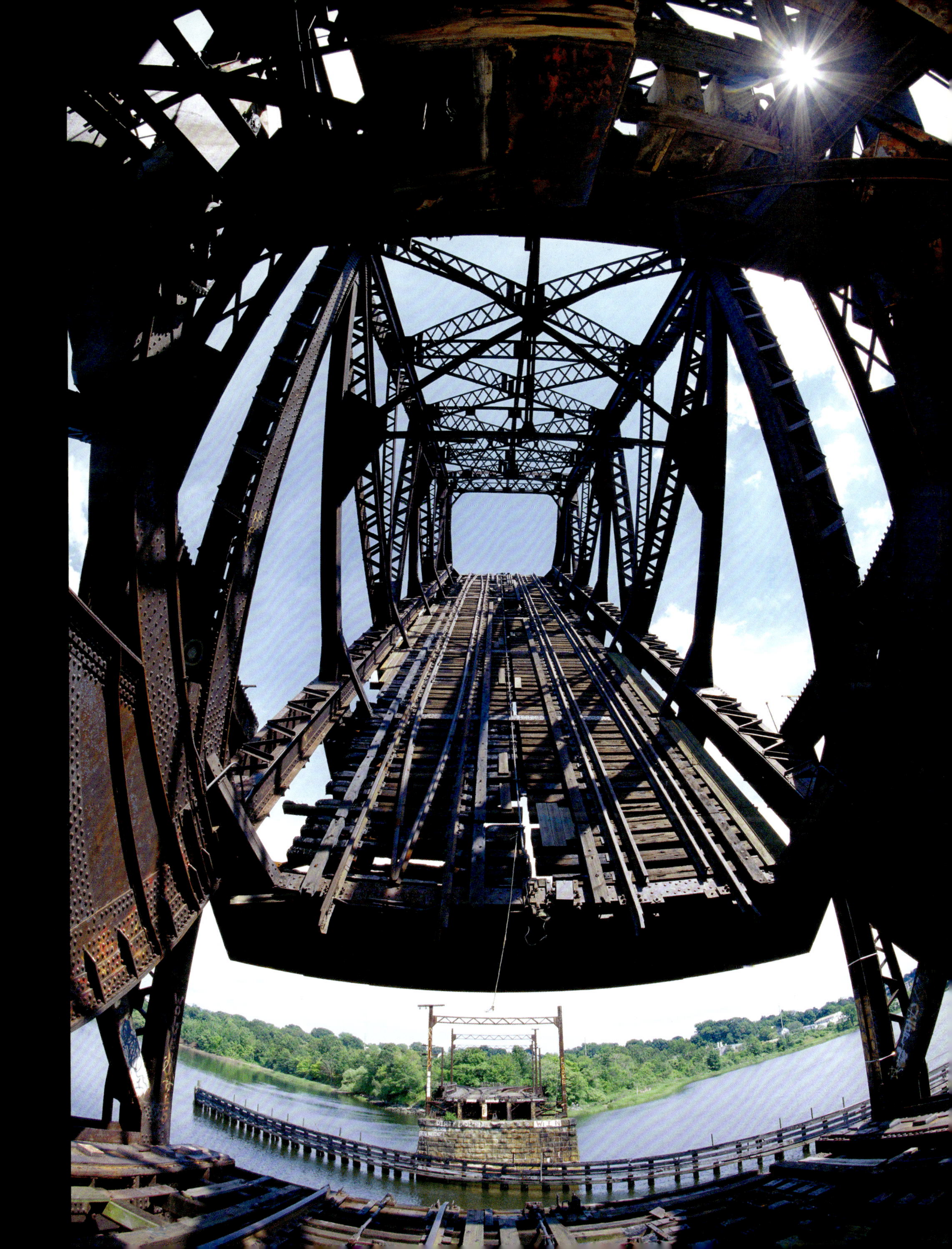

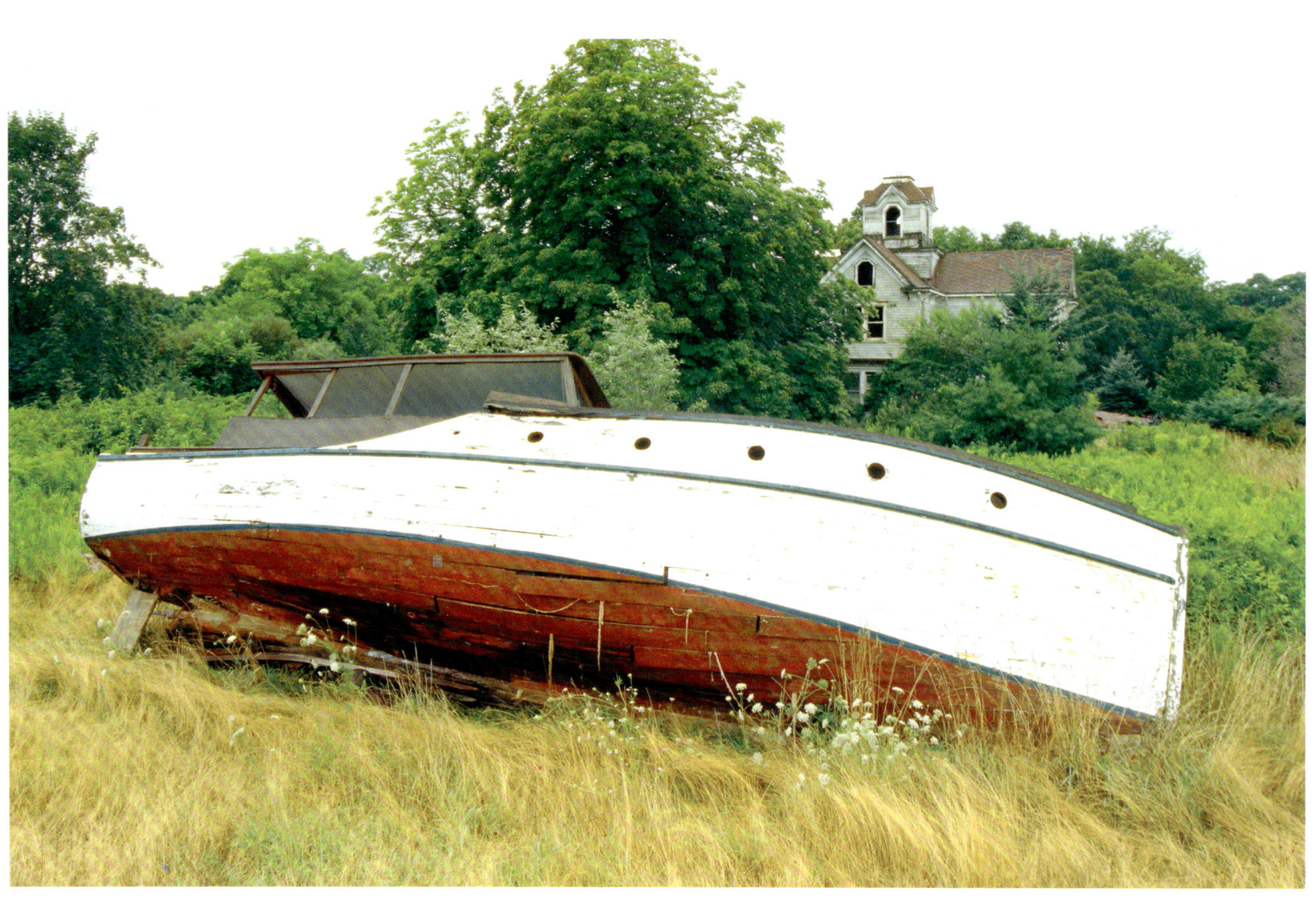

Back in the Roaring Twenties, Scott and Zelda Fitzgerald and their swanky friends might have enjoyed wild and elegant boating and lawn parties on this very spot.

RARITAN RIVER | *New Jersey*

Lying askew in the mud—colors fading, paint peeling, and metal rusting—this ferryboat holds within it a million stories—stories of the people who gazed out its windows while chugging between New Jersey and New York City.

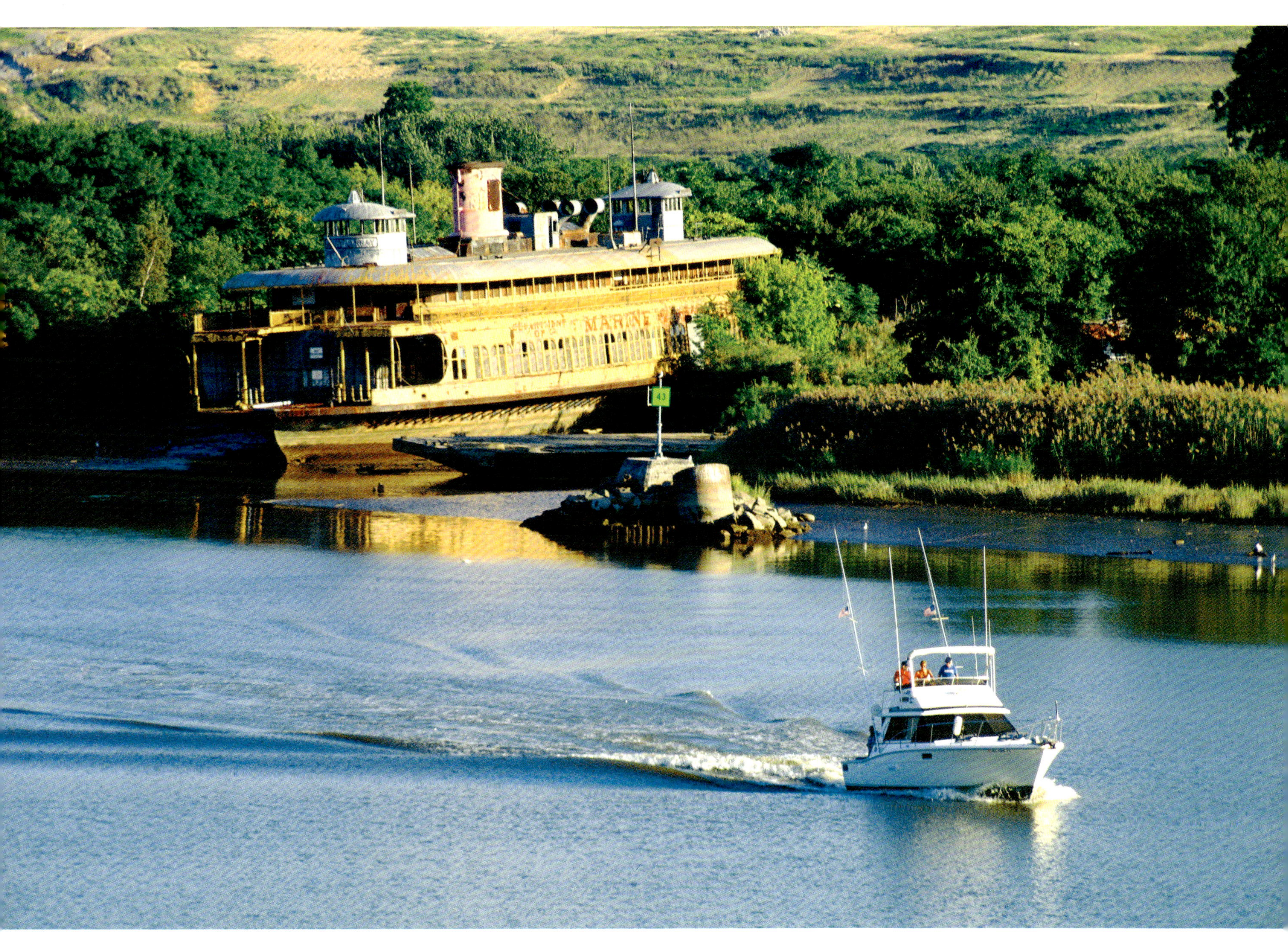
MARINE
43

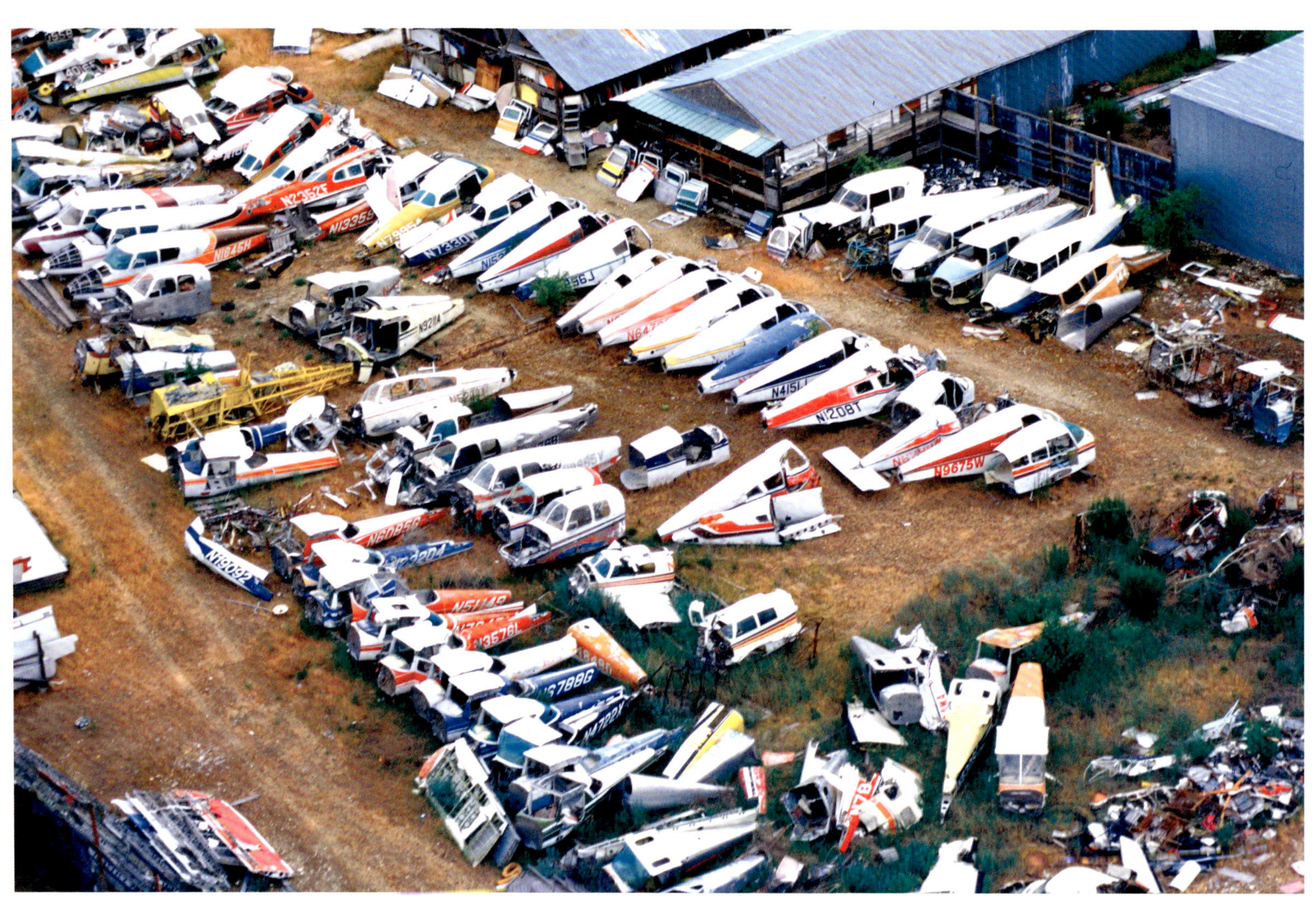
N2352F
N1846H
N9211A
N4151J
N1208T
N9675W
N19092
N6085G
N5114B
N3576L
N4722X

About 100 fractured fuselages lay next to a tiny
one-strip runway used primarily by crop dusters.
"Where do you store the propellers?" I asked the graveyard's owner.
"Don't have any. They always break when the planes crash."
"You're not tellin' me that all those planes crashed?"
"Yeah. All of 'em."

Culebra | *Puerto Rico*

At the conclusion of *Planet of the Apes*, astronaut Charlton Heston, believing he is on another planet, rounds a bend on a beach and is shocked to find the ruins of the Statue of Liberty partially buried in the sand. It was less melodramatic, but nonetheless startling, when I turned a corner and found this Sherman tank, battered by military target practice and corroded by salt water.

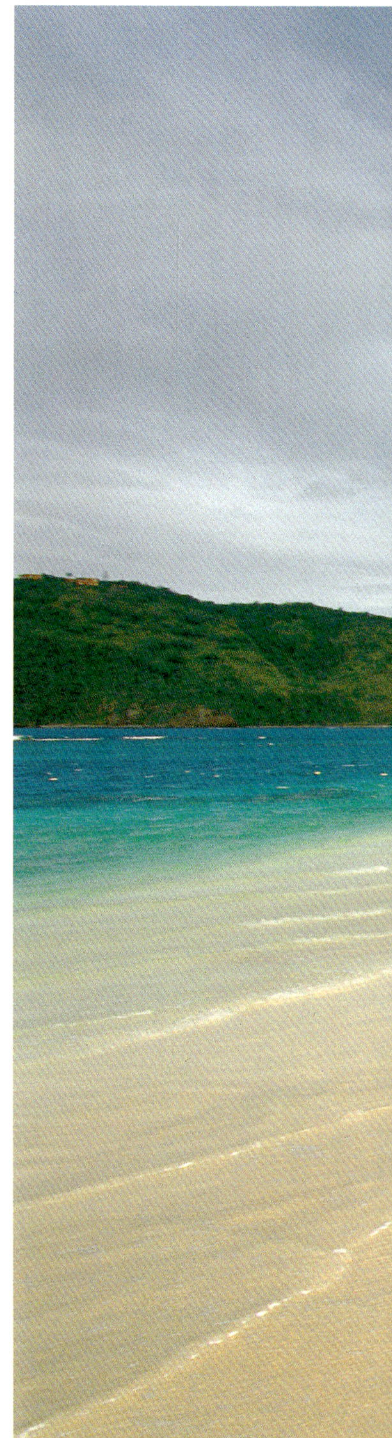

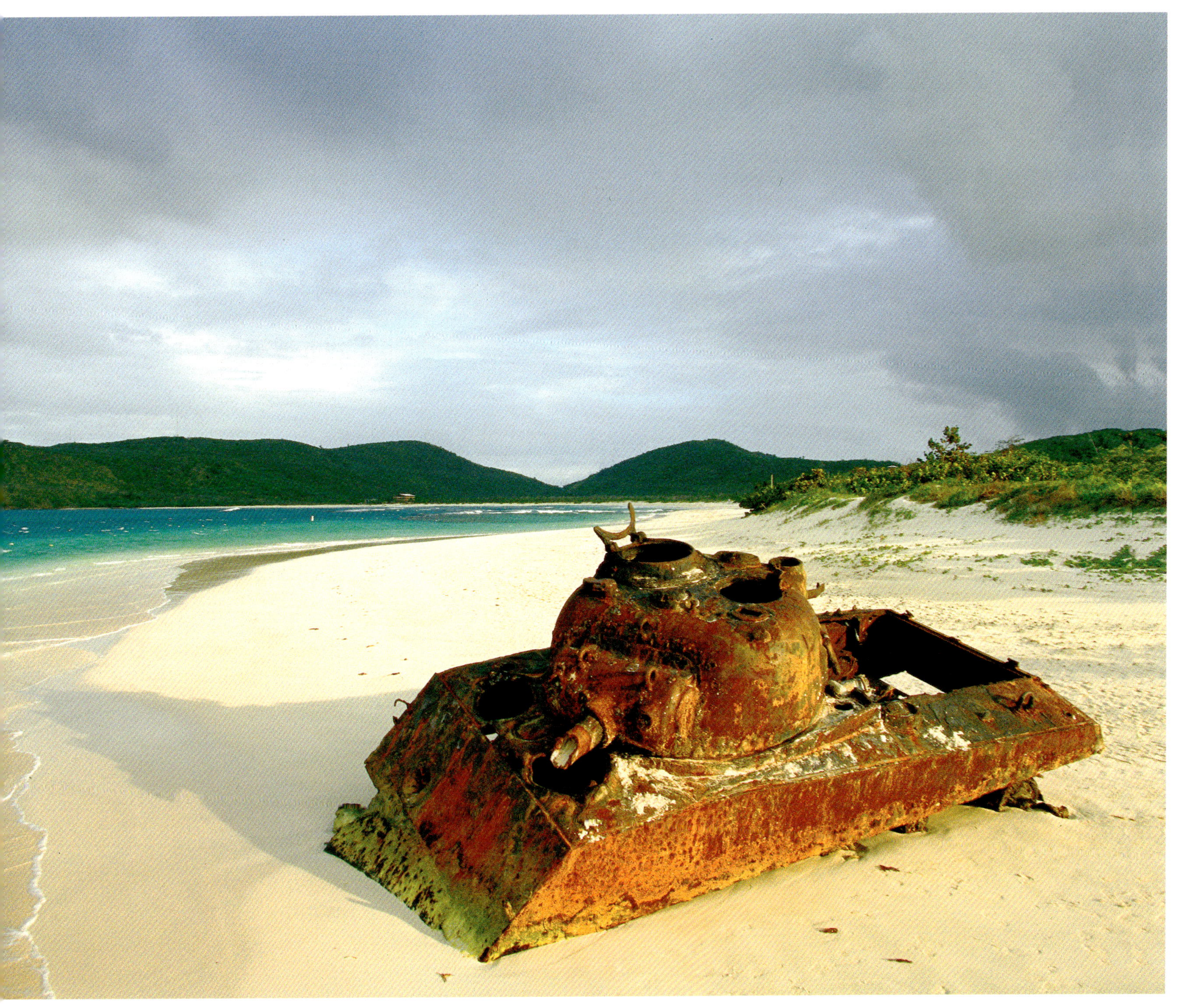

Signs & Facades

I missed the coming-of-age experience of taking a date to a drive-in, yet that activity is so embedded in the collective American consciousness that I easily envisioned myself as an 18-year-old at this drive-in, popcorn in my lap, my right hand tentatively wandering. You might call this "faux déjà vu": an experience you're *not* having today triggering the memory of an experience you did *not* have in the past.

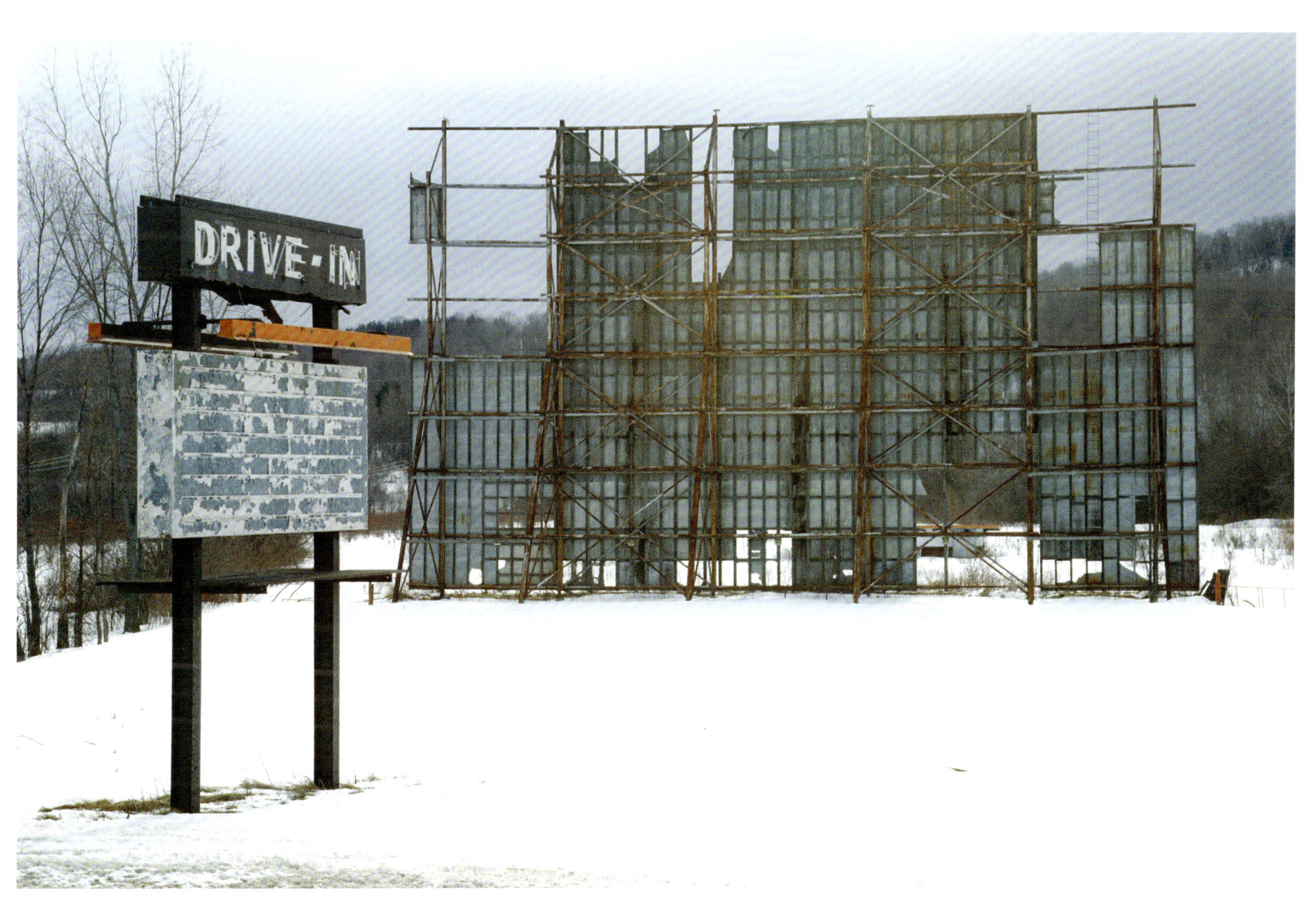
DRIVE-IN

There was no house on a nearby hill, but WHIT'S so closely resembled the Bates Motel I wondered: was this motel driven out of business when Hitchcock's *Psycho* hit the screen and terrified the entire nation?

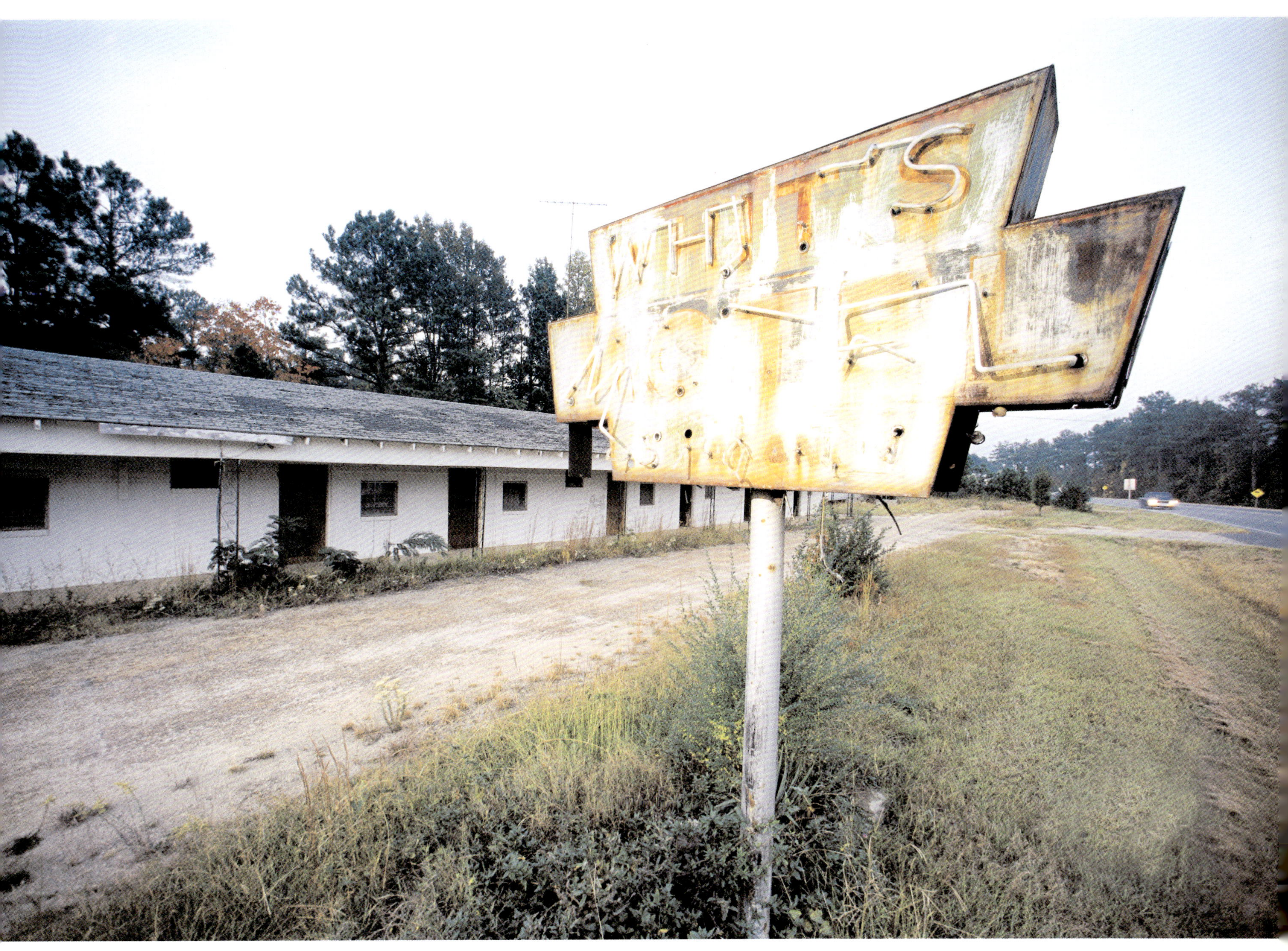

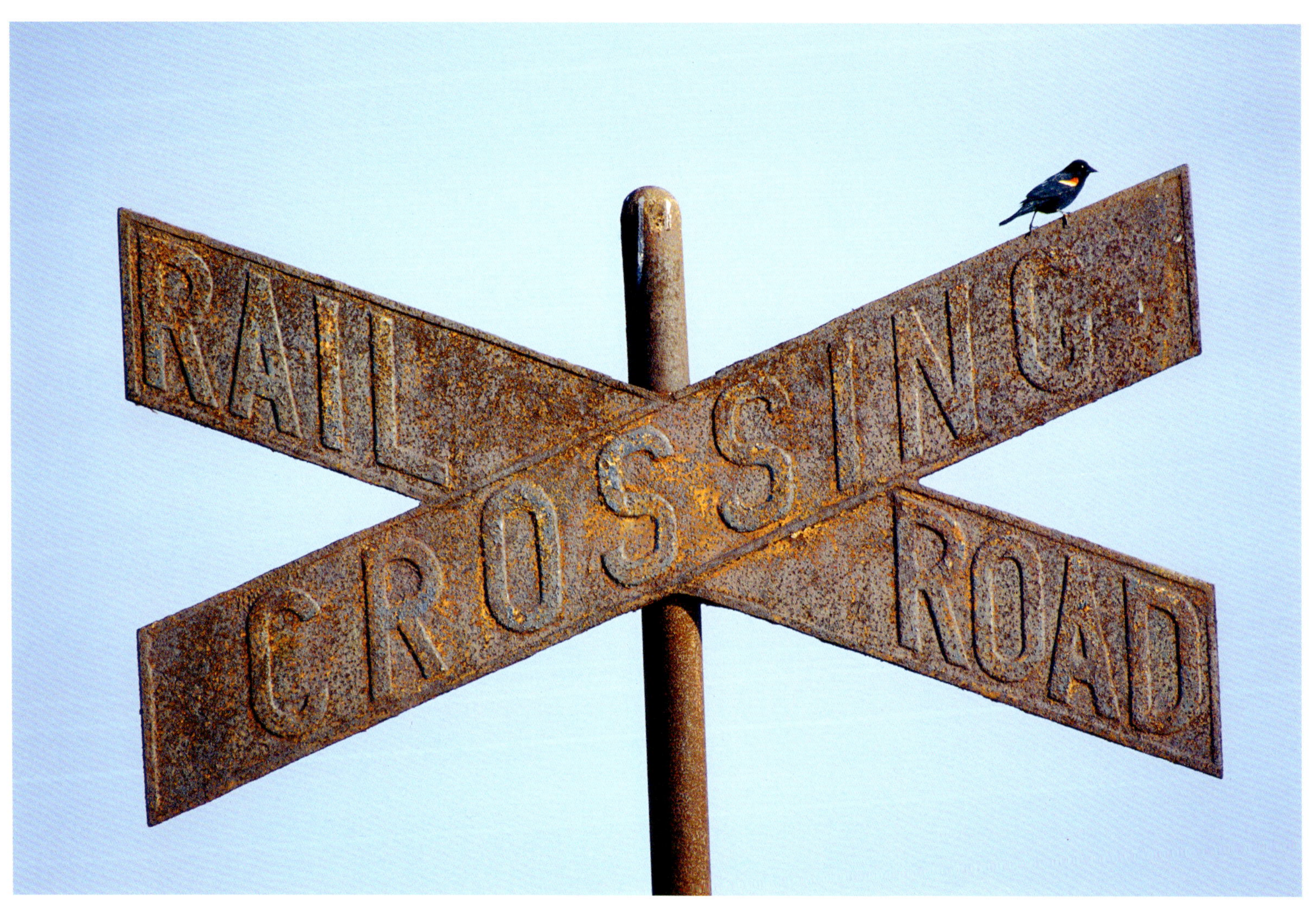
RAIL ROAD
CROSSING

This red-winged blackbird was perched in a perfect position, but just a few decades too late, to spot steam trains coming down the tracks.

I once toured inside an active pulp mill similar to the one I found abandoned in Lawrence. Harsh chemicals saturated the air like tear gas and after just a few minutes' exposure I aborted the tour and escaped to the outside with one overriding thought: I must take a shower!

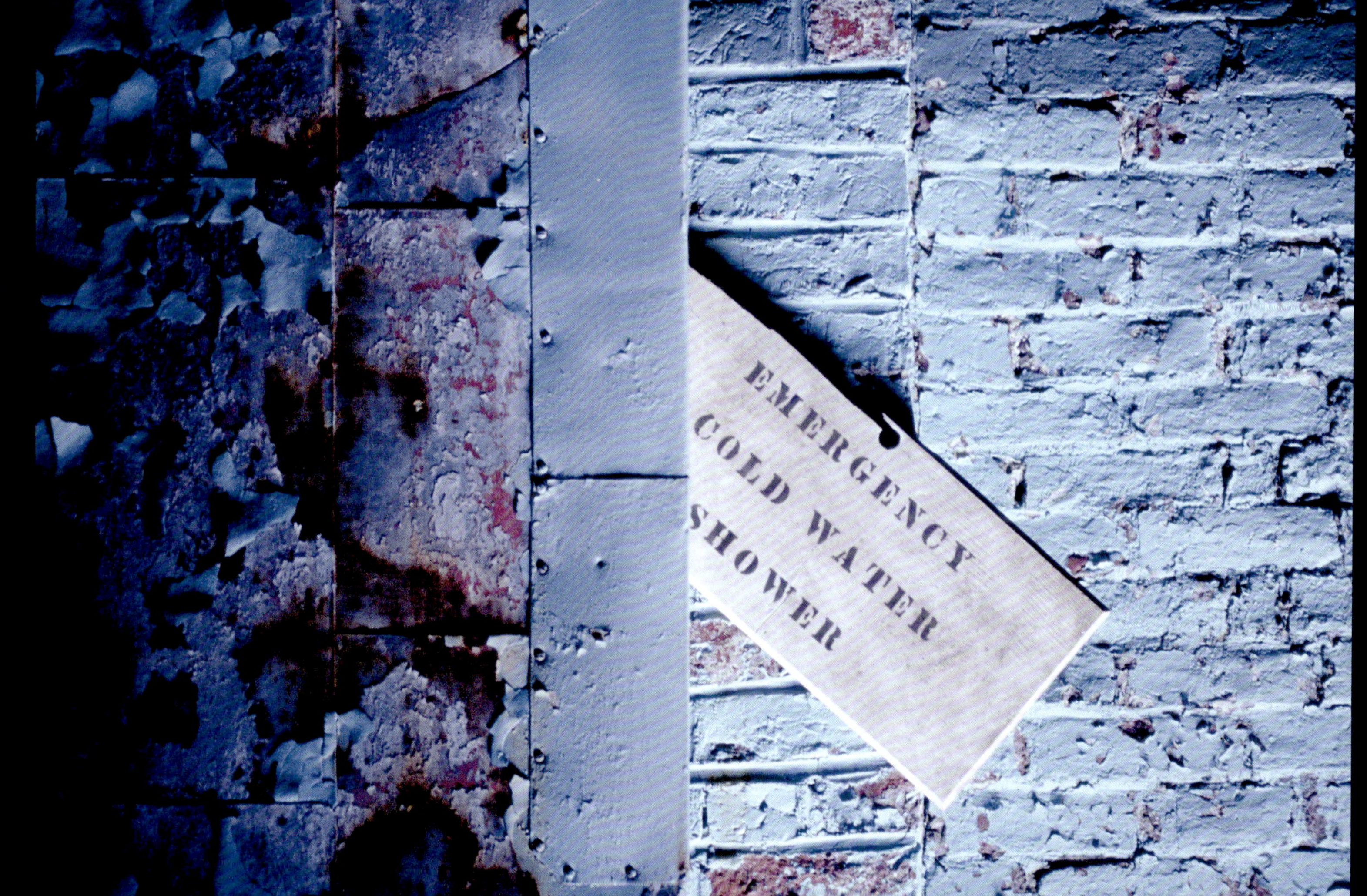
EMERGENCY
COLD WATER
SHOWER

122

Lost Springs | *Wyoming*

This town was comprised of three houses, including the one in the photograph. I saw no evidence of spring water.

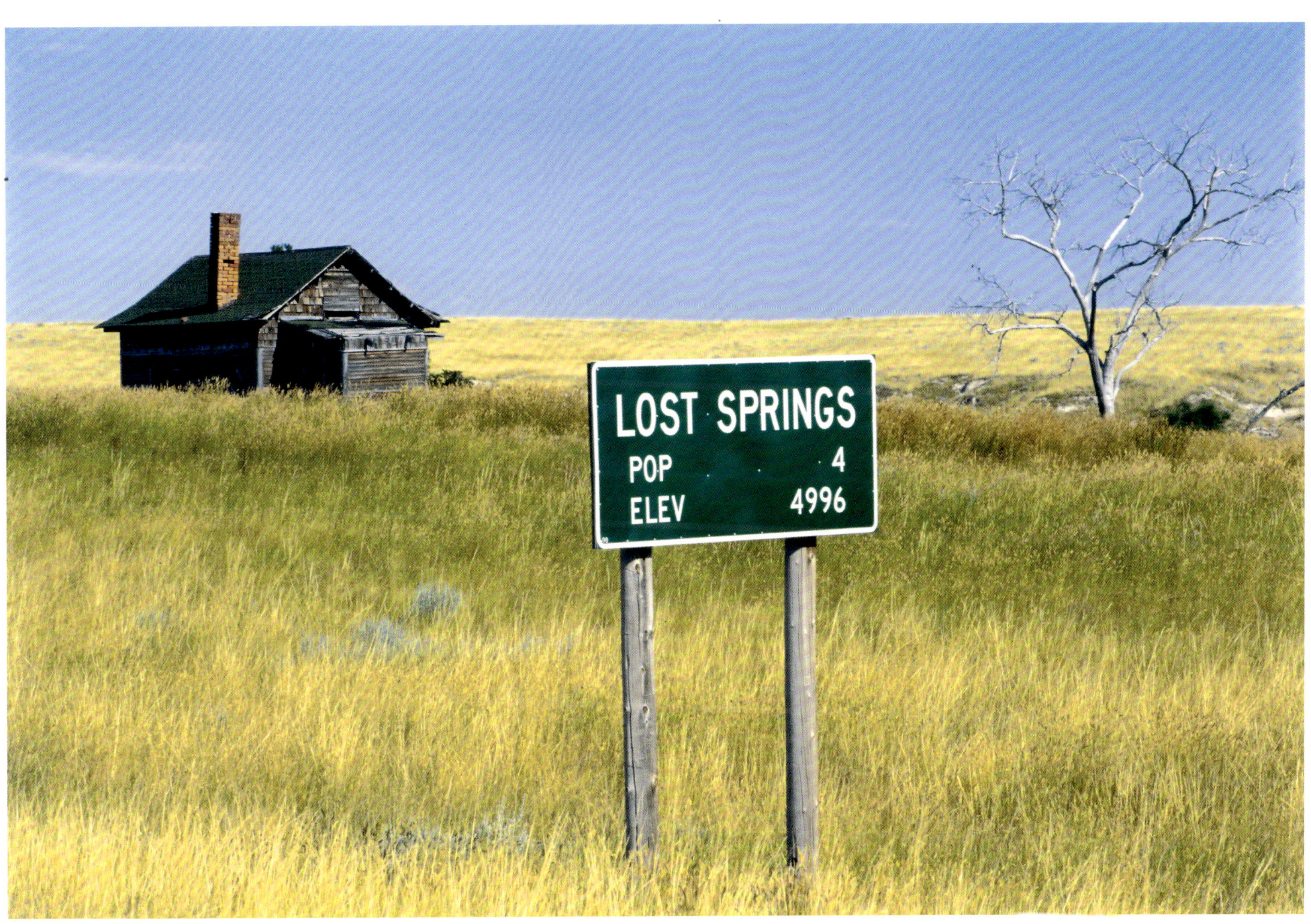
LOST SPRINGS
POP 4
ELEV 4996

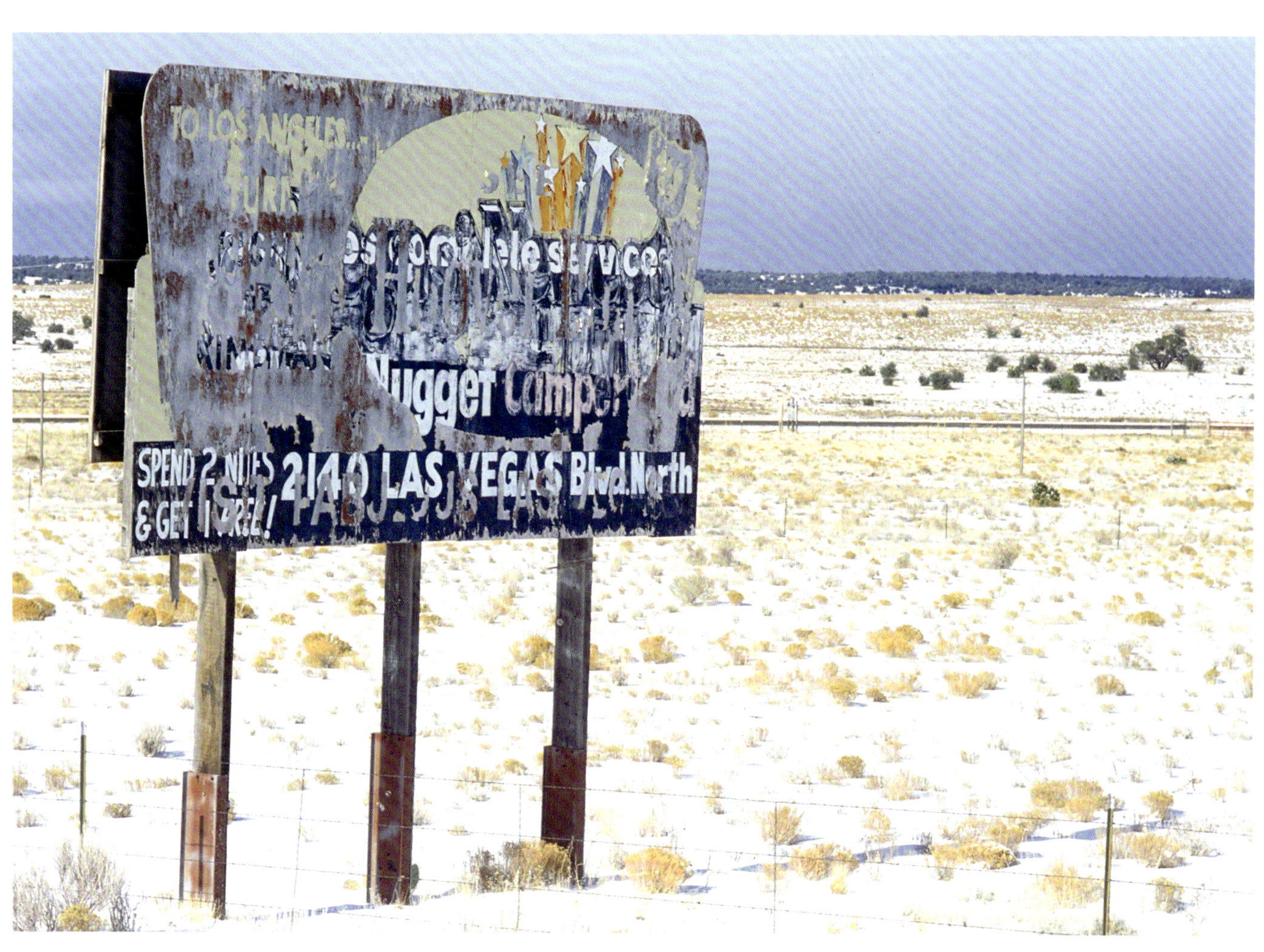
TO LOS ANGELES...
Nugget
SPEND 2
2140 LAS VEGAS Blvd.North
& GET

After a nearby interstate highway was completed, this billboard on an old state road had few eyes on it.

Johnson City | *Tennessee*

He had the face of a prophet and the clothes of a pauper. I asked him to pose for me by leaning on the wall of a 1930s warehouse. "You probably think I'm some kinda bum," he declared, "but if you got to know me you'd be surprised." How right he was. We spent the day together scouting for photos along Tennessee back roads, all the while absorbed in fascinating conversation.

"Can I send you a print of you and the Coke sign?" I offered.

"Nope," he replied, "I don't have an address."

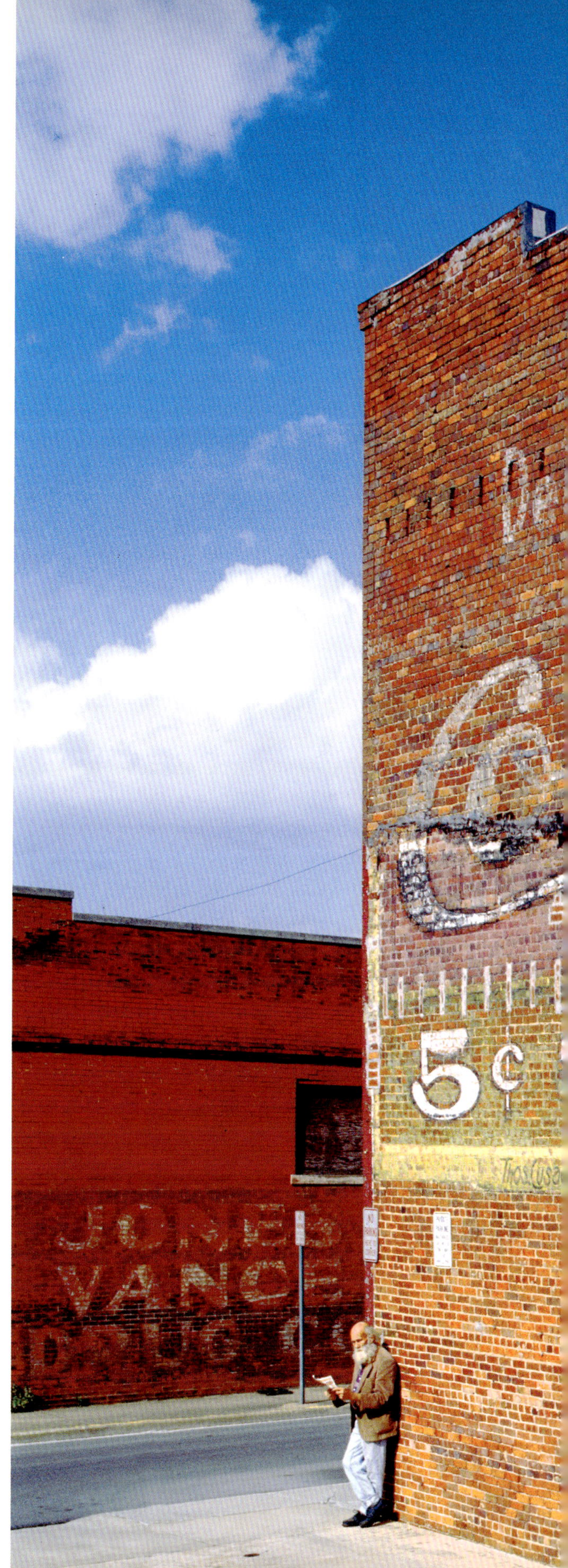

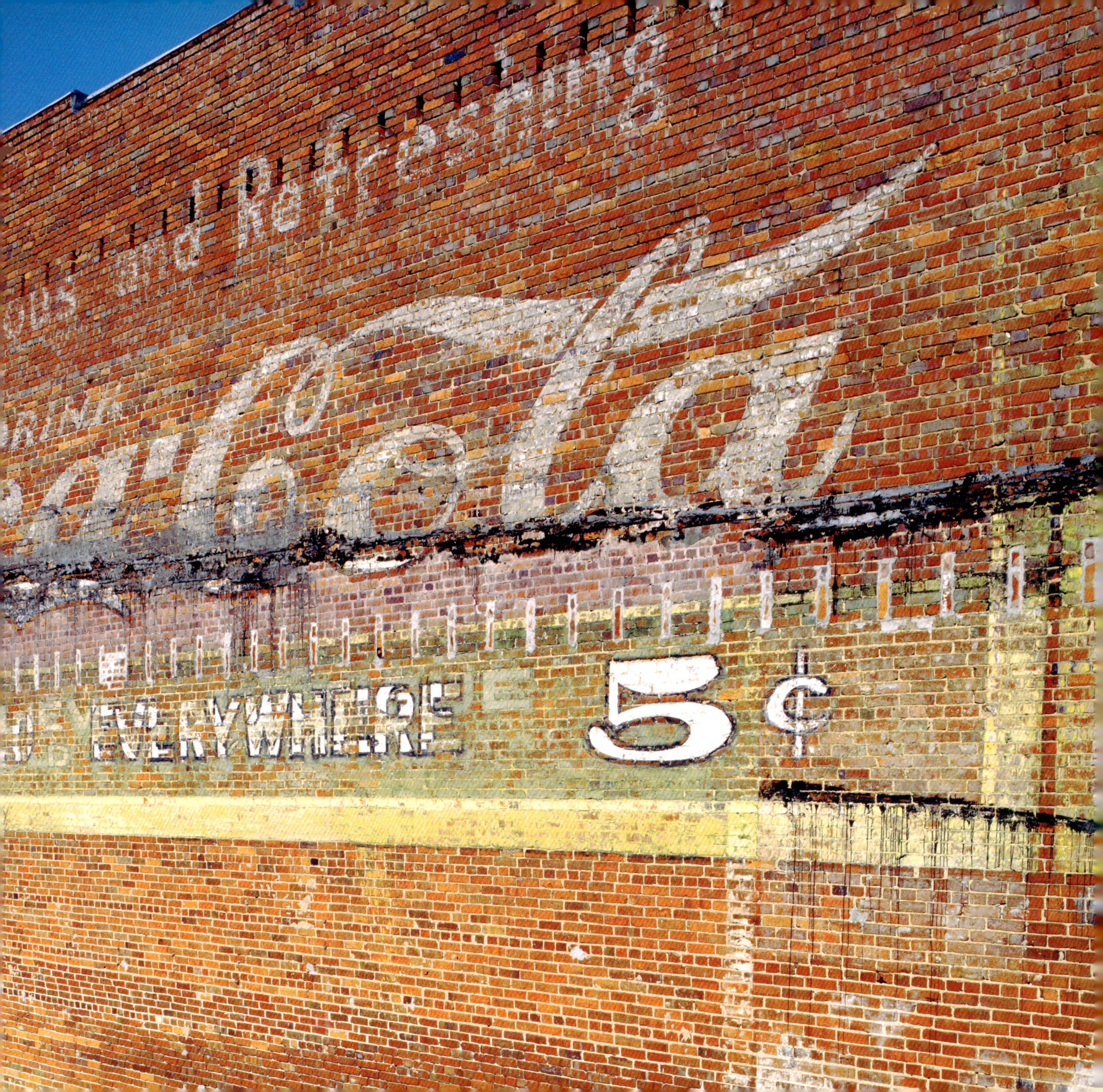
and Refreshing
EVERYWHERE
5¢

CENTREVILLE | *Mississippi*

The urbanization, suburbanization and Walmartization of America was a body blow to many an American Main Street. While many town centers were wounded, the majority have survived, a few have even prospered. Alas, some have not.

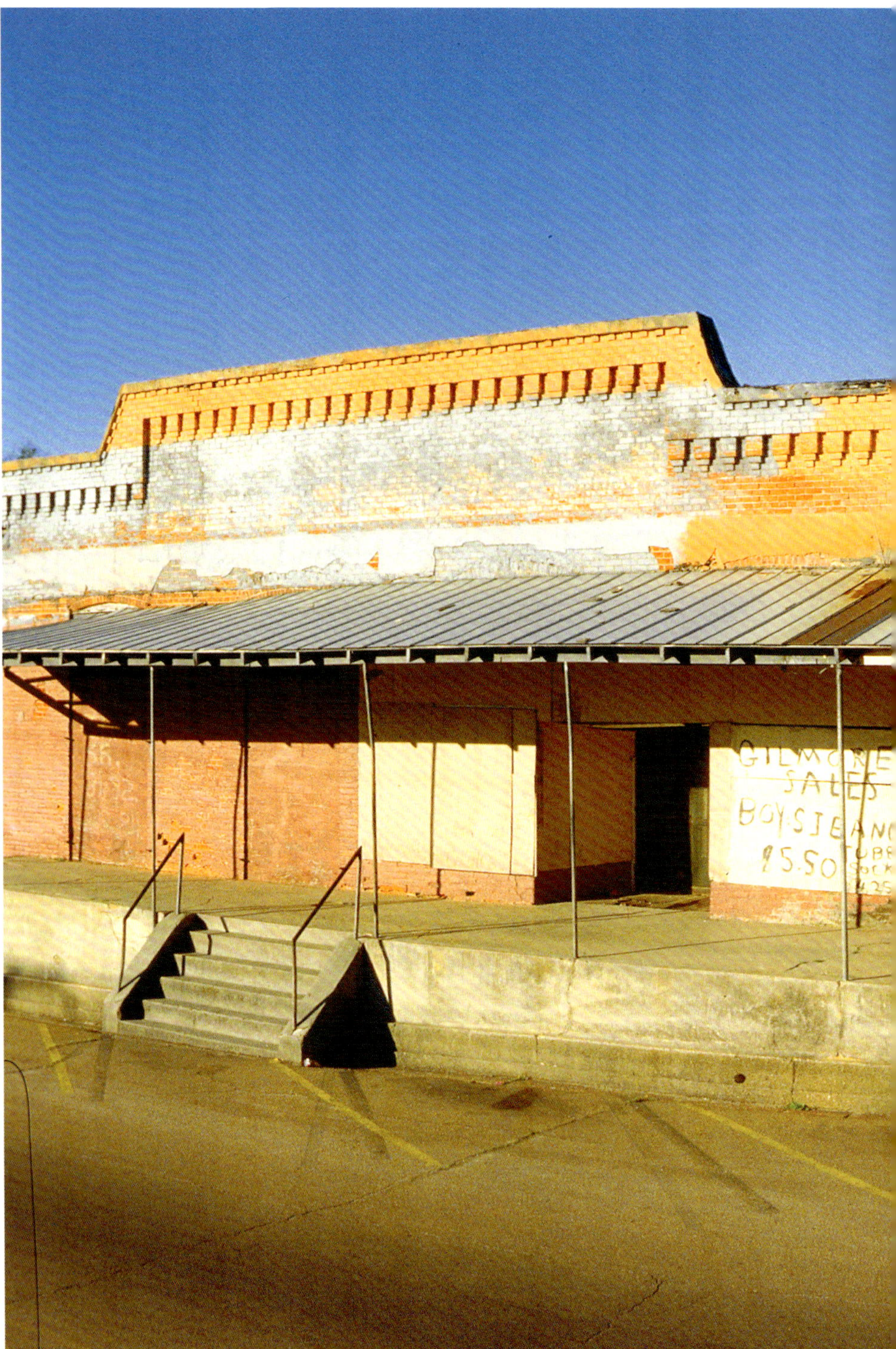

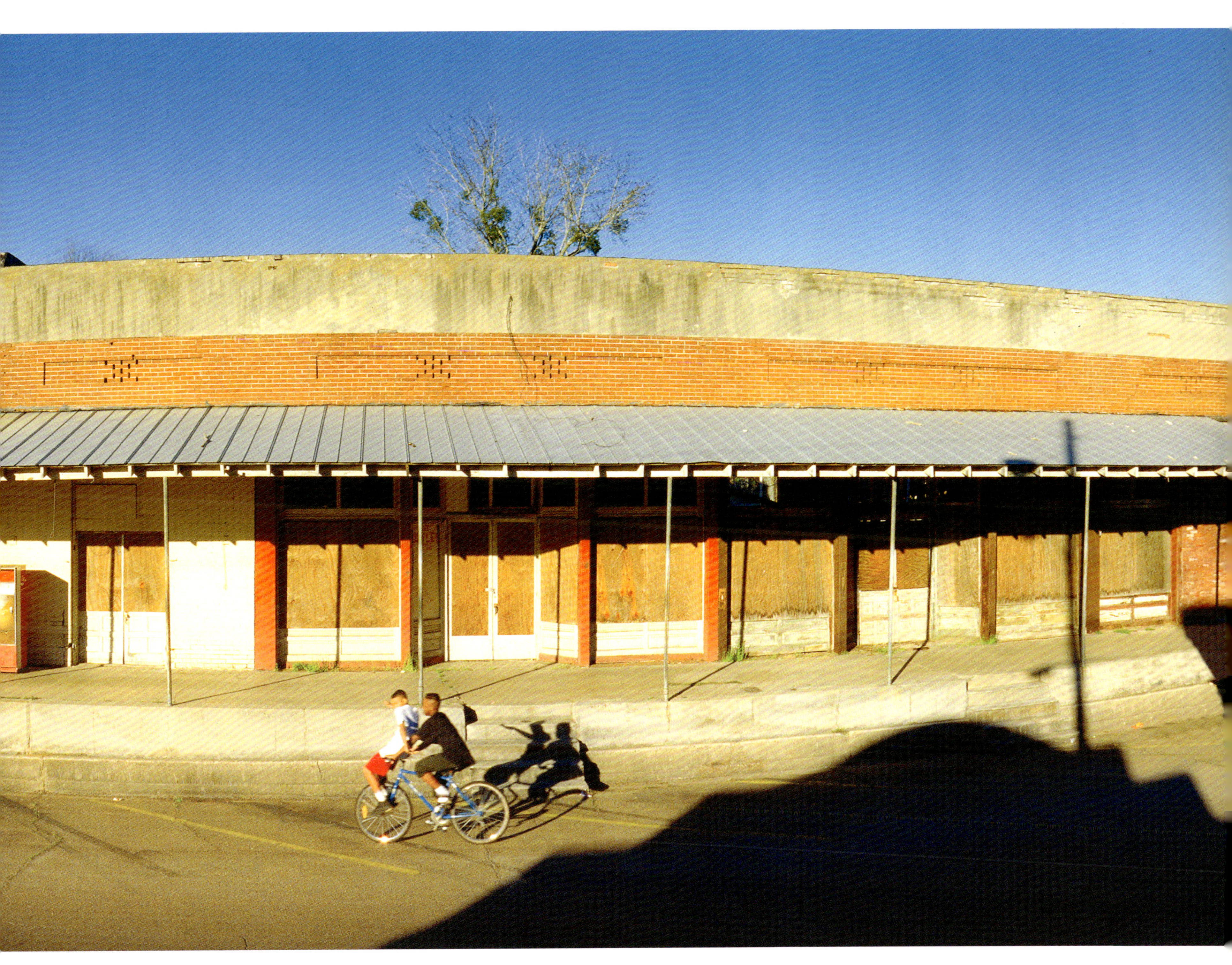

CUSTER COUNTY | *South Dakota*

Decades before self-serve, credit card payment, and mini-marts, I stood at a station just like this one near my grandfather's house and watched gasoline flow through the small glass bulbs near the top of the pumps.

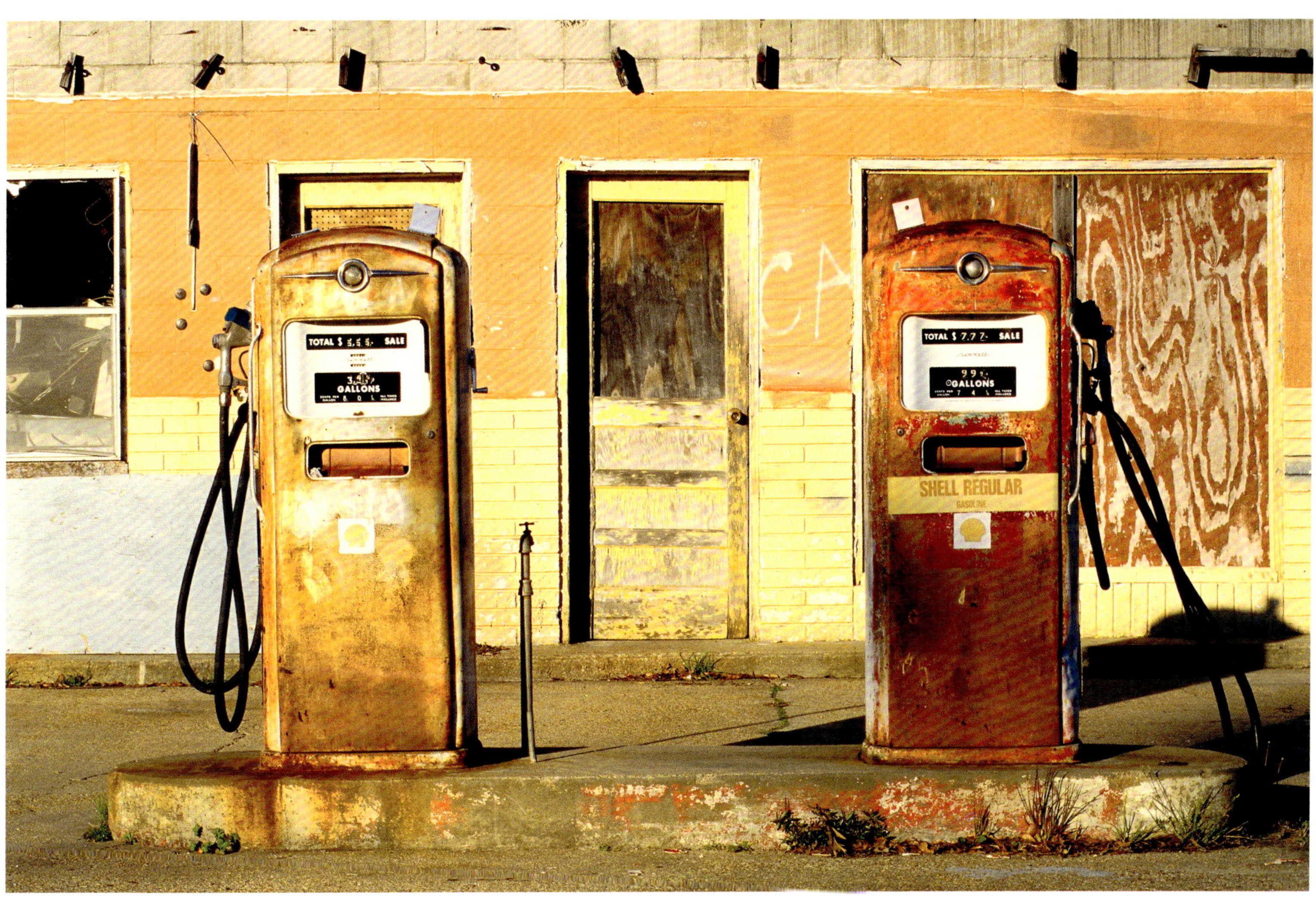
TOTAL $ SALE
GALLONS
TOTAL $ 7.77 SALE
GALLONS
SHELL REGULAR
GASOLINE

Asbury Park | *New Jersey*

I lost many a quarter on Asbury Park's bustling arcade in the late 1950s when this architecturally majestic hotel must have sparkled. A decade later the town lost its lure and became a ghostly presence, sandwiched between beautiful ocean beaches and wealthy neighborhoods.

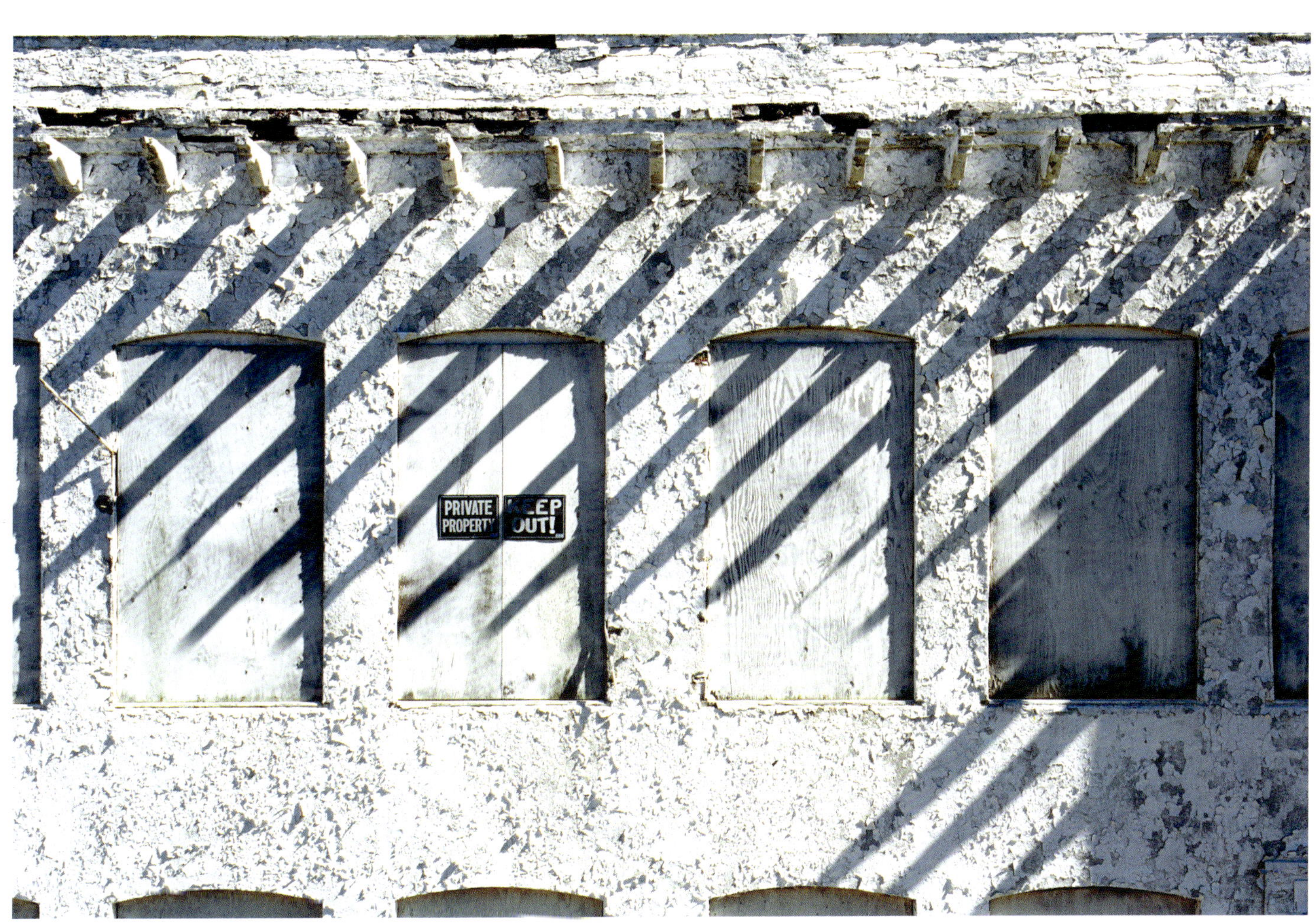
PRIVATE
PROPERTY
OUT!

ASBURY PARK | *New Jersey*

From the old Paramount dance hall veranda, the ocean appears like a *trompe l'oeil* in reverse—something *real* that *looks like* a painting.

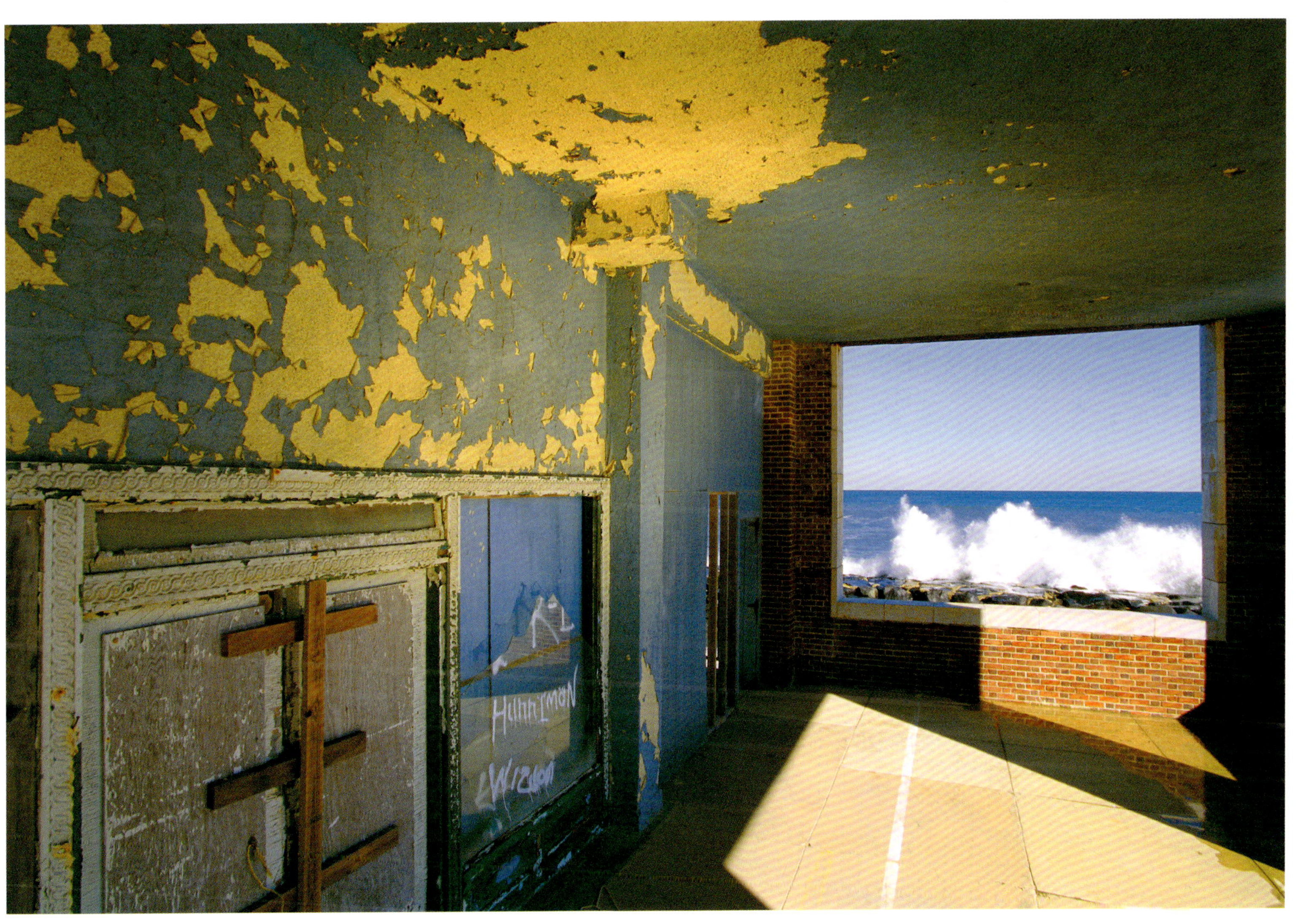

Rocky Point | *Rhode Island*

Situated on a beautiful peninsula in Narragansett Bay, the Rocky Point Amusement Park had its origins before the Civil War. It was closed recently to make way for residential development. After a very long run, this house no longer haunts.

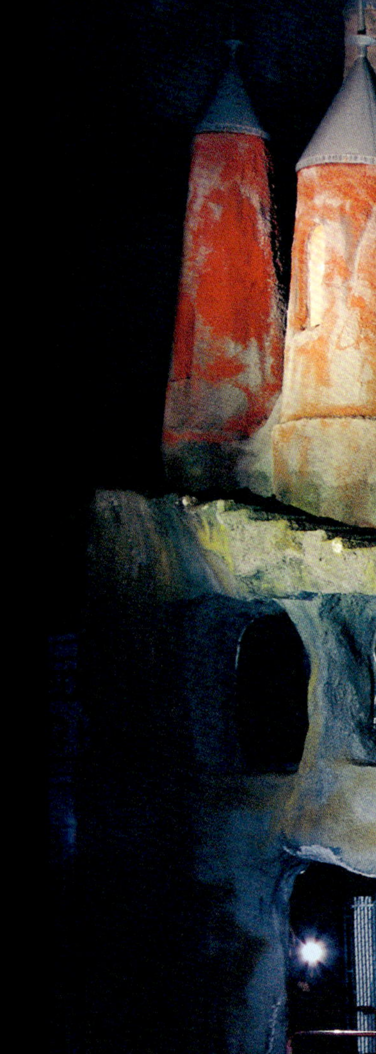

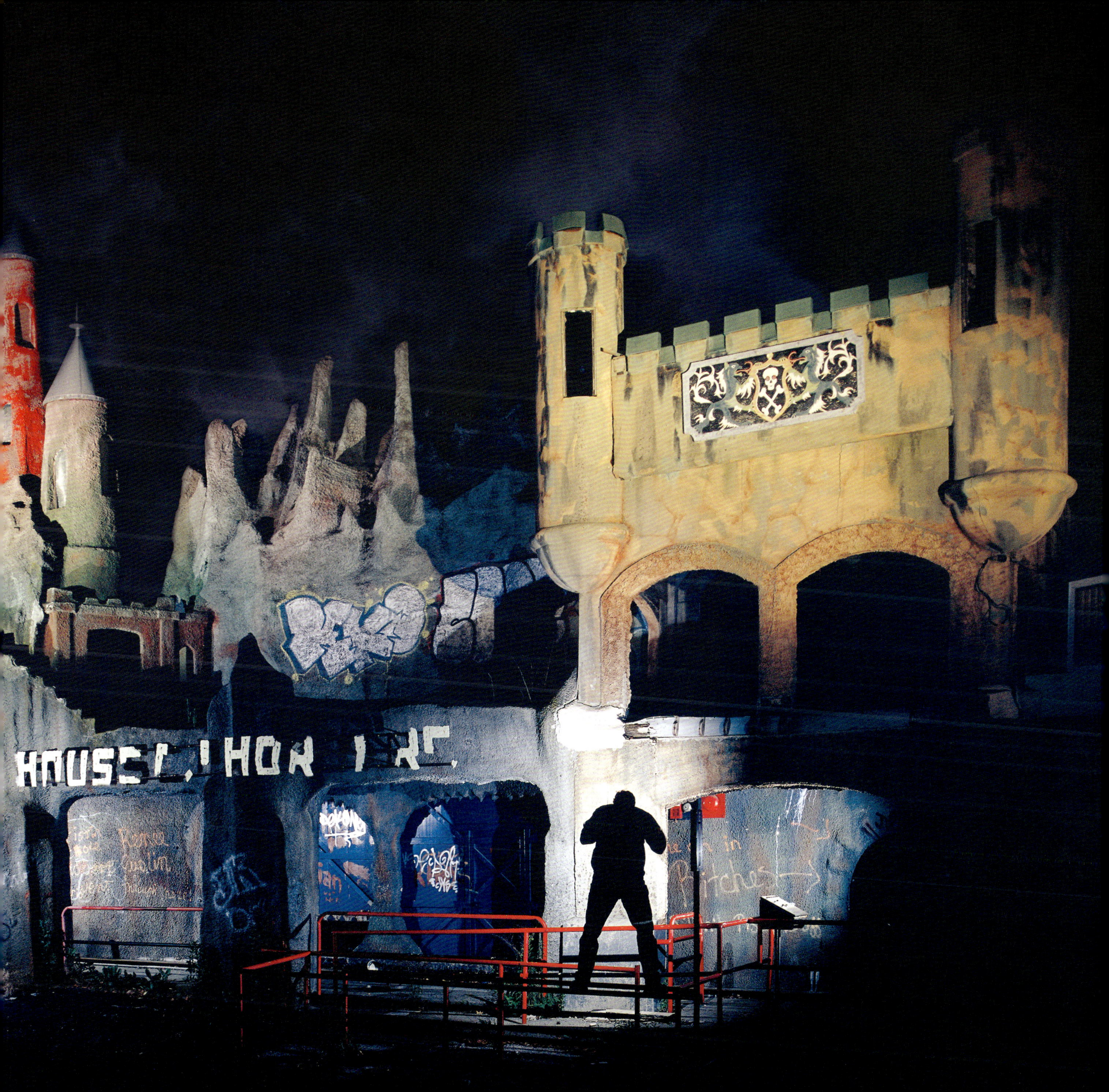

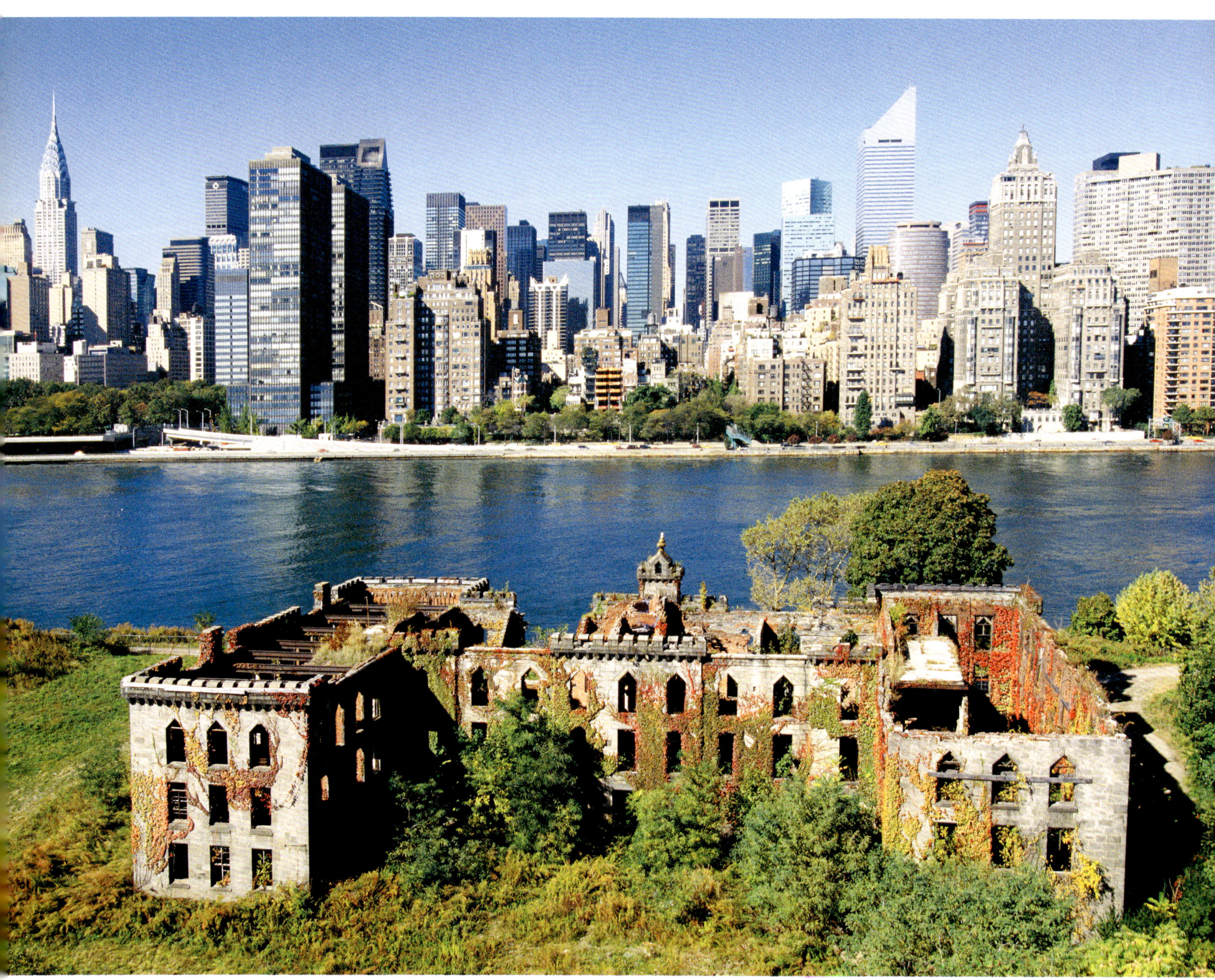

No sooner are Manhattan's buildings abandoned than they meet with wrecking balls and construction cranes. But just short yards away from the city's steel and brick giants—on the tip of adjacent Roosevelt Island—the shell of a psychiatric hospital has been left undisturbed for decades. (The vantage point is a helicopter about 100 feet over the East River.)

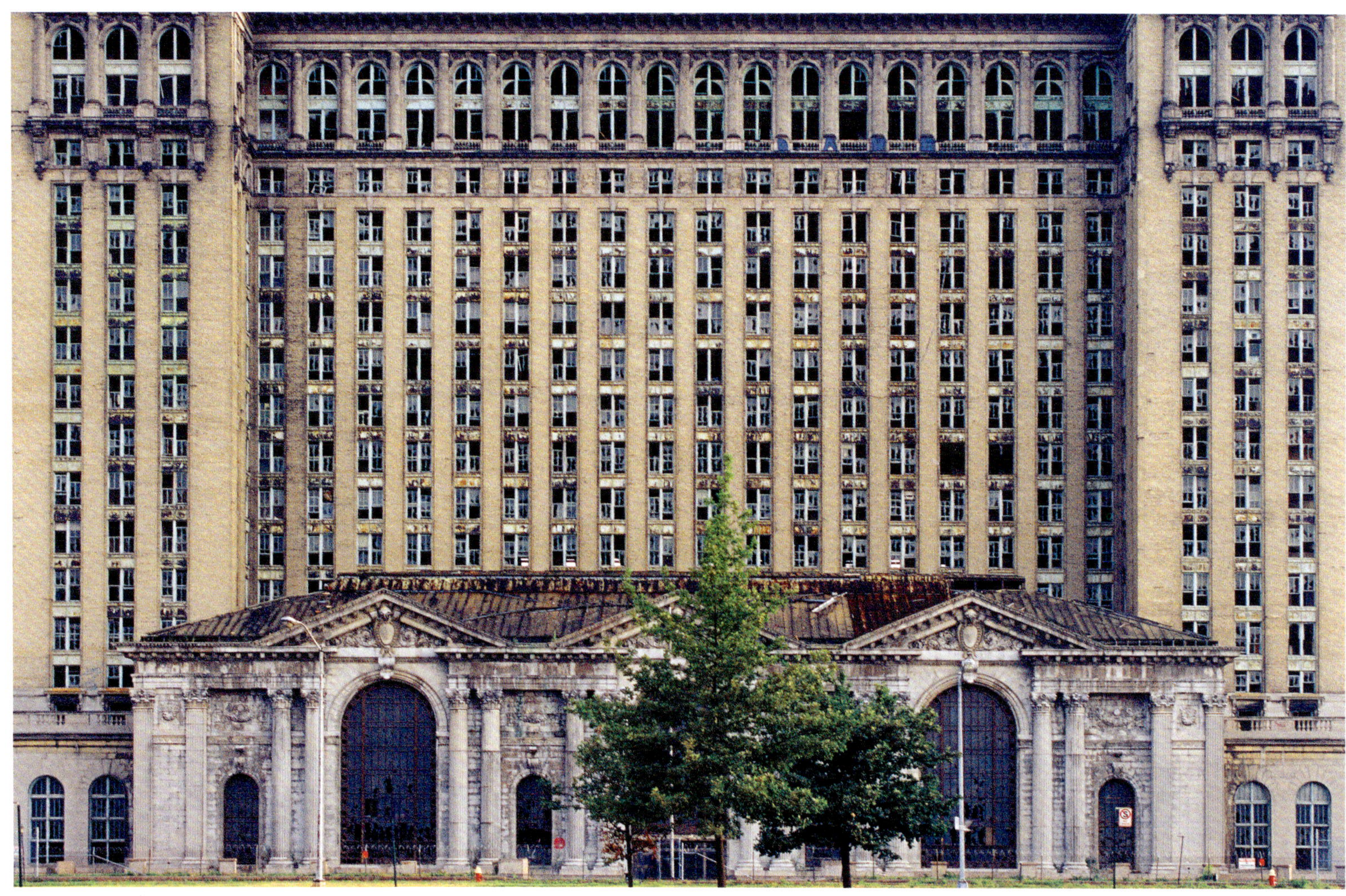

DETROIT | *Michigan*

Detroit's City Council has proposed demolishing the Grand Trunk Railroad building, which served as both train station and corporate headquarters. Inside and out, this is the most breathtaking abandoned building I've ever seen. Detroiters arise...save your extraordinary landmark!

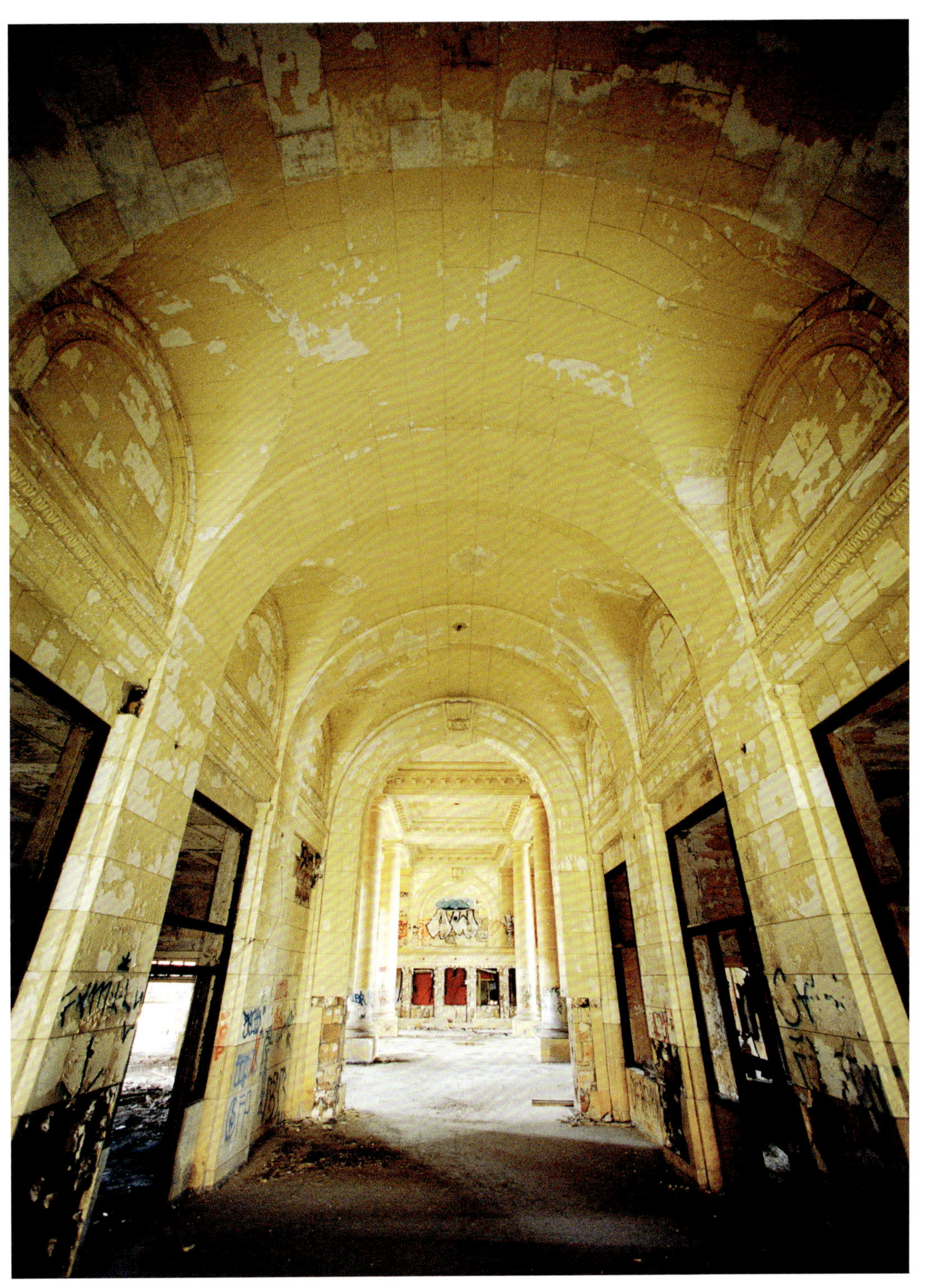

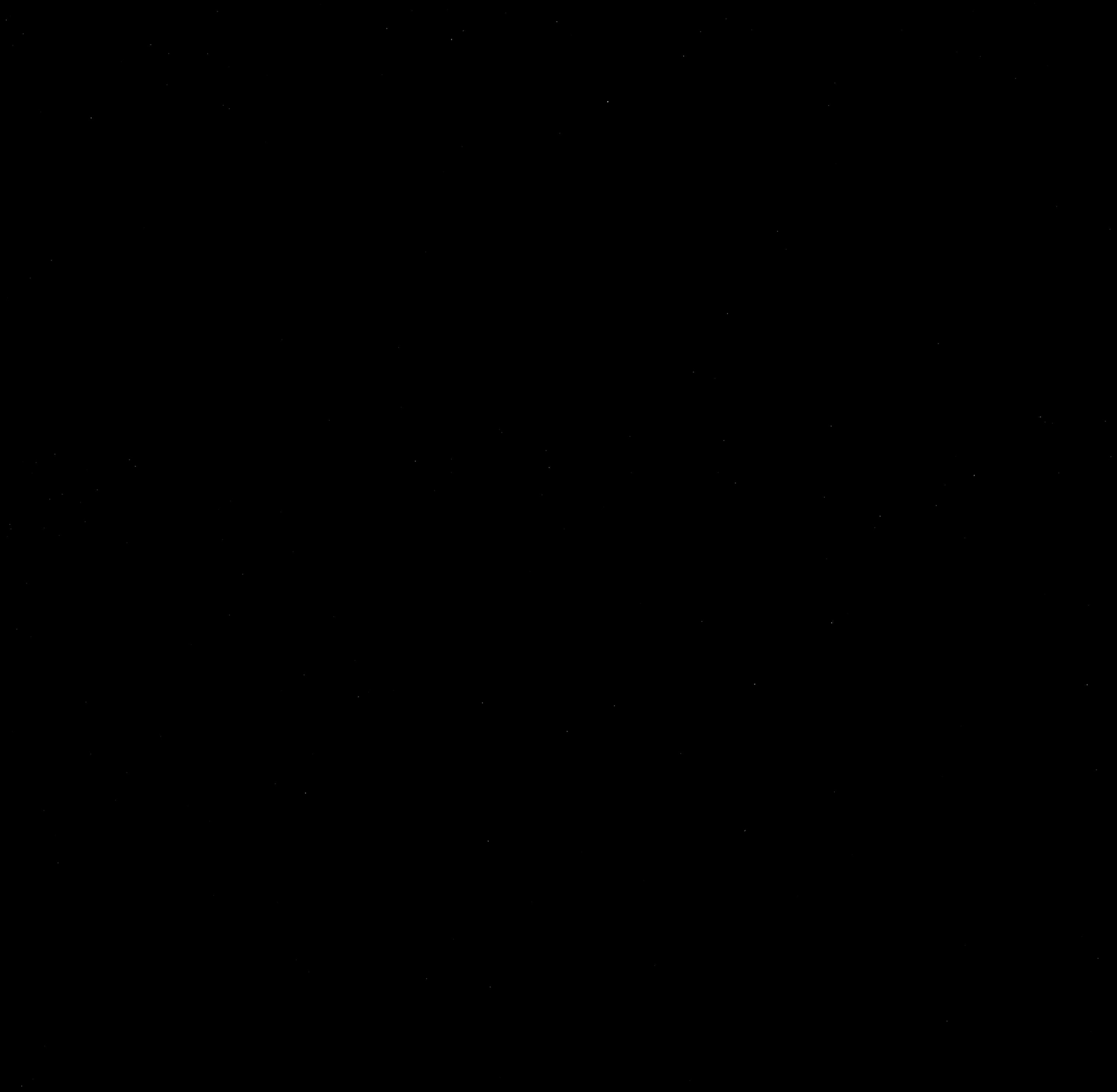

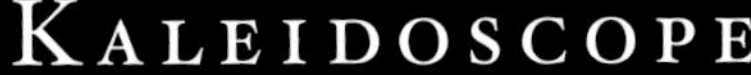

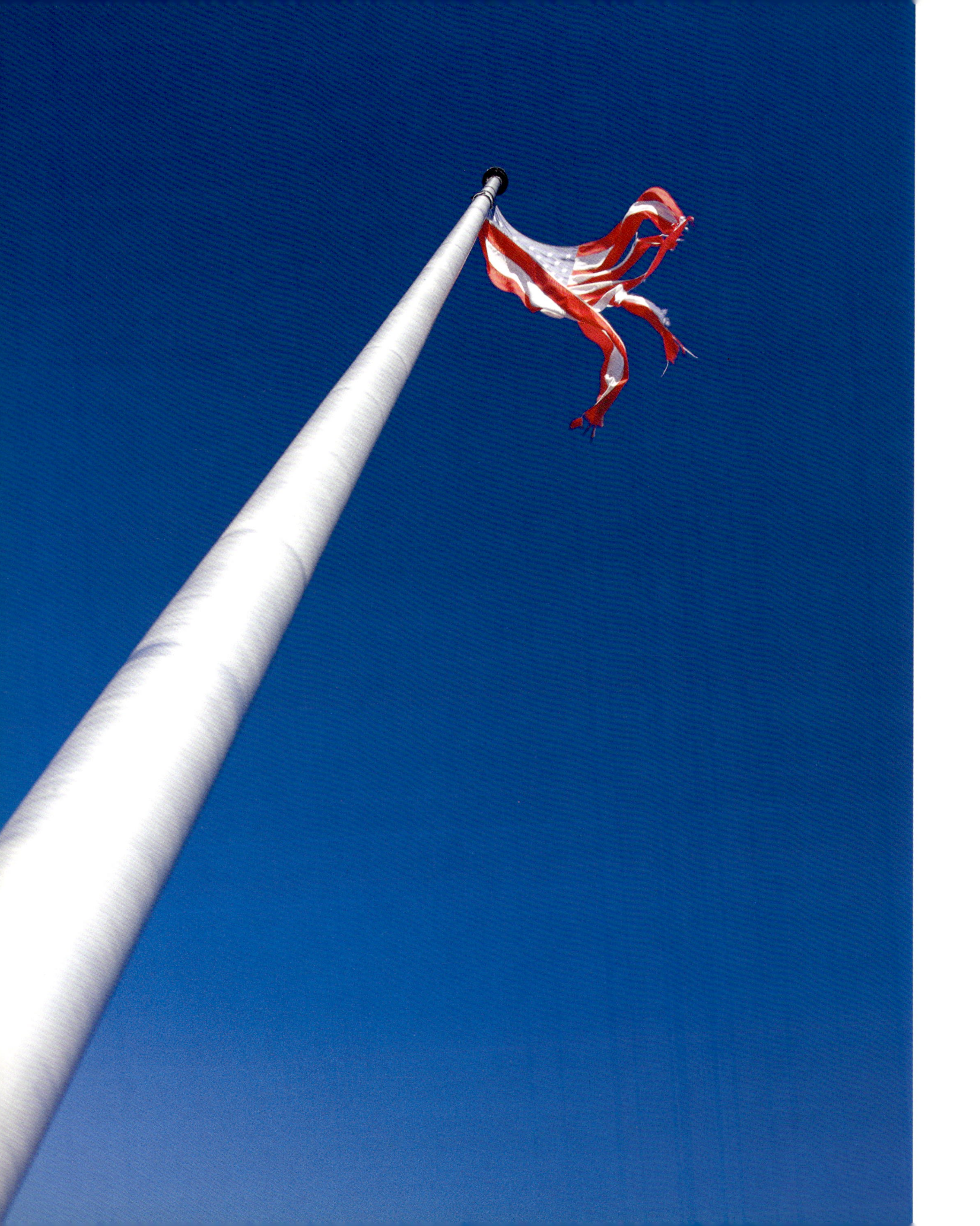

Someone taped the rope to the top of the pole, so that the flag—ironically situated on government property—could not be lowered. The strong breezes coming off New York City's harbor whipped it to tatters.

Some front page stories had historic significance—the Battle of the Bulge, the Kennedy assassination, Watergate—but most were of no particular import. So what could explain a living room filled with dozens of large bundles of newspapers and magazines, dating from 1944 to 1977, tied up ever-so neatly as if the owner were just about to haul them off to a recycling center?

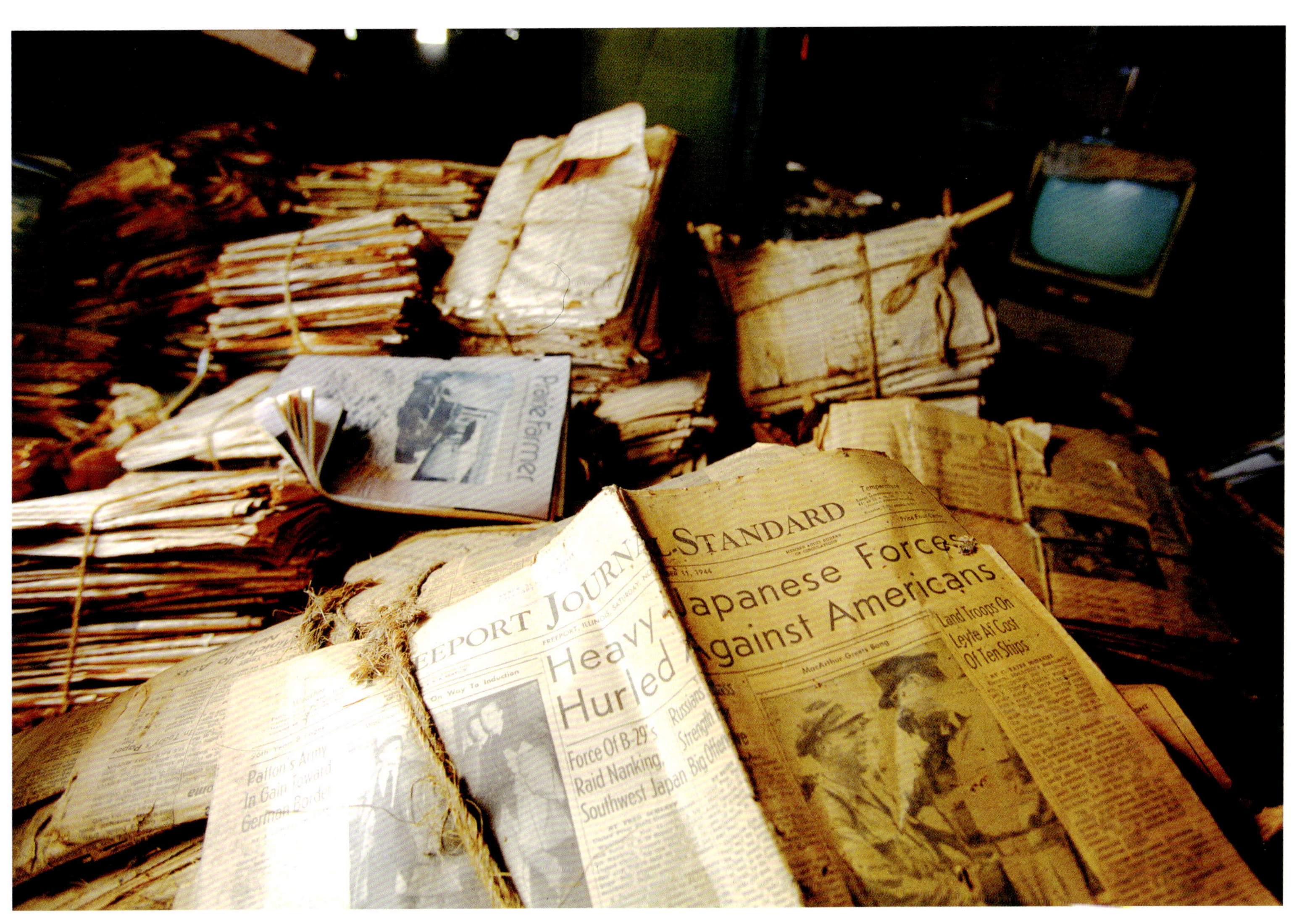
Prairie Farmer
STANDARD
EEPORT JOURN
Japanese Forces
Against Americans
Heavy
Hurled
Land Troops On
Leyte At Cost
Of Ten Ships
MacArthur Greets Bong
On Way To Induction
Force Of B-29's
Raid Nanking,
Southwest Japan
Russians
Strength
Patton's Army
In Gain Toward
German Border

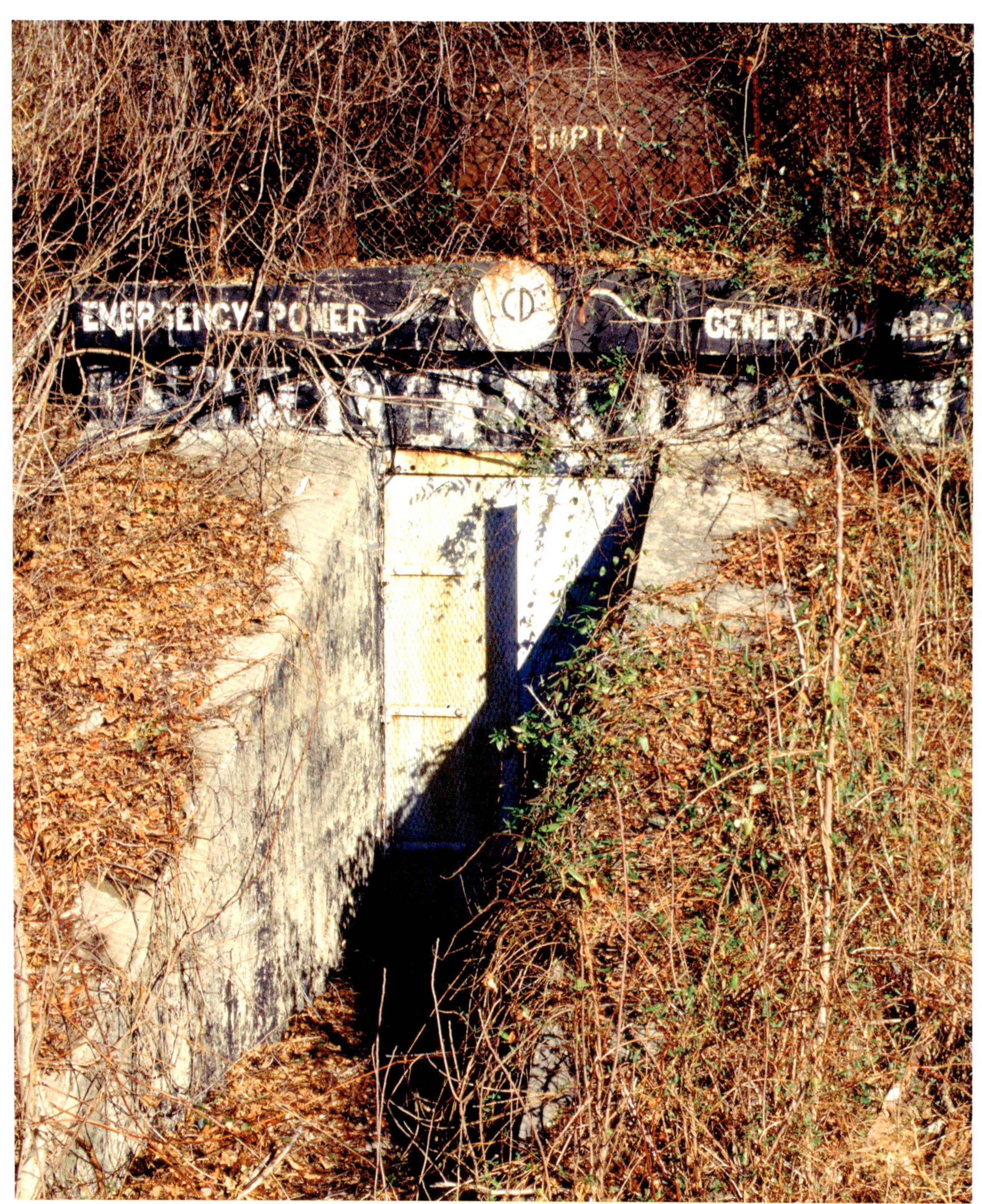
EMERGENCY-POWER
CD

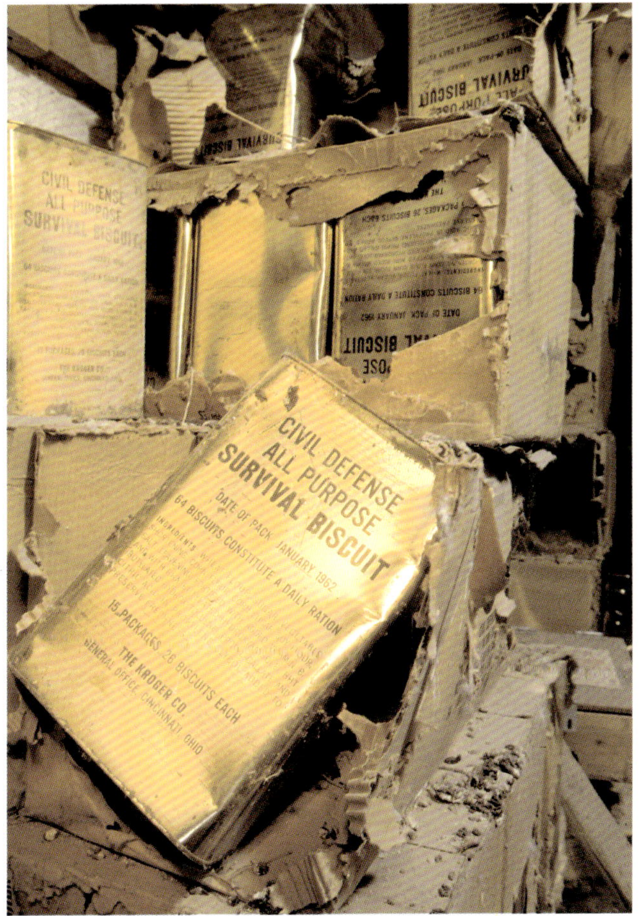

New Castle County | *Delaware*

Nampa | *Idaho*

Ah, the good old days. The days of the Cold War. The Cuban Missile Crisis. The nuclear arms race. Fear of Armageddon. The days when some Americans believed they could retreat into so-called "Civil Defense fallout shelters," live on crackers and water, and then, when radiation levels subsided, return safely to the outside world. Ah yes, those were the good old days.

150

Hudson River | *New York*

As a youngster, I was awed by colossal ocean liners towering majestically beside piers so massive they seemed part of the land itself. Just a few of those piers survive, some as rusted skeletons, decomposing under the forces of rain, ice, fire, and corrosion.

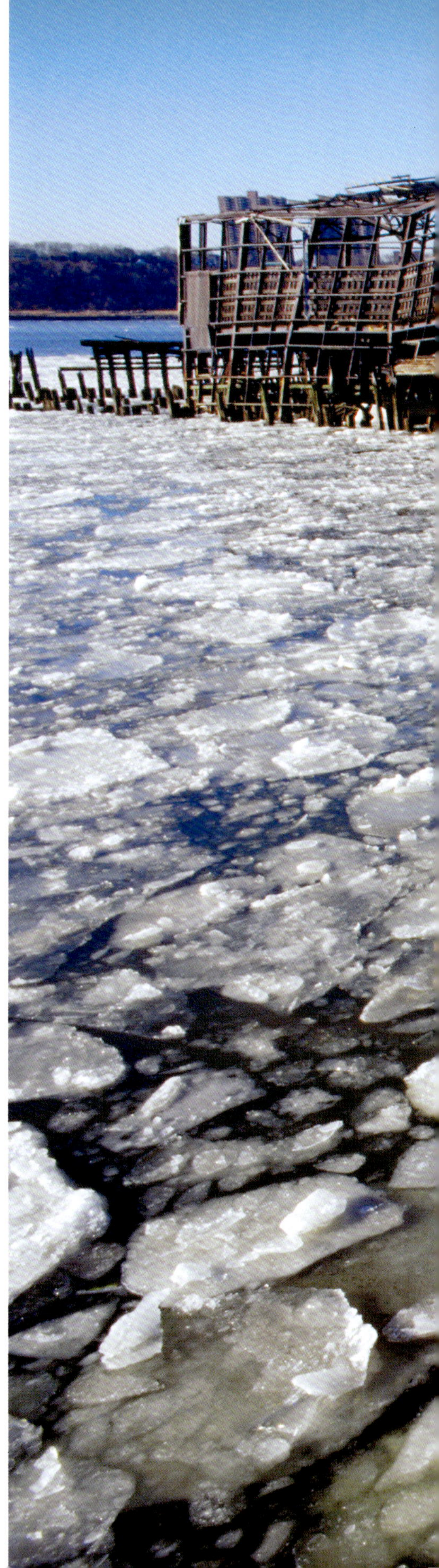

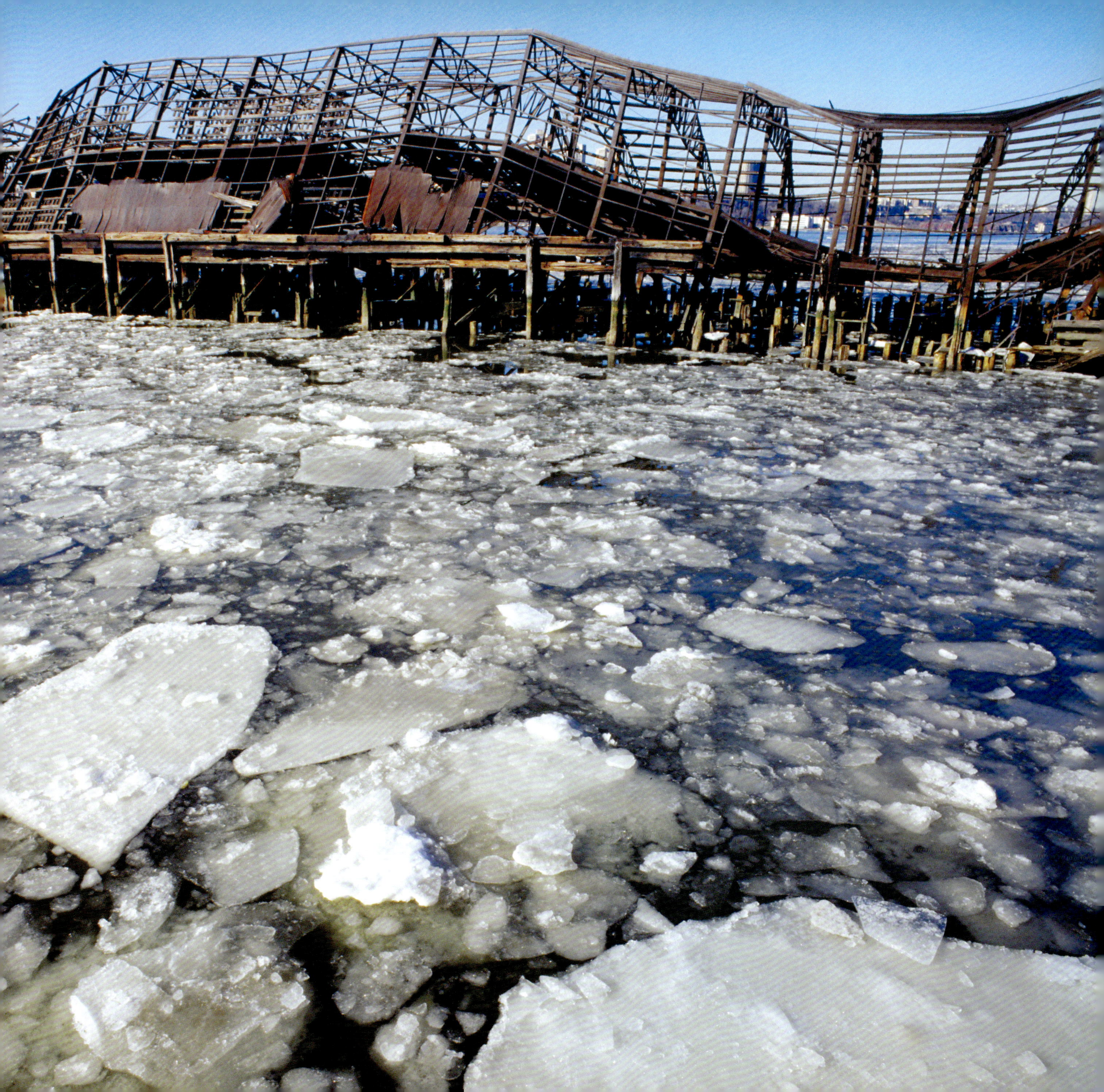

ACCOMACK COUNTY | *Virginia*

As a rule, cemeteries are respectfully tended even when the living have no idea who's buried there. Near the Chesapeake Bay I found an exception to that rule.

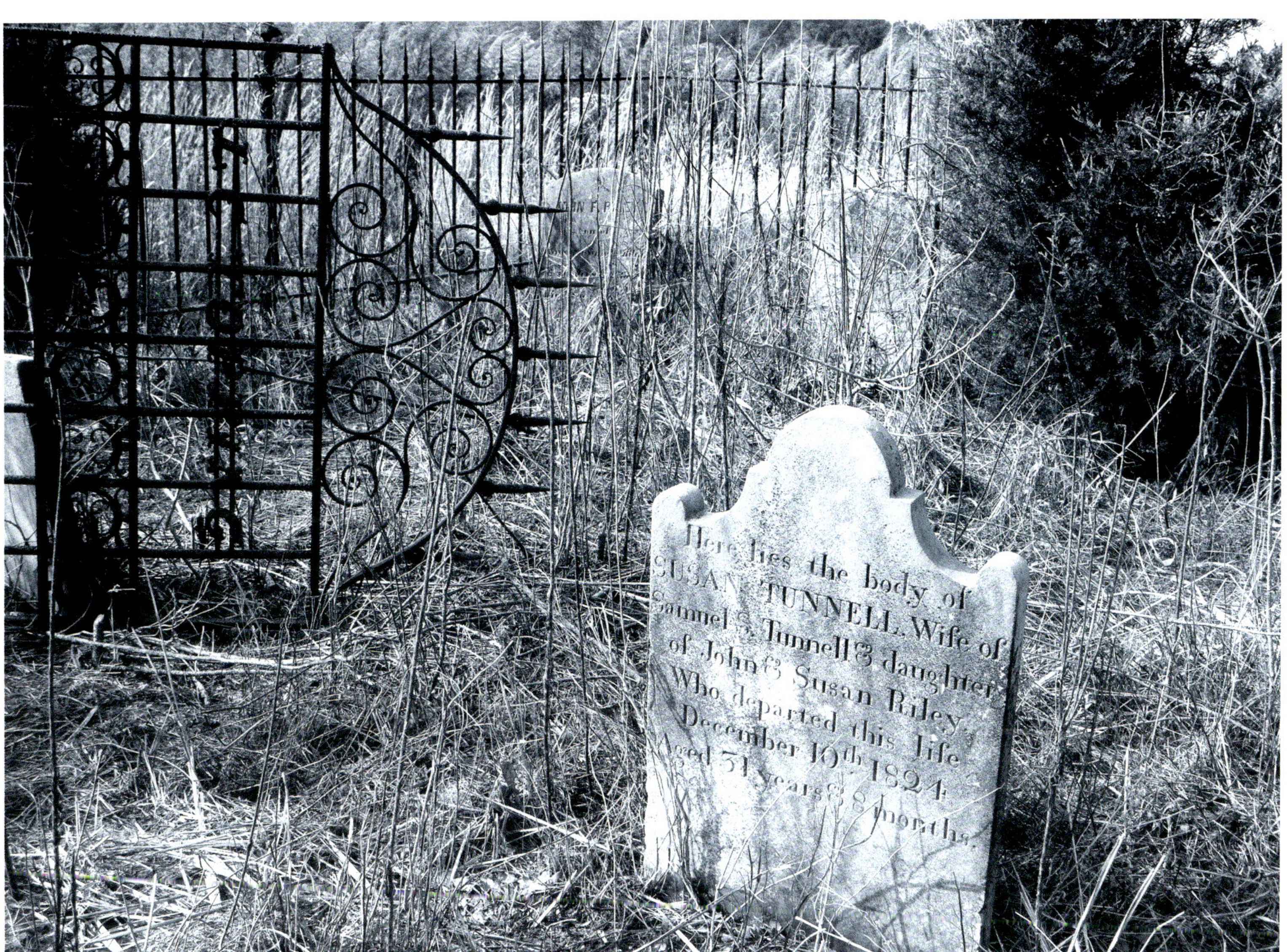
Here lies the body of
SUSAN TUNNELL, Wife of
Samuel Tunnell & daughter
of John & Susan Riley
Who departed this life
December 10th 1824
Aged 31 years & 8 months

The owner was startled to find me, my camera, and my tripod inside the long-abandoned house he once called home. After forgiving me for trespassing, he offered some history:

–His grandfather bought it in 1927 when it was already "real old."

–It was built on the very spot where the Pony Express once stopped.

–He and his four siblings were all born inside.

–His father abandoned it in 1957.

–He had recently given up any thoughts of renovation and planned to tear it down soon.

–The dolls had belonged to his sister.

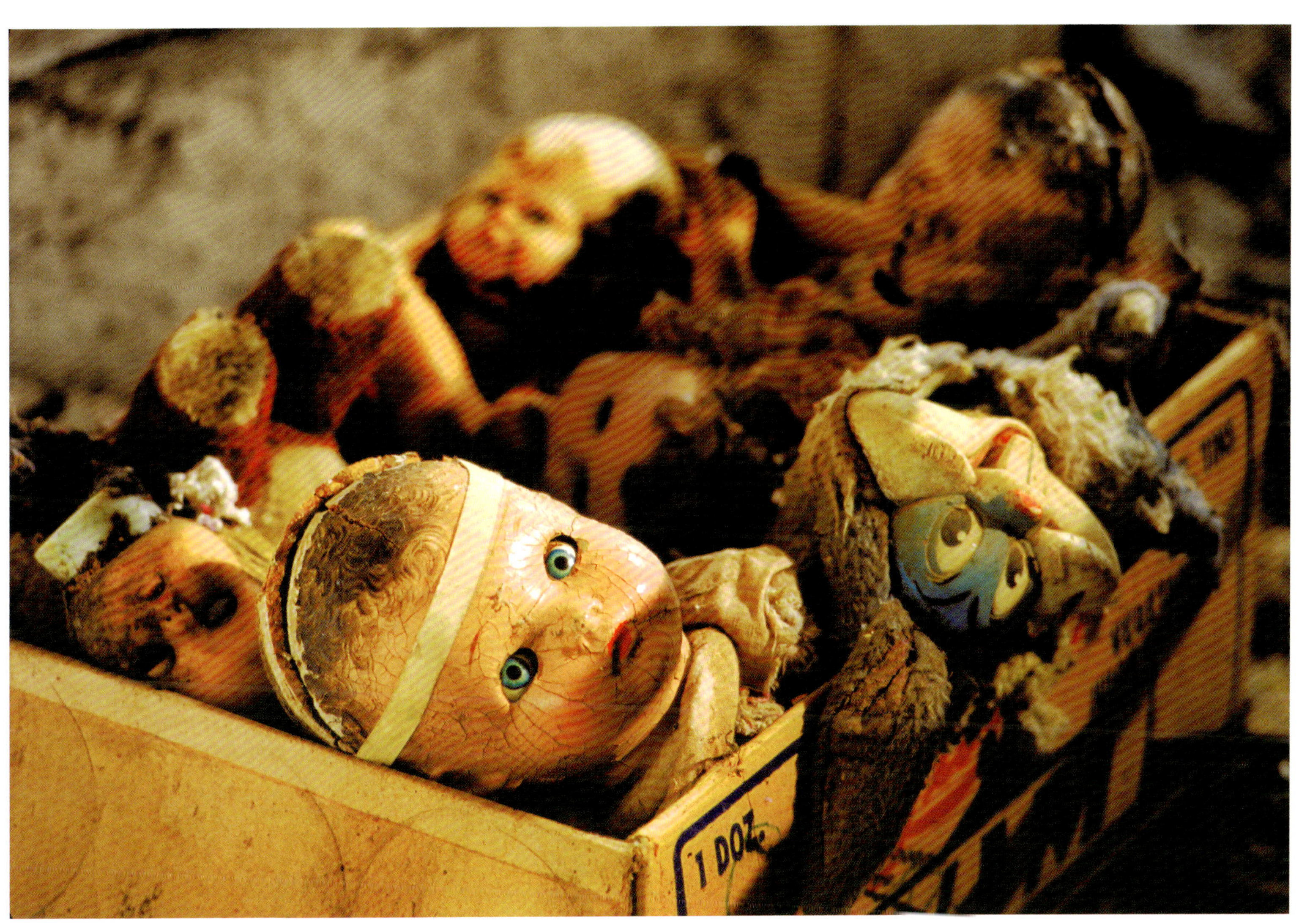
1 DOZ.

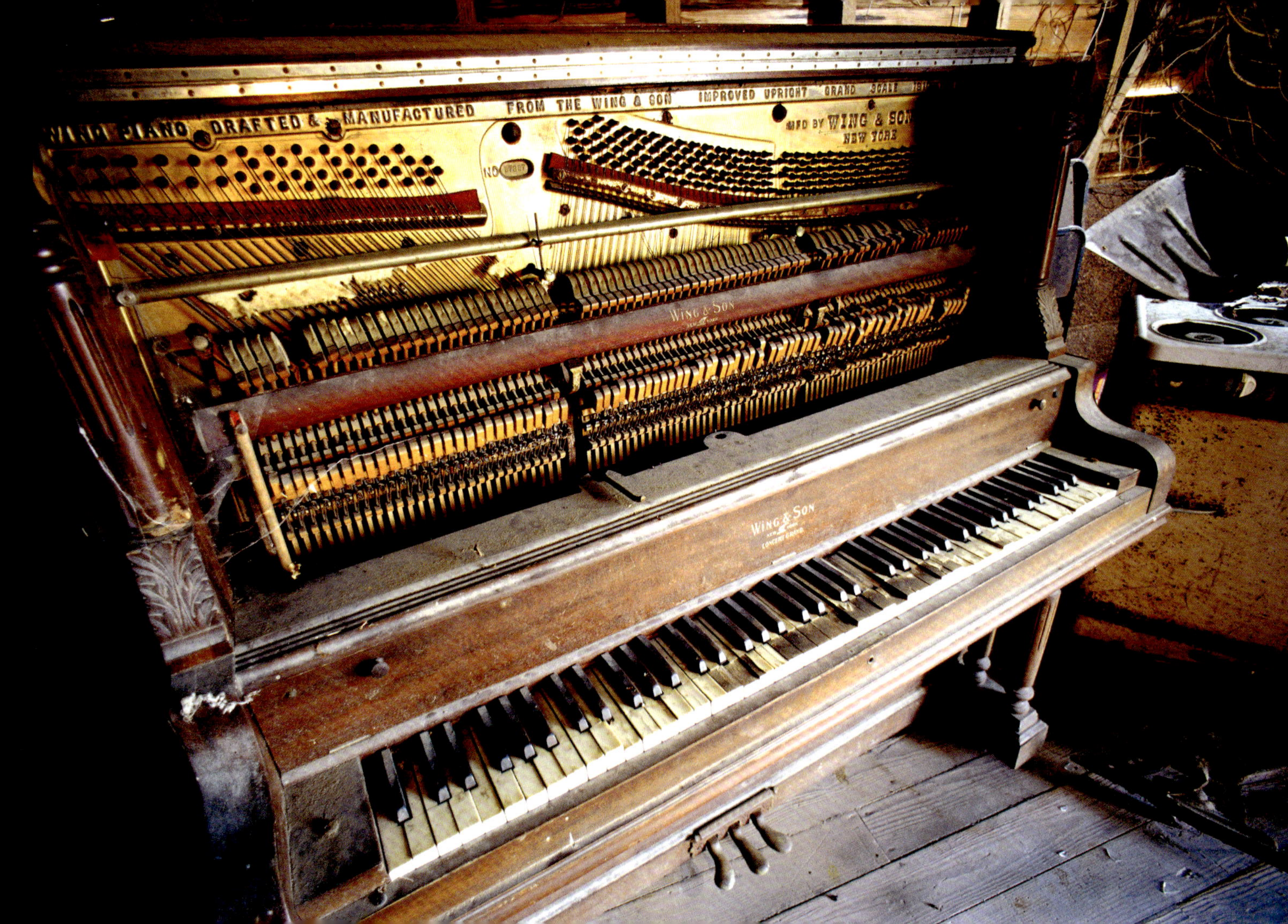
DRAFTED & MANUFACTURED
FROM THE WING & SON
IMPROVED UPRIGHT GRAND SCALE
WING & SON
NEW YORK
Wing & Son
Wing & Son

Poking one's nose into old barns generally yields such everyday items as horse stalls, metal poles that restrain cows during milking, and bales of hay. Occasionally serendipity strikes, as in a barn in the middle of a Carolina tobacco field.

A 78 rpm record, circa 1950, and a 1966 Rhode Island license plate are unlikely items to find juxtaposed, but not in the storage shed behind Cookie's Junk Shop. At 92 years of age Cookie's strength is his folksy charm, not his organizational skill.

For those unfamiliar with Rogers & Hammerstein's *South Pacific*, the cobwebbed tune is "There Is Nothin' Like a Dame."

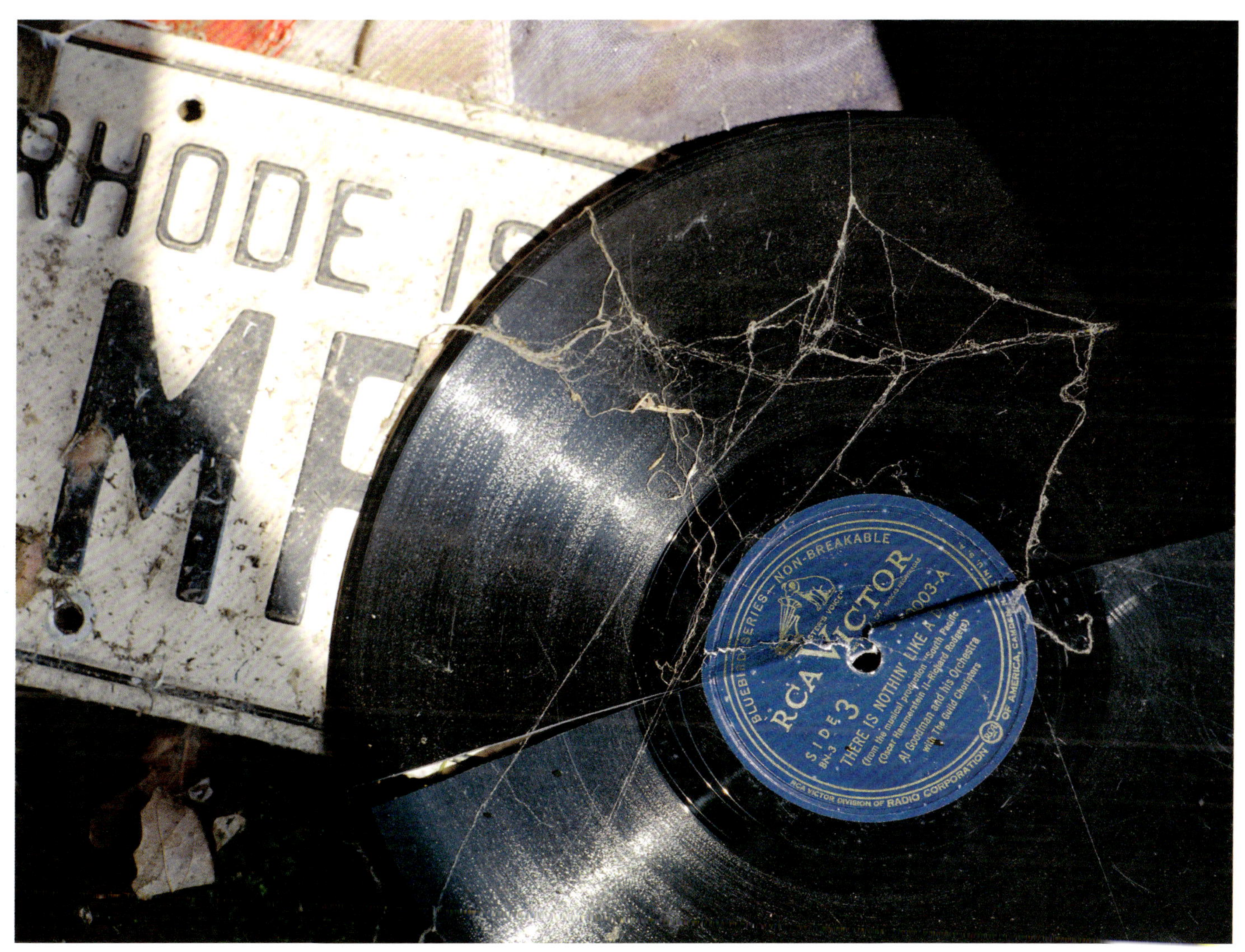
RHODE IS
NON-BREAKABLE
RCA VICTOR
SIDE 3
BN-3
THERE IS NOTHIN' LIKE A
Al Goodman and his Orchestra
with The Guild Choristers
RCA VICTOR DIVISION OF RADIO CORPORATION OF AMERICA

Washington County | *Pennsylvania*

This mailbox—which had become a shelter in which squirrels cracked their nuts—was actually in better shape than the home that went with it.

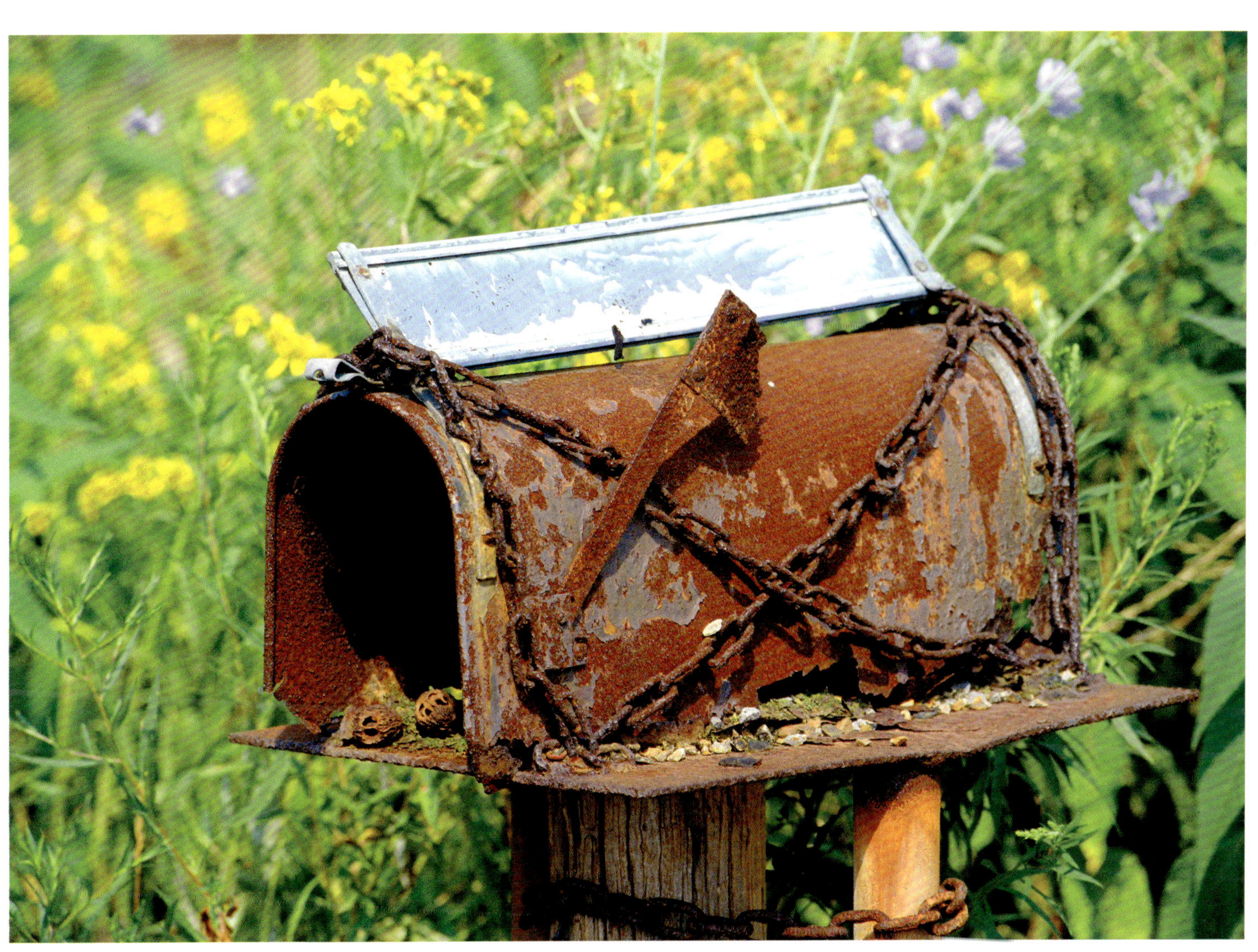

ARMSTRONG MILLS | *Ohio*

Dreamland:

A well-worn wall

of an abandoned store

on a narrow street in a quiet town

that time forgot after the train station closed.

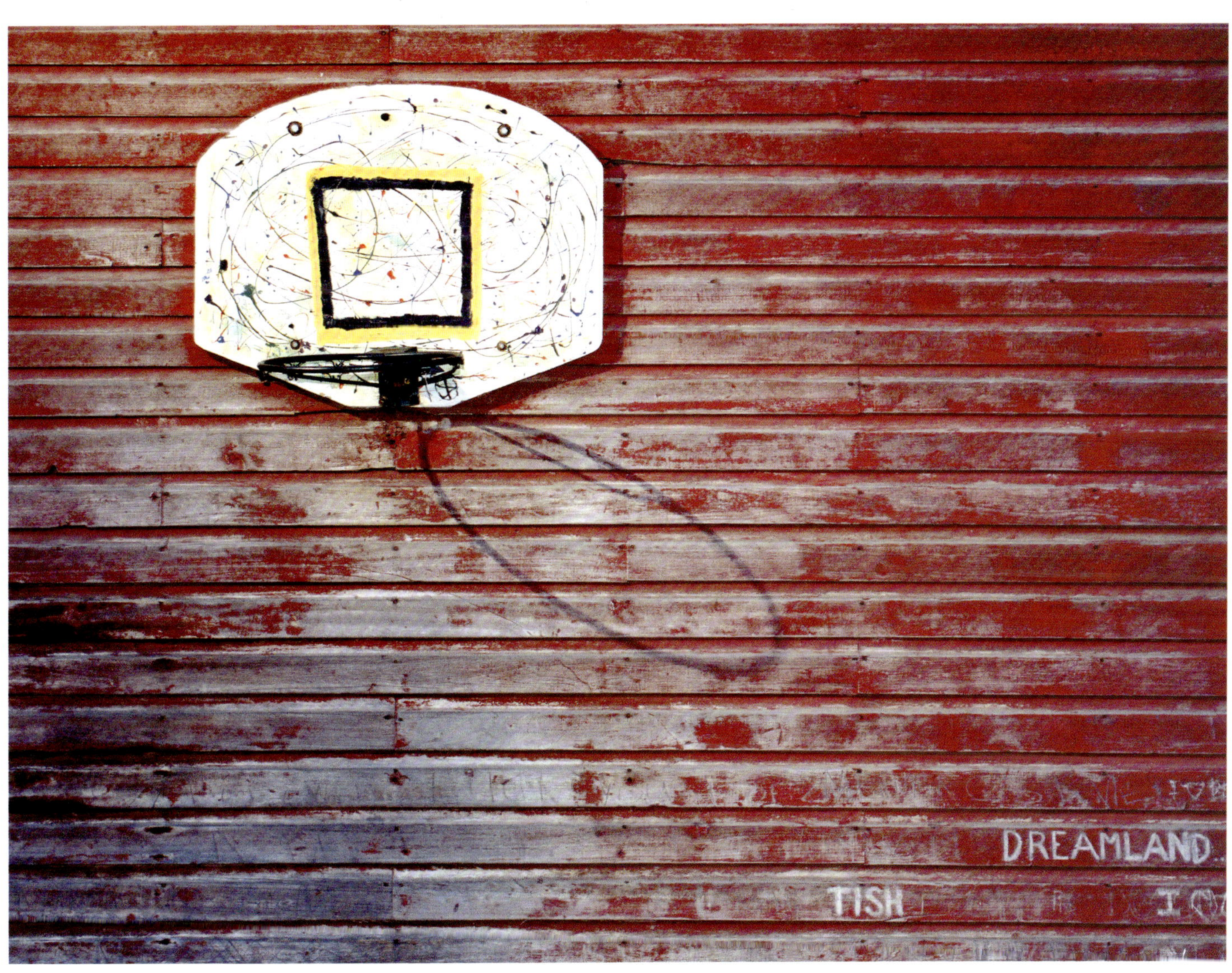
DREAMLAND
TISH

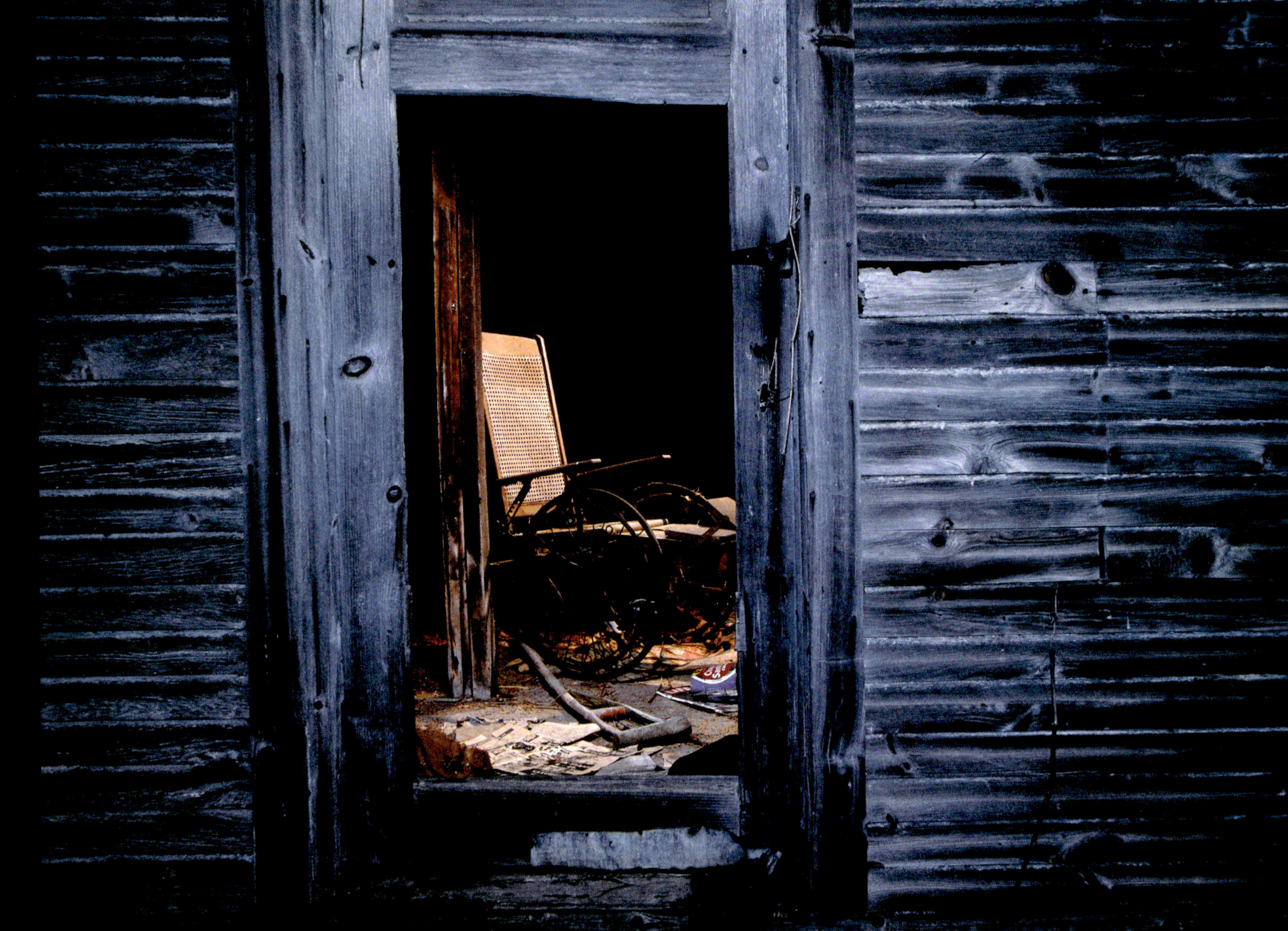

"It was forty-three years ago that I last set foot on the farm. The padlock on the front door was rusted, but miraculously my old key still worked. Standing there, gazing into the room, stirred memories of that hot, broken-legged summer: little circles imprinted on the underside of my thighs from the wheelchair's wicker; the smell of Chase & Sandborn coffee; leafing through a *Life* magazine—the one with Steve McQueen on the cover—at least 50 times. I recalled how clever my father was to improvise a crutch from a dead branch, but why didn't he make a ramp for the door? I guess there was no place for a wheelchair-bound boy to go..."

Opening of an (unfinished) short story

For how long had grass been growing between the chair slats? One clue: inside the mining shed was an enormous stack of sepia-toned newspapers; a *Denver Post's* headline at the very top announced the resignation of Spiro Agnew, Richard Nixon's vice president.

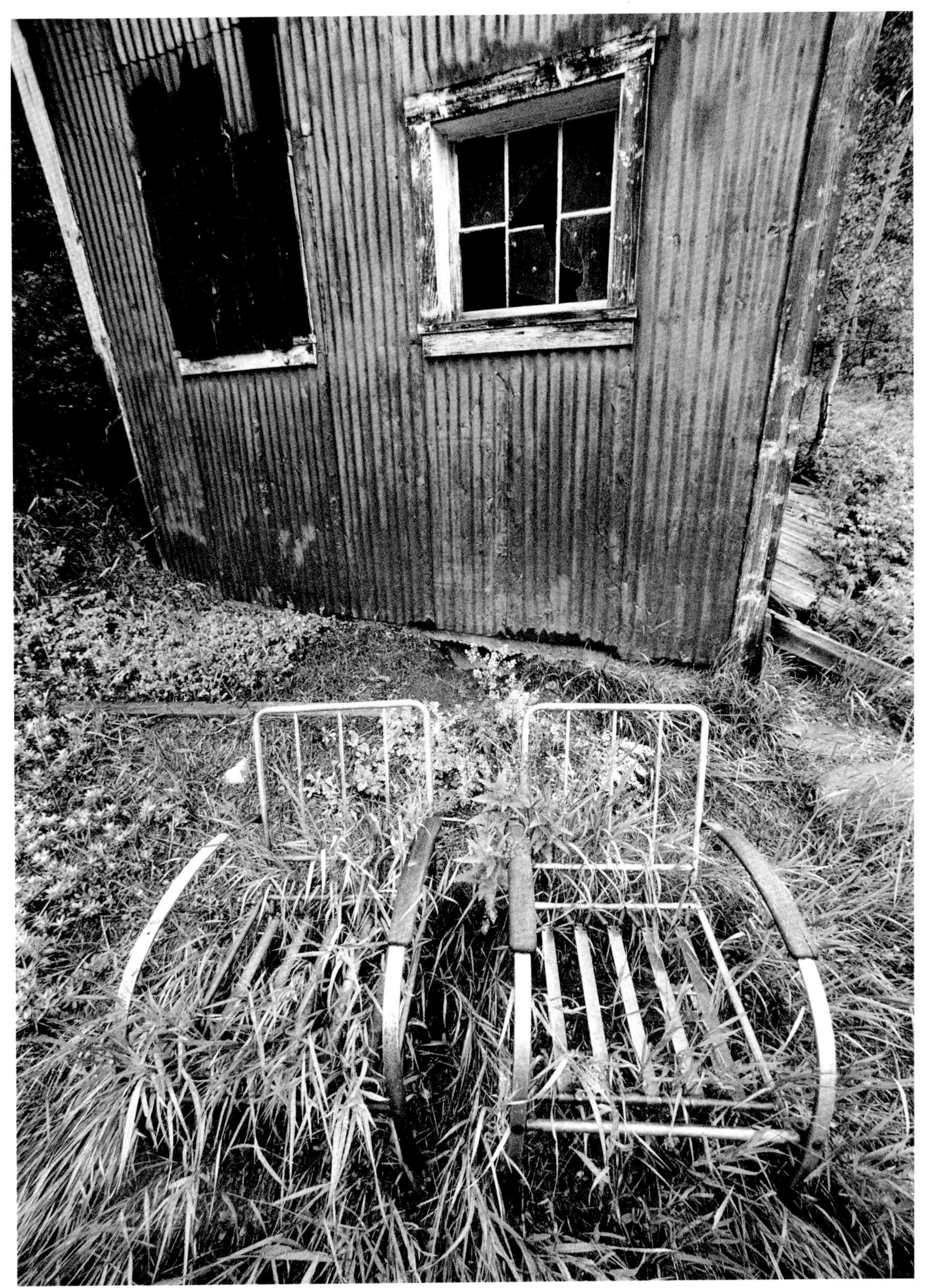

NORTHAMPTON | *Massachusetts*

Henry David Thoreau once observed: "I had three chairs in my house: one for solitude, two for company, three for society." These seven chairs in the courtyard of a mental hospital seemed to answer all those needs: their gentle arc allowed each sitter to be alone, or to connect easily with a neighbor, or to be part of the entire group. The legs of every chair had sunk deep into the earth, as if each had for many years been occupied by a ghostly weight.

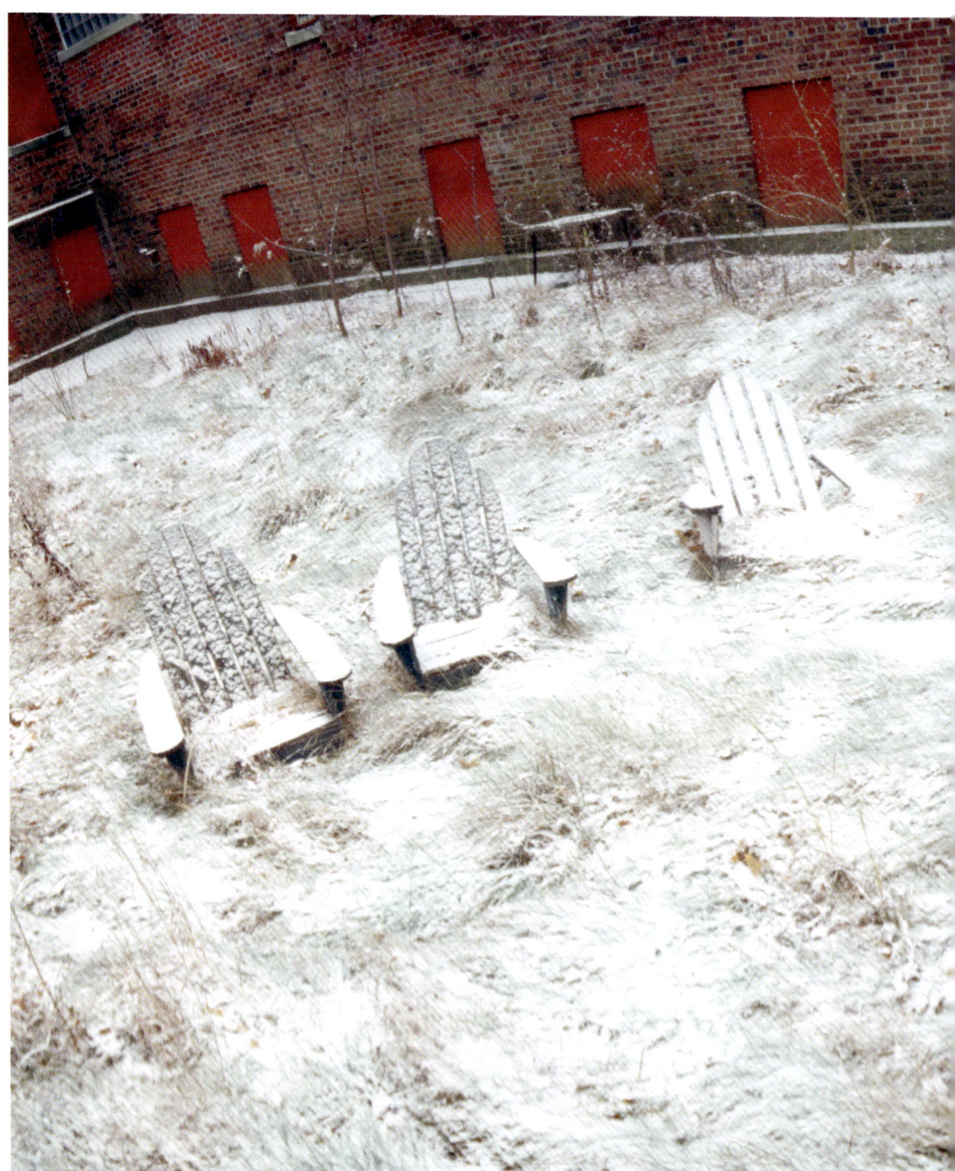

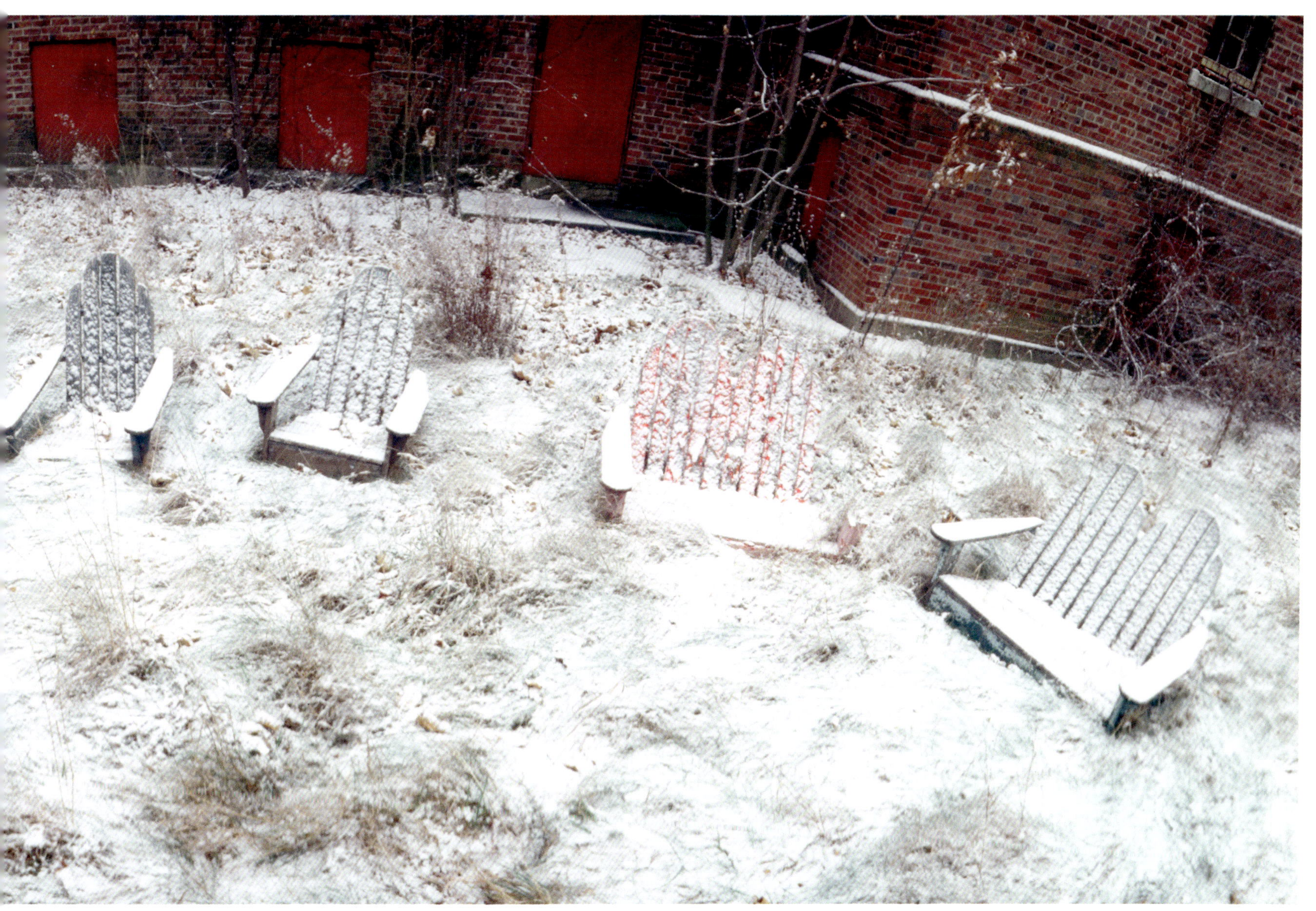

Brookfield | *Connecticut*

I once loathed the typewriter. During high school, college, law school, and the 10 years I practiced law before becoming a photographer, it represented compositions, term papers, legal briefs, and the oppressive deadlines that accompanied them. But after I became a photographer and life no longer depended on the written word, sitting at the keyboard became a joy. So I was especially sad to find this "Woodstock" amidst the remnants of a burned home.

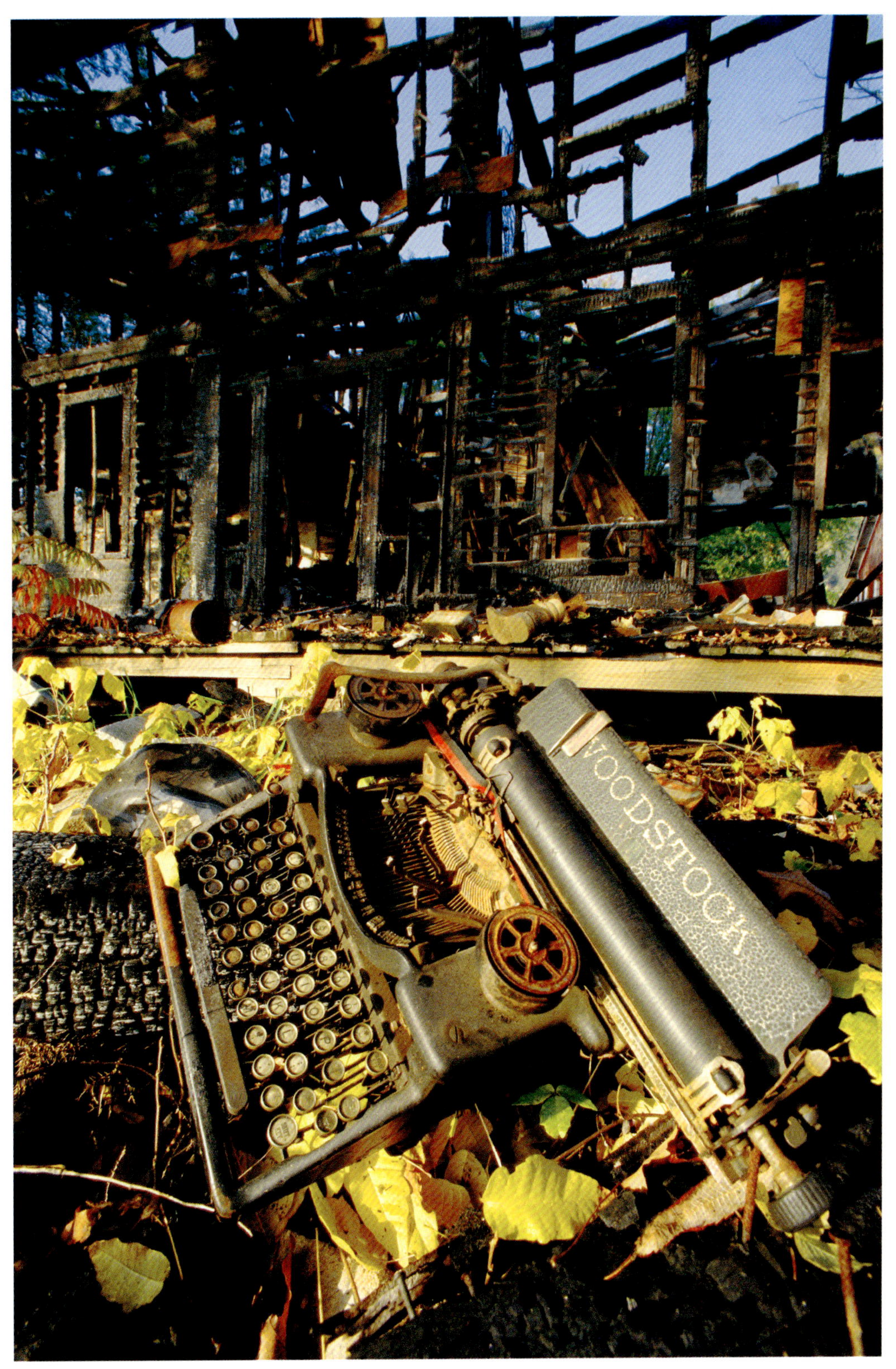
WOODSTOCK

Uvalde County | *Texas*

After many hundreds of rolls of film exposed and many thousands of miles traveled over a period of many years this portfolio comes to an end—but my odyssey in search of great abandoned subject matter continues...

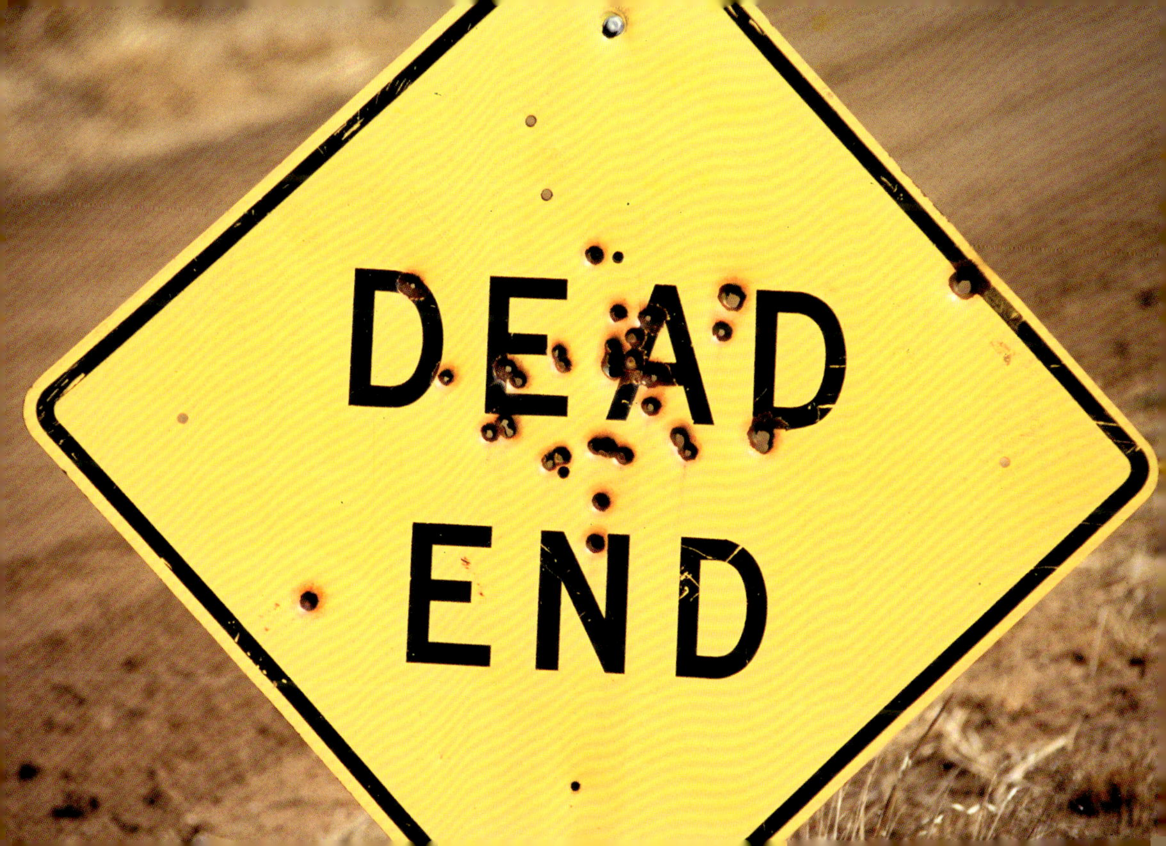
DEAD
END

Technical Notes

Most of the photographs in this book were taken with the brilliantly designed, ever-reliable Nikon cameras and Nikon lenses, ranging from 14 mm to 500 mm, including three zoom lenses covering the focal lengths from 20 to 200 mm. I generally keep color film in two bodies, black and white in a third, while a fourth is adapted for a Polaroid attachment which enables me to instantly check the effect of flash. I also use the Mamiya 645, a lightweight, easy-to-handle medium format (2¼) camera, with lenses ranging from 24 mm fisheye to 300 mm. Most of the panoramic shots were taken with the Widelux 35 mm camera, whose moving lens encompasses 140°.

I love the many complexions of natural light but nature often needs a helping hand, particularly since I often lack the time to remain in one location for the right atmospherics to develop. Over one-third of the pictures in this book have utilized flash (Nikon and Sunpak...as many as five at a time) which is filtered to be compatible to, or occasionally contrasting with, the available light. For kicking light into selected places, reflectors—silver, white, and gold—are also handy.

I have relied on Kodak film since the beginning of time—more than 20 different varieties have wound through my cameras over the years. My current preference is Ektachrome 100VS, a transparency film which provides rich, vibrant colors, and Ektachrome 100SW, which is similar to VS but with a pleasing warm cast. Both films have a superfine grain structure which allows for strikingly sharp enlargements.

The photographs were prepared for this book by scanning them and then importing the digitized images into my computer. Using Adobe Photoshop,® images were cropped and color adjusted when needed, and distractions, such as telephone lines, were sometimes removed...but for the most part, what you see here is essentially what I saw on the processed film.

Steve Gottlieb has traveled through all 50 states photographing people, architecture, and landscapes. His award-winning pictures have been published in hundreds of magazines, advertisements, and annual reports worldwide. Murals from his first book, *Washington: Portrait of a City*, form the core of a permanent exhibit about our capital city at the National Building Museum. His second book, *American Icons*, is a visual celebration of our nation's most widely recognized symbols. A graduate of Columbia College and Law School, Gottlieb labored for 10 years as a lawyer, after which he turned his lifelong hobby of photography into a second career. Gottlieb lives in Manhattan.